Christmas at River Cottage

To my parents,
who taught me the
meaning of celebration

Christmas at River Cottage

Lucy Brazier

with seasonal notes and recipes from
Hugh Fearnley-Whittingstall

Hugh Fearnley-Whittingstall's
RIVER COTTAGE

BLOOMSBURY PUBLISHING
LONDON • OXFORD • NEW YORK • NEW DELHI • SYDNEY

Contents

Foreword

In recent decades, Christmas has become a little stretched out of shape, all of us pulled this way and that by the pressure to buy endless stuff and put on a perfect, sparkling performance of gifting, decorating and entertaining. At its worst, it descends into a festival of waste, of expense and ephemera, epitomised by panicky supermarket shopping trips, heaps of plastic and fractious tempers.

In our hearts we all want a Christmas that's the opposite of that. Whether you celebrate the Christian festival that anchors the season or whether its significance lies elsewhere for you, this is a time when every wise and compassionate value that underpins our society – and certainly the values that we hold so dear at River Cottage – can come to the fore. So it counts for a lot that we can find practical, dependable ways to make that happen.

For me, the essence of Christmas is best expressed by bringing people together in a spirit of generosity and hospitality, and giving them just what they need to cast their cares aside and talk, laugh and eat. Some of that involves planning and doing and buying – but those activities should always be secondary to the people themselves. A quiet frosty walk with someone you love, a mince pie and a chat with an old friend, a gathering with neighbours to toast the season with a few special snacks laid on – these are the things that truly comfort and enrich us after a long, busy year. If we can frame those interactions with good food and drink, simple gifts and beautiful, natural decorations, then who needs more?

Of course, it's one thing to wax lyrical about such a warm and nourishing Christmas, quite another to deliver it. Take on too much and your festivities can be spoiled by stress. But approach it as Lucy Brazier suggests here – with a sense of kindness to yourself, as host, before you worry too much about everyone else – and the result can be a Christmas that people talk about for years to come for all the right reasons.

I have worked with Lucy for a long time now and I was delighted when she established our Christmas Hamper courses at the River Cottage Cookery School, events from which students always emerge full of inspiration and glowing with good will – and possibly a tot or two of Lucy's sloe gin. But even if we hadn't secured her for the course, she'd still be the person I'd choose to write this book; she embodies more than anyone I know the warmth and generosity at the heart of Christmas.

Lucy is also endlessly creative and imaginative, fascinated by the traditions that weave through the year and lead us to this seasonal apex, and passionate about the foraging, baking, preserving and infusing that pay such delicious dividends come December. An invitation to a solstice bonfire or Christmas Eve drinks at Lucy's is something to covet...

It's been such a pleasure to hear in detail how Lucy does Christmas. And it's an honour to add a few of my own insights, family traditions (and foibles). Blame me for all the bits with this rosy tint behind them – together they make up my Christmas trifle.

If you want to host a large festive gathering, Lucy will show you that it's well within your capabilities. It needn't mean a sit-down three-course lunch for fifteen, if that's not your thing. There are other ways to bring your dearest ones nearer and enjoy the experience. Lucy urges us not to forget the natural season within which Christmas sits because the beauty of December is all part of the joy of it, whether you breathe it in on rosy-cheeked winter rambles, or bring it inside in the form of fresh greenery. Remember the simple pleasures, she bids us – the satisfaction in sending a home-made card, the licence Christmas grants us to curl up and read a book *in the daytime!*

And then, of course, there is the festive food, something about which Lucy and I are endlessly enthusiastic. We love sharing celebratory recipes and, again, she's been kind enough to invite me to include some of mine in these pages. And so you'll find a few of my favourite edible gifts, seasonal salads and meaty centrepieces dotted among Lucy's family favourites and the River Cottage Christmas classics.

I love the way Lucy demonstrates that a year of seasonal cooking, foraging and preserving – just a little

here and there – can come to glorious fruition as we gather for Christmas. And I love her celebration of the many fine fresh ingredients to be had at the year's end too. Midwinter festival it may be, but Christmas can be a time of seasonal abundance, with so much produce still in excellent condition from the farm or the market. Take home knobbly walking sticks of Brussels sprouts, purple-whorled red cabbage and vivid orange clementines. Load up on earthy-sweet nuts and intensely flavoured dried fruit; inhale the evocative scents of warm spices and evergreen herbs.

If you enjoy meat, now is the time to indulge, with plump poultry and well-aged beef ready to be relished and the all-important gravy to be made. And, arguably best of all, there are the post-Christmas Day leftovers to look forward to, those low-effort meals of tossed-together bits and pieces, never precisely the same, always delicious and utterly comforting.

I hope this is all starting to sound like the sort of Christmas you want to enjoy: one that is simple, natural and joyful, rooted in the season as it turns quietly through the solstice, allowing time to celebrate but also time to talk and to rest. In these few precious and special weeks, let's put aside the concerns that drive us through the rest of the year and come together with those we hold dear, to light the candles, pour a drink and share good things.

The very best of the season to you!
Hugh

Introduction

CHRISTMAS AT RIVER COTTAGE is the much-anticipated festive climax of the year. It is a joyous blend of celebration, seasonality, tradition and sustainability – themes that run through Christmas as they do through River Cottage itself. For me, River Cottage is a place where Christmas is its truest self, where Hugh and the team embrace the spirit of the season through their commitment to local ingredients, ethical sourcing and generous feasting, something I have been lucky to be part of for many years.

I love Christmas and its mass of contradictions. I am seduced by the intoxicating combination of food, drink, people and ritual. Yet I also crave the simplicity of a bleak midwinter landscape, bracing walks, quiet days and suppers of leftovers. The vivid red of high-kicking decadence paired with the peaceful green of the rejuvenating natural world. The trick is to strike the right balance, and I hope that is what the pages ahead will give you. I also sincerely wish that you may, just for a brief time, tap into that feeling of pure excitement about Christmas you had as a child. Not just vicariously through any children that may be around you, but for yourself. Maybe you will find it while tucking into the first mince pie, hearing the solo to 'Once in Royal David's City', picking up a copy of the Christmas *Radio Times* or reading a few pages from *A Christmas Carol*. Savour those moments that bring you closer to the essence of the season.

My particular passion for Christmas was nurtured by my yuletide-obsessed mother and grandparents. Our tiny terraced London house and sparse budget both burst at the seams come Christmas, our celebrations a wonderful cocktail of Victoriana and 1970s kitsch. My grandmother made the same plum pudding every year based on a recipe passed down from her mother, which was then passed on to mine and now to me. My grandfather couldn't invite people around without it becoming a party, and when it became a party he had to take the doors off every room to create as much space as possible. On Christmas Day, every place around the dining table was filled and there was often a second table squeezed in to accommodate more. It instilled in me a hospitable core and a festive spirit (and a hatred for washing up).

As a grown-up, I still consider old family traditions while creating new ones for my own children. Food and drink are at the centre of it all. The feasts of dishes, joyful hours in the kitchen with annual recipes, *Carols from King's* on the radio, the bare bones of a jigsaw waiting for a quiet moment with a fresh ginger tea and a wedge of crumbly fruit cake. There are jars of preserves, bottles of home-steeped booze, a pile of dried orange slices and a large bowl of heavenly scented paperwhites bowing under the weight of each other. I chop, fry, bake, roast and ferment, knowing that if I put the time in on the lead-up there will be plentiful leftovers to carry us through the holiday with little further effort.

As well as reflecting my own affection for this time, I want this book to capture the wonderful experience of a River Cottage Christmas – the food, drink, decoration and merriment of it all. Sustainability is at the heart of everything River Cottage do and there is no better example of this than at Christmas, when we buck the modern trend of excessive, wasteful consumption. Many of us are trying hard to reduce our waste and embrace a more sustainable way forward, but these intentions can be seriously tested over the festivities, even for the most committed. We are preoccupied by time-saving quick fixes and affordable solutions, which results in shocking but unsurprising statistics: we create an additional 30 per cent of rubbish over the festive season. Plastic packaging from gifts is a big problem, and the roughly 270,000 tonnes of festive food thrown away, much of it still edible when it is put in the bin, is nothing short of shameful.

At this time of year, it feels harder to continue our war on waste but it is imperative that we do, and it's easier and more heart-warming than you may think. There will be advice throughout the book to help you achieve a sustainable approach, whether this is preserving the harvest, creating edible gifts, cooking ahead or celebrating the major feast days and loving your leftovers. The recipes in the book echo this and the seasonal rhythm from the end of summer through to Twelfth Night. Also woven through are historical gems and nuggets of folklore revealing national and global customs as well as craft and decoration ideas too, drawing on the natural world rather than the high street.

Christmas is about belief. From pagan stirrings to the Christian nativity and the impatient wait for Father Christmas, this festival is rooted in spirituality, faith and a little bit of magic. It is about tradition, a familiar and reassuring structure of rituals that take us from one year to the next. It is also about generosity – sharing our hospitality and our homes. Last, but not least, it is about people and the importance of spending time with family and friends. It's an amazing mix but it all adds up to an awful lot of expectation. It is unsurprising that the most wonderful time of the year can also be the most exhausting, and there is a particular type of melancholy that belongs to this season too.

It can be a terribly hard and lonely period for many, one that intensifies ongoing challenges – the loss of a loved one, a difficult home life or health issues, perhaps. The financial cost of Christmas can weigh heavy, whatever our situation. The value of the season is not in how much we spend, it is in how we approach the celebration with thought and care, for others and for ourselves.

I have been labelled Mrs Christmas over the years, by my family, friends and the RC team. Probably because I have never made any secret about my love for the season. But in truth I don't much like this epithet: it makes me sound like I know it all and I don't. I am still happily exploring ways to create a better, harmonious, more sustainable celebration each year and I am immensely proud to be able to share this with you in this book.

It has been an absolute pleasure to be joined by Hugh too and discover more about what Christmas means to him, both at home and in the River Cottage world he created over 21 years ago. My sincerest thanks to him and each of the brilliant River Cottage experts who inspired and supported me over the years – their knowledge and insight echoes throughout. I am a home cook and novice veg grower who took on the challenge of a new life in the country, and fell into the safest hands.

So, let us raise a glass to festive cheer. I wish you the Christmas you wish for yourself. For me, I would like a crackling fire, a pair of hand-knitted wool socks, a pile of new books, a glass or two of something home-steeped and the people I love. Here's comfort and joy to you all.

1
Planning Ahead

IN THIS CHAPTER, we are going back before we go forwards. I think you will be glad because a little regular effort over the summer and autumn will have you reaping the rewards of a full larder by Christmas (and if you are first reading this in December, don't worry – your preparations for next year can begin in the coming spring!). Much as I love Christmas, I don't want to spend half the year speeding towards it. But neither do I want to be caught out with the stress of a last-minute panic. So, I focus on a few early preparations that are both a pleasure to undertake and a useful way to take advantage of seasonal gluts and natural bounty. They give a nod to the festive season without feeling like I am eating mince pies in August.

While the autumn equinox, around 22 September, marks the official start of the season, traditionally autumn began on 29 September, known as Michaelmas. Once a holy day, it was an important date in the farming calendar, marking the end of the harvest and signalling the time for account settling and hiring fairs. These days it carries very little significance but I love any excuse for a celebration so I embrace it, with foliage picked from the hedgerows, a crumble made using the last of the blackberries and, if I am really lucky, a dinner of Michaelmas goose.

Autumn is also one of the busiest times of the year at River Cottage, when the gardeners are picking the late summer bounty of fruit and veg, but also nurturing the winter crops and even sowing for the following spring. The kitchen at Park Farm effortlessly steps into a new season, excited by the abundant harvest and keen to preserve it for the tougher months ahead. The larder is a vital resource for River Cottage as a working smallholding with sustainability as its core ethos, but it should be important to us all. There is such basic comfort in fully stocked shelves.

Whether we grow produce ourselves or source it locally, making sure we have something extra for the months ahead is useful, practical and rather satisfying. And when I say larder, I don't just mean in the physical sense, although how lovely if you have one. Many of us don't – but a lack of space needn't stop you. There is almost always a shelf, cupboard or corner somewhere that can house a few pots of chutney, a Kilner jar of sloe gin or a carefully wrapped Christmas cake.

So here I will talk about preserving produce, growing vegetables, sourcing ingredients and stocking up with good things both for yourself and as gifts for others. I'll look at the tradition of Stir-up Sunday, and the eminently sensible idea of getting ahead with some simple baking. The relative calm before the fairy-light twinkling storm.

Growing your own produce

Imagine popping out to the veg patch in your dressing gown on Christmas morning, to pull up some leeks, shake the soil off a bunch of carrots or cut down a stalk of perfect Brussels sprouts… It's more than possible! Growing part of your Christmas lunch – even just one element of it – is a worthwhile aspiration, and home-grown produce can be turned into gifts too, from mint jelly to blackcurrant jam. You can also grow flowers that you can collect seed from, and gift those seeds too.

The space you have will dictate what you can grow, of course, but even a few sprigs of rosemary or bay from a pot are rewarding. Unless you have an allotment or several robust raised beds, pick a few favourite vegetables, a couple of preferred fruits and a selection of herbs, and concentrate on those. It's amazing how many people seem to focus on what they think a veg patch ought to include, rather than what they actually want to eat. If you have a balcony or windowsill then select evergreen herbs such as winter savory, thyme, rosemary, sage and chervil. Container gardeners should have good results with lots of veg and fruit, including beetroot, carrots, chillies and currants.

Don't forget flowers that give you bang for your buck too, like the hard-working nasturtium, which adds vibrant colour to your garden, helps to ward off aphids from your beans and gives edible flowers for your summer salads. If that wasn't enough service, you can then collect seed pods as they fall (leave some if you want a return crop in the same place) and either save them to give as gifts or pickle them and use as you would capers.

I love calendula (technically a herb) for similar insect fighting and salad reasons, but the flowers are also powerful as a natural medicine or in a tea. Harvesting flower heads and seeds to dry is a mindful early autumn activity. These cheery flowers give so much all summer and produce a mass of seeds that make you feel like you are giving away kernels of pure sunshine at Christmas.

One of the best things about growing your own is being able to enjoy produce that isn't widely available in the shops, so sample some heritage varieties such as purple-podded peas, Black Russian tomatoes and jostaberries. Choose versatile produce that works for preserving as well as eating fresh. And since you will no doubt find yourself wishing for a crop of something you haven't got space for, I highly recommend setting up an arrangement with a friend or neighbour to swap or barter produce. Over the next few pages, I'm offering some ideas for your fruit and veg patch, whether you want to preserve or grow for the winter months.

Summer and autumn harvests

Courgettes Easy to grow and prolific – green, striped, yellow or globe – courgettes really are the gift that keeps on giving throughout the season. Sow the seeds under cover in early spring and wait until the final frost before planting out, making sure you give them enough space to thrive. In return, you will be rewarded with flowers to stuff and fry, early courgettes to eat raw, and gluts to preserve as chutneys. Remember to keep picking them and not to let them get to a tasteless, bumper size. If you are looking for a marrow (and I always am), try the Tiger Cross variety, which can be picked as a courgette or left to transform into marrows. These make a delicious Provençal-style stew, are sturdy enough to stuff and the star of my relish recipe on page 31.

Runner beans These remind me of my childhood and picking them straight from my grandparents' overgrown bamboo cane tunnel. They would be pushed through the stringer, blanched and then swirled in a generous coating of melted butter. It was like eating a pile of slippery green worms with a touch of crunch! There was often a runner bean pickle for the Cheddar cheese sandwiches in our school packed lunch, too. They are just as important to me now and I grow a tepee of them with whatever other beans I may be seduced by – broad, French and borlotti, usually. Sow under cover or direct in early spring. You'll find they need very little attention, last longer than the good weather and add beauty and height to your plot. The best beans to pickle are the early, small ones.

Tomatoes I don't think I need tell you how much tastier home-grown tomatoes can be compared to some insipid shop-bought varieties. A grow-bag of Gardener's Delight, a hanging basket of Tumbling Toms or a couple of pots of Oxheart in a sunny spot require regular watering and the occasional feed. The reward is fruits that can be eaten straight from the vine and used in a myriad of recipes. Preserving these bursts of sweet red sunshine is one of the kindest things you can do for your winter self, whether in chutney, ketchup or, my favourite, a rich garlicky passata. The plum tomato, San Marzano, is perfect for this.

Mulberries In the middle of the old walled kitchen garden at River Cottage sits a magnificent mulberry tree in a purpose-built raised bed. It was planted when Hugh and the team first took on the farm over 15 years ago and it took a few years to bear fruit, but has been a trustworthy producer ever since. These are my favourite berries and I include them here because they are pretty impossible to buy, due to their fragility and quick demise once picked. Plus, the tree is a small, hardy, attractive

accessory to a garden. You do need to be ready to pick the berries before the birds strip the tree and, once you have, they really do not keep – so eat them for breakfast, lunch and dinner. I would recommend making a batch of jam and bottling some mulberries in gin or vodka (much like my cherry vodka recipe on page 49), so you can savour them again through the bleakest months.

Plums Including greengages and mirabelles in this category, plums are wonderful to pluck straight from the tree and pop into your mouth – but great for cooking and preserving too. As with berries and currants, they are sublime in baking and make the most delicious jams for your larder. If you are tight for space then I would highly recommend an espaliered plant that spreads along a wall or fence. Popular varieties include Marjorie's Seedlings and the blush-coloured Opal. I am also a huge fan of damsons – while the flesh is quite sour they are a preserver's dream for jams, jellies and chutneys.

Quince As ancient as life itself, it is thought this was the 'apple' referred to in the Bible that Eve tempted Adam with. It is a hard, knobbly pear-shaped fruit, which is impossible to eat raw but transforms beautifully when cooked. Once the height of fashion, quince is now often overlooked in favour of apples and pears and the trees are consequently harder to find.

A quince tree is an easy, if still unusual, addition to your garden and fruit bowl. The fruits can sit happily in your kitchen for several weeks before you use them and give the most fragrant scent – a sign of what they will taste like. If this appeals, take a look at the Champion variety, or the smaller and slightly russeted and dimpled Serbian Quince (Hugh's recommendation).

What happens to quince is nothing short of magical when you poach, roast, steep, jelly or bake it. In its natural state, plucked from the tree, it is inedible, but give it a little heat or alcohol and this remarkable fruit generously shares its pear-like texture and sweet, floral notes. The Victorians grew quince in their gardens and companion planted them in orchards, but their popularity subsequently declined, partly because they were considered 'not worth the trouble'. Perhaps the quincemas cake (on page 47) and quince ratafia (on page 55) will be enough to convince you otherwise. Plant your own quince if you can, make friends with someone who has a tree or talk to your local greengrocer. It deserves a big audience.

Winter veg

Brussels sprouts Straight off the stem and eaten raw, thinly sliced or shaved, these are a revelation – trust me, sprout-haters! The plants need to be started early, around the same time you would plant many summer seeds. Sown under cover in spring and planted out in early summer, they need plenty of space. Idemar is a relatively new but already popular variety. Cut the sprouts off the stem as they mature or take the top off one entire plant in October and leave it – the leafy tops themselves make a delicious winter green. By Christmas all the sprouts on that plant should be ready to eat. Nature works in mysterious ways.

Parsnips Sown direct from March to May, these mainstays of winter feasting are easy to grow and require very little attention. Favoured varieties at River Cottage are Aromata, and Tender and True. You can begin to harvest late autumn but the parsnips will always be sweeter after the first frost. Leave in the ground until you need them but don't let them become giant and tasteless. As well as roasts and soups, they shine in warm winter salads, giving pulses and leaves a delicious rooty focus.

Swede A personal favourite of mine and much maligned. Sown direct between April and June, it can be pulled up through the winter. Lomonde is a popular variety for its hardiness, resistance to mildew and attractive purple and yellow colour. For those of you who consider this rooty delight a waste of space, bear in mind that, if you pick carefully, you can cook with part of the leafy top while the plant is still growing (swede is one of few vegetables that will allow you to do this). Once picked, peel, boil and mash with butter and black pepper. If you are still not convinced, add more butter and pepper. Swede also makes a delicious soup, and roasts surprising well – especially when mixed with other roots and chunks of apple (add these halfway through).

Leeks An aesthetic and delicious addition to your winter veg patch, this allium needs to be started under cover by April and planted out in July to be ready for harvesting in the autumn. The leeks can be left in the soil until you need them. River Cottage Head Gardener, Adam Crofts, prefers the Giant Winter and Blue Green Winter varieties. They need watering early on but are hardy soldiers of the vegetable world and a deliciously versatile crop to reap.

I use leeks in so many different recipes but one of my favourite ways to enjoy them is sliced and sautéed in a little butter along with a pile of shredded fennel. They also combine brilliantly with cabbage (shredded, blanched and then stirred through almost-cooked leeks), or in a gratin with cauliflower florets and a garlicky breadcrumb topping.

Kalettes The love-child of kale and Brussels sprouts, these are a relatively new but very wonderful addition to the Brassica family. They look like tiny cabbages, or sprouts wearing ruffled shirts, and taste sweeter than either of their parents. They are really versatile: whether raw, steamed, stir-fried or roasted, they keep their shape and flavour. Plant out as seedlings in May and you should be guaranteed a crop from November. They may even convert the sprout dodgers!

Carrots Sown direct as late as June, these can be pulled up on Christmas morning. However, if they are ready before then or need protecting after a wet autumn, they can be pulled and stored (unwashed) in sand or sacks. I grow carrots as much for their frondy tops as their crunchy bodies, and make pesto and salsa verde with the leaves. Autumn King, Amsterdam Forcing and Nantes 2 are regular varieties in the walled kitchen garden at River Cottage.

Winter cabbages These need to be sown under cover in the spring and then planted out in the summer. They do hog the soil somewhat but can be forgiven as they are relatively low maintenance and make the perfect addition to the autumn veg patch. Choose varieties like Deadon, Winter Paresa and Vertus; you will find they are so much tastier than those stocked in the supermarkets.

Kale This can be an almost year-round joy. I am looking at you Cavolo Nero, Red Russian and Red Bore. For a winter harvest sow under cover in August before planting out around 6 weeks later. The plants take a while to get going but are ready to pick after 3 months. Annoyingly, the birds (and caterpillars) are rather partial to them too, but kales are robust, long-lasting and not bothered by frost so make the ideal cut-and-come-again leaf. I fill half of a raised bed with them so I always have something green to add to a dish from late autumn through to spring – the (surprisingly long) 'hungry gap'.

Beetroot These can also be sown and harvested throughout much of the year. They are one of the most versatile, nutritious vegetables we have (the leafy tops as good as the roots) and they deserve to be celebrated more than they are. Take a look at varieties like Boltardy, Golden and Chioggia. Sow direct in July for a winter crop (if earlier sowings are overwintered they can develop a slightly harsh tannic note, though it mellows with cooking).

This is the vegetable most synonymous with River Cottage as we often have it growing in the walled garden, ready to be transformed into hummus, salads, ferments and krauts, roasts, pizza toppings and even cakes. The River Cottage beetroot brownie is legendary.

Sourcing the best produce

Whether you are reaping the rewards of your own kitchen garden, making the most of a gifted glut or buying produce, provenance is key. You want the freshest, best, pesticide-free fruit and veg that are seasonally and locally available. This is as pertinent if you are preserving produce as it is if you're eating it straight away.

The easiest way to know where your fruit and veg come from, and the soil they have been produced in, is to grow them yourself if you can. Supermarkets are getting better at responsible sourcing and transparency with their customers but there is still much work to be done in this area.

For the veg you can't grow (and for some that's all of your veg), the best options are to head to your nearest farm shop or independent food store, sign up for a veg box scheme or keep an eye out for a farmers' market or honesty box. These are some of the best (and most enjoyable) ways to access fresh, seasonal ingredients and support the local producers who work so hard to provide them.

Then, of course, there is food for free. What could be more satisfying than sourcing food in the wild? The spring hedgerow has rich pickings, like nettles and Alexanders, followed by the elderflowers, but the busiest time for the enthusiastic forager is surely from early September for a couple of months. Gathering a wild harvest at this time is a good way to gently start preparations for the festive season while still enjoying autumn's precious weeks of mellow fruitfulness.

As an entire month, October is my favourite – the burnished landscape, ribbons of wood smoke over roof tops and pots of rooty soups and stews blipping away on the stove. It's the best time to get out blackberrying and sloe-picking too. I am always tempted to return with a stepladder but I leave the highest, plumpest berries for the birds.

Good foragers follow a clear code of conduct that focuses on the conservation and protection of wildlife and the natural world. This includes picking from a good crop not a sparse one, only taking a little of something, never pulling up whole plants, and only cutting a few leaves or taking fruit that leaves the plant to thrive… and not trespassing.

These wild ingredients will only remain free and abundant if we gather them responsibly. If not, then we risk losing species and reducing biodiversity with long-lasting effects on our environment. There never seems to be any fear we will run out of blackberries though. The hedgerows in the lanes and bordering River Cottage are laden with them from August to October.

I dream of verbena

Fruits and vegetables are not the only home-grown harvests that get preserved with Christmas in mind. One of my favourites is a herb – the aromatic arrow-headed leaf, lemon verbena. The Latin name is Aloysia Citrodora – and what's not to adore?

With notes of citrus zest, ginger and bay, it makes the most delicious tisane, fully flavoured from just 5 or 6 fresh leaves steeped in a mug of boiling water. Put a lid on that, and give it at least 3 minutes, for full intensity. We drink it several times a week from June through to October, when the leaves are abundant.

And so vigorous and abundant is our (now 10-year-old) shrub, that even after that relentless summer and autumn pillaging, it is still heaving with leaves (and often flowers too) by late autumn. I preserve them in the simplest possible way – by drying them. Some Sunday in November I will massively prune the bush, tie the leaf-laden branches together in bunches and hang them inside the kitchen window, where sunlight and the heat of the Esse (the thinking person's Aga) will make short work of drying them to curled and rustling stability.

Even dried to a crisp, the leaves are robust enough to stay mainly whole, as I strip them from branch and twig, pile them into jars, tamping them down as I go to just-short-of-crushing point. Like this, they keep for ages. I know from retrieving a lost jar at the back of the larder shelf, that even after 3 years their aromatic intensity is still intact, ready to be released by boiling water. As with the fresh leaves, half a dozen dried leaves does the job.

As well as making a lovely tisane, lemon verbena is a versatile herb, not deployed often enough in our kitchens. It is brilliant added to a compote of Bramley apples (a dozen dried leaves to a kilo of apples) and makes the gorgeous Bramley apple festive fumble on page 112 even more celebratory. I also use it with fish, where that sophisticated blend of bay, citrus and ginger notes works very well indeed.

There's one more thing I really love to do at Christmas with my hefty harvest of dried verbena leaves – and that's to give them away. A well-stuffed jam jar of leaves will be good for dozens of infusions. Of course, it's a good idea to know that the recipient isn't already in possession of a productive lemon verbena plant themselves. But on receipt of such a delightfully fragrant and versatile gift, it's a pretty sure bet they soon will be. And within a few years, they will be spreading the verbena love themselves, participating in an exponential outpouring of aromatic joy. **Hugh**

Preserving

Naturally, I embrace the River Cottage philosophy of SLOW food – seasonal, local, organic and wild. Inherent in this approach is also the principle of wasting nothing: every glut or surfeit of produce is an opportunity, a harvest waiting to be transformed into jams, pickles, drinks and ferments, creating an enviable winter supply.

While I am always on the lookout for a preserving opportunity, the real action starts in late spring and the most bountiful months are from early summer to the depths of autumn. The arrival of the first runner beans means an early batch of pickle. When a friend gives me a tray of pink cherries from her tree, we eat handfuls of them and the rest I plunge into a large jar of vodka, sugar and bay leaves and label 'Do NOT touch till December!' My jam efforts start with June strawberries and end with September damsons, each ingredient saved and celebrated in some way for the colder months ahead.

As well as making a fantastic selection of preserves for your own celebrations, it is a great idea to make extra to share in hampers, stuff into stockings or give as individual presents. I can think of few things better to give or receive than a lovingly made, edible treat. Recipes can be adapted for specific dietary needs or personal tastes and a few jars or bottles kept in reserve in case there is somebody you have forgotten.

Jam The season starts for jam makers with strawberries and moves on to soft fruits including cherries, gooseberries, loganberries, mulberries and black-, red- and white currants. Around July or August the raspberries appear and many varieties overlap with the autumn arrival of orchard fruits – plums, damsons, medlars, apples, pears and the ancient quince. Catch them while you can and make as much jam, curd and jelly as you have the energy for. I always make a couple of traditional preserves as well as experimenting with herb, spice or alcohol additions to time-honoured recipes. If you are intending to keep them for Christmas, consider the flavours that will appeal at that time. You may want to conjure a memory of summer with strawberry and basil jam, or you may fancy something richer and spiced, like a clove-scented crab apple jelly.

Pickles A spoonful of home-made chutney, pickle, ketchup or relish will elevate many a meal and can be endlessly useful for those seasonal leftovers. A cold buffet in our house is an excuse to crack open the malty chutneys, spicy relishes and fruity jellies. The infamous glutney often makes an appearance too. It is exactly what it says on the label, a chutney made from a glut (or gluts). The formula adapts with the seasons and works with almost any veg (and fruit) that you can think of. I have created the ultimate Christmassy version (see page 32).

Booze Christmas traditions are awash with alcohol from champagne corks popping to spiced wine mulling on the stove, and sticky sweet liqueurs we probably wouldn't touch at any other time of the year. We stock up the drinks cabinet, decant the port and leave Father Christmas a tipple for his trouble. It's particularly pleasing if some of your libations have been made by your own hand. I am a great fan of home-steeping, a lazily effective way of turning wild fruits, soft fruits or citrus into treats and gifts. I have included several recipes in this book for you to try. All you need is a bottle of spirit (most commonly gin or vodka), a couple of handfuls of fruit, a smattering of herbs or spices, some sugar... and time. In recent years sloe gin has become ubiquitous but there are so many other recipes to explore. The hardest part of the process is the wait as the combined ingredients work their magic. Home-steeping requires at least 3 months and ideally a year or more maturation; in most cases the longer the wait, the more your patience will be rewarded.

Non-alcoholic drinks Habits are changing and more people are drinking less, if at all, but the festive season can be a tough time to avoid booze. This is a wonderful opportunity to experiment with traditional home-made methods for syrups, cordials and non-alcoholic fermented drinks.

Syrups and cordials There is some debate about the difference between a syrup and a cordial. They are both an extract of an ingredient, usually a fruit, combined with a water and sugar base. The flavour is achieved by either simmering all the components together and creating a purée from the fruit (usually termed a syrup), or boiling the sugar and water and then infusing the key ingredient (more often called a cordial). Whatever term or technique you use, these are quick and easy consumable gifts to make, without the artificial additives or excessive sugar of mass-produced versions. I always make a ginger syrup at Christmas (by dissolving 250g sugar in 200ml water, adding 250g roughly chopped ginger and simmering for 15 minutes then leaving to steep off the heat for a couple of hours before straining). The resulting syrup works just as well diluted with hot water as it does in soft drinks or alcohol. You can store cordials and syrups in sterilised bottles for around a month in the fridge or freeze them in ice-cube trays. Or, for a longer life, add citric acid.

Fermented drinks An ancient practice, fermentation has exploded back onto the food and drink scene in recent years. It combines a passion for preserving with a focus on well-being and health because beneficial live bacteria are often involved. Kombucha and Jun drinks need a SCOBY (symbiotic culture of bacteria and yeast). These drinks are pleasingly tart, interestingly flavoured, and much lower in sugar (or calories) than soft drinks and even fruit juice. They lend themselves to great non-alcohol cocktails too. For this reason, they are an excellent festive option for adults who are planning a no- or low-alcohol Christmas. Hugh talks more about this on page 28.

Preserving kit

Preserving pan One of these large, robust pans is incredibly useful if you plan to make jam or chutney regularly. Not only does it allow you to cook a good quantity, but the design of the pan and the way the heat disperses through it guards against sticking and burning on the base – a risk when making jam in standard saucepans. A preserving pan has slanted sides and ample depth for safely cooking boiling, bubbling, sticky liquid.

Jam jars Save these throughout the year, or buy from your local hardware store or online. To sterilise them before potting, wash them thoroughly in hot, soapy water, dry them well and then place in a low oven (120°C/Fan 110°C/Gas ½) for 20 minutes (or put them through a hot dishwasher cycle). Metal lids can be sterilised in the same way but rubber seals can crack in the oven so are better submerged in a bowl of just-boiled water. Put hot jam or chutney into your jars while they are still warm and seal straight away.

Kilner jars A range of Kilner jars of different sizes – from 500ml to 1.5 litres – is useful for home-steeping fruit recipes like sloe gin (page 106) and cherry vodka (page 49). Sterilise the jars and lids by washing them in hot, soapy water, rinsing well then putting in a low oven (at 120°C/Fan 110°C/Gas ½) for 20 minutes to dry out then leave to cool before filling.

Cook's thermometer While not essential, it is handy to have one of these to check your preserves are at setting point. A digital thermometer is brilliant for this and makes a great cook's tool for many other things, like judging roast meat.

Jelly bag This purpose-made item is useful for straining the precious liquid from the fruit when you are making jellies, though you can use a muslin cloth instead. Muslin and jelly bags can be cleaned for reuse – by boiling them or putting in a hot laundry wash.

Wide-based metal funnel For easy pouring of lava-hot preserves into jars, one of these is highly recommended.

The gutsy gift that keeps on giving

As you may already know, I'm a bit of a kombucha evangelist. I think this Far Eastern fermented tea, swimming and brimming with beneficial bacteria, is the most brilliant 'functional drink'. I've only known kombucha for a few years, but it's so much a part of my life now that I can't imagine being without it.

For me, despite it being 'good for you', helping us to maintain and develop a healthily diverse gut biome, drinking it is not in any way a virtuous chore; it's a genuine pleasure. The light tartness and subtle sparkle make it a pleasingly slow drink; and because it's not overly gluggable, it's not over too quickly either. And, of course, it can be flavoured with all kinds of diverting aromatics, including my beloved lemon verbena (see page 24).

I drink kombucha most days. And on some of those days I am drinking it, in part, because I am *not* drinking wine – or any other alcohol. This is something I attempt on a minimum of 2 days, and ideally 4 days, per week. And it is kombucha that gets me (and my wife) past the 'chopping board hump'. That's the moment when, customarily, supper prep starts, and the knife hand likes to be in easy reach of a glass of something cold and uplifting. And it turns out that is a job kombucha can do.

Impressively, kombucha can also deliver for the 'pre-supper pause', when the second glass (okay sometimes third) is gratefully enjoyed on the sofa, perhaps in front of the fire, before we gather for the family feud. I mean food. It's quite a tribute to kombucha that it can support us through these critical moments of the late day, which traditionally we have asked wine to help us with. And I'm eternally (and internally) grateful.

We try to take a proper break over Christmas and New Year, with at least a week or ten days of not much that could reasonably be described as work. And with all the festive food and party mood that's buzzing around the house, it can be a little more challenging than usual to squeeze in some alcohol-free days, and to navigate those crucial moments of expectation.

So that's when I ask kombucha to up its game, participating in a number of seasonally-oriented and celebratory dry cocktails. I tend to avoid the word 'mocktails'; too often with such concoctions of fruit juices and cordials it's your tastebuds that are mocked – and your guts sugar-rushed. Kombucha on the other hand lends itself brilliantly to mixological prestidigitation – as you will see from my trio of festive kombocktails on pages 194–5.

But, of course, kombucha isn't just for Christmas, it's for life! And unlike the proverbial puppy, you can give a 'pet SCOBY' away as a present without too much weighing on your conscience. This 'Symbiotic Culture of Bacteria and Yeast' is the kombucha equivalent of the sourdough starter. And in much the same way, a chunk of your lively SCOBY may be very gratefully received as a gift.

And then again, it may not – but therein lies the art of Christmas giving. It is in itself a bit of festive fun to intuit which of your friends has the interest, inclination and, frankly, the caring qualities, to take responsibility for a SCOBY and raise a weekly batch of 'buch. And if you get it wrong, well, a dead SCOBY is a shame, but it's better than a dead Scooby Doo.

So, for me a SCOBY-to-go is another great 'jam jar' Christmas present. In the few weeks before Christmas I can usually separate and nurture enough of my SCOBY to put together 3 or 4 jars for gifting. The struggle this year, I suspect, will be to find 3 or 4 more friends who look like they have the tenacity to succeed in kombucha culture. I have them ear-marked, but I sense I may be scraping the barrel.

Frankly, they should be grateful they are not getting frogspawn. That's the Easter jam jar present, of course. Not unlike a SCOBY, as it happens, but with added black dots... Both blobs are primed to perform one of life's little miracles, and I for one plan to keep on marvelling at them. **Hugh**

Marrow & Chilli Relish

For some people, marrows generate the heart-sinking feeling that they didn't catch a good courgette in time. Not me. I have a passion for them, and also for the roadside honesty boxes where you often find them. One happy day, driving down a Cornish lane with a friend, children and several surfboards, I screeched to a halt outside a farm honesty stand to buy eggs, honey and a pot of marrow relish. It was the best I had ever eaten and I vowed to create my own version. This is it. Never wonder what to do with a marrow again. The relish also works well with courgettes, of course. Make it when they are in season, around 4 months ahead of Christmas.

Makes 4–5 x 250ml jars

1kg marrow
2 tbsp salt
2 onions, finely chopped
2 garlic cloves, crushed
1 fresh or dried red chilli, deseeded
   and finely chopped
1 tbsp rapeseed oil
1 tbsp yellow mustard seeds

1 tbsp cumin seeds
200ml white wine vinegar or
   cider vinegar
150g granulated sugar

You will also need:
A preserving pan (or similar)
4–5 sterilised 250ml jars

Peel, deseed and chop your marrow. Place in a bowl, sprinkle with the salt and give everything a good stir. Tip the marrow into a colander placed over another bowl, cover and leave for a few hours to draw out excess water.

Rinse the marrow with cold water and set aside to drain. In a food processor, blitz the onions, garlic and chilli together to form a chunky paste. Set aside.

Heat the oil in a frying pan. Add the mustard and cumin seeds, toss well and fry for 1–2 minutes until they start to pop. Stir in the onion paste and fry for a few minutes to drive off any excess liquid; don't let it burn.

Pour the vinegar into a preserving pan and add the sugar and spiced onion paste. Now add the marrow and give everything a good stir. Bring almost to the boil, then turn the heat down to low. Leave to simmer for 40 minutes until the marrow is soft, stirring occasionally.

If you prefer a less chunky relish (as I do), blitz briefly in a food processor or using a hand blender. Spoon the warm relish into sterilised jars (see page 27) and seal with vinegar-proof lids. Store in a cool, dark cupboard. Refrigerate after opening and use within a couple of months.

Christmas Glutney

A chutney by any other name, this is a version of Hugh's glutney recipe, ideal for transforming a glut of veg. It is a River Cottage staple, whether made with an early-summer harvest of green beans and courgettes, late-summer tomatoes and plums for a fruity number, or late-autumn robust veg with festive spices (as I use here). Feel free to adapt the recipe – as long as you keep to the quantities you can swap any of the ingredients out for preferred alternatives. The chopping takes time but once everything is in the pan it will blip away happily, filling the kitchen with the fizzy scent of vinegar for a couple of hours. Make it at least 8 weeks before Christmas.

Makes 10 x 250ml jars
1kg pumpkin or squash
500g onions, finely chopped
750g pears
750g quince
500g sultanas
500g light brown sugar
700ml cider vinegar or white wine vinegar
2 tsp dried chilli flakes (optional)

For the spice bag:
2 cinnamon sticks
2 star anise
50g fresh ginger, roughly chopped

You will also need:
A square of muslin, for the spice bag
A preserving pan (or similar)
10 sterilised 250ml jars

To make the spice bag, place the cinnamon sticks, star anise and chopped ginger in the centre of the muslin square. Gather the corners and tie with string. Now tie to the handle of your preserving pan so the bag will be immersed in the mixture (or it can simply be put straight into the pan).

Peel, deseed and dice the pumpkin or squash and put into the preserving pan with the onions. Peel, core and dice the pears and quince and tip into the pan. Add all the other ingredients and bring gently to the boil, giving an occasional stir. Turn the heat down to a simmer and leave to cook gently, uncovered, for 3 hours. During this time stir regularly to stop it burning.

Once the liquid has reduced and the chutney is glossy and thick, it should be ready to jar up. To check it is, draw a wooden spoon through the middle of the chutney to create a parting – it should be a few seconds before it closes over and covers the base of the pan again. Take out the spice bag. Spoon the warm glutney into sterilised jars and push down to make sure there are no air pockets. Seal with vinegar-proof lids. Store in a cool, dark place for a couple of months before opening. Eat within a year or so.

Damson & Star Anise Jam

Sadly, I do not have a damson tree. But a couple of generous local friends do. Each summer, I watch the plump fruits begin to drop and bounce across the lane, waiting impatiently for the invitation to pick them. Eating the fruit raw is a taste roulette of sweet and sour – but they always make the most fabulous preserves. This jam is an excellent Christmas gift for any damson addict who, like me, does not have their own harvest to revel in.

Plums make a good alternative to damsons, although they can take longer to cook and are often sweeter, so you may want to adjust the sugar (only by 50g). You could also swap the star anise for a cinnamon stick.

Makes 4–5 x 250ml jars
1kg damsons
3 star anise
Juice of 2 lemons
600g granulated sugar

You will also need:
A preserving pan (or similar)
4–5 sterilised 250ml jars

Cut a slit in each damson and count them so you know how many stones you will need to fish out with a slotted spoon at the end of the process. It will save a lot of time later! Chill a plate in the freezer (unless you have a digital or jam thermometer to check the set).

Put the damsons, star anise, 100ml water and the lemon juice into your preserving pan and bring to a simmer, stirring regularly to make sure the fruit doesn't catch. Once the fruit has begun to soften, after 10 minutes or so, add the sugar. Give everything a good stir and turn the heat up to dissolve the sugar and get your jam to boiling point. Keep it at a rolling boil for 15 minutes before checking that it is ready.

If you're using a cook's thermometer to test the jam, it should register 105°C. Alternatively, as the jam starts to thicken, carefully take a teaspoonful of it and place on the chilled plate. Push with your finger. If it begins to wrinkle then you have reached the right set. If not, continue to boil the jam for another 10 minutes or so and test it again. (It may take up to 30 minutes in total, depending on the ripeness of your damsons.)

When the jam is ready, take the pan off the heat and fish out the star anise and damson stones with a slotted spoon. Carefully pot the jam in sterilised jars. Store in a cool, dark cupboard and refrigerate after opening.

For me, a bit of duck or goose at Christmas is a must – the meat is rich and rewarding and just feels right for a celebration. So, if I'm not having a lovely roast goose (see page 259) on Christmas day, then I will at some point pop open a jar of confit duck legs, prepared well in advance. After cooking them, you can keep them in the fridge, completely covered in goose or pork fat (lard), for up to 3 months – either set by for your own celebrations or as a special foodie gift.

The meat is incredibly tender and tastes wonderful crisped up in the oven, served with simply cooked Puy lentils and a zesty, crunchy winter salad (like the red cabbage, carrot and clementine salad on page 221). A dab of glutney (page 32) doesn't go amiss either.

You can buy free-range and organic duck legs, or whole ducks and remove the legs for confit. Roasting the rest of the birds whole is a lovely treat, and you can save the fat for the confit – though you'll probably need some in addition. Jars of goose fat are easy to buy, or ask your butcher for some spare free-range pork fat to render at home.

One confit duck leg is a very generous serving as a main course, and if you shred the meat off the bone, it will do two people nicely as a starter. **Hugh**

Confit of Duck Legs

Serves 4 as a main, 6–8 as a starter

4 free-range duck legs (with as much fat as possible)

Finely grated zest of 1 orange
4–6 large garlic cloves, peeled

For the seasoning paste:
40g flaky sea salt
1 good tsp freshly ground black pepper
A few sprigs of thyme or rosemary, leaves picked
4 or 5 bay leaves, shredded
1 star anise, ground

For the confit:
About 600ml rendered duck or goose fat (or pork fat, or a mix)

You will also need:
A 1.5 litre Kilner jar (or lidded plastic container with a similar capacity)

For the seasoning paste, using a pestle and mortar, crush all the ingredients together, including the orange zest and garlic, to form a rough paste.

Rub this aromatic paste thoroughly into the skin and meat of your duck legs. Put them into a roomy container, put the lid on and leave in the fridge for about 48 hours, giving the duck legs another massage with the salty mixture after 24 hours.

When you're ready to cook the duck legs, preheat the oven to 120°C/Fan 110°C/Gas ½. Take the duck legs from the fridge, scrape off the seasoning paste and set it aside. Heat a little duck or goose fat in a heavy-based pan over a medium heat. Add the legs, skin side down, and brown thoroughly, then turn and repeat on the other side.

Transfer the duck legs to a small ovenproof dish in which they fit snugly. Add the fat from the frying pan and the reserved seasoning paste and then pour on enough rendered duck or goose fat to cover (or almost cover) the meat. Place in the oven and cook for at least 2½ hours, until the meat is almost falling from the bone. If the legs are not quite covered by the fat, turn them carefully a few times during cooking. Remove from the oven and leave to cool.

You've got two options now: either leave the legs smeared with some of the set fat and store them in a covered container in the fridge (for up to 2 weeks) or, if you want to keep them for longer or turn them into a gift, you can completely submerge them in fat. For the second option, pack the duck legs snugly into a large Kilner jar (or a plastic tub with a lid) and pour over enough warm duck or goose fat (or pork fat) to completely cover the meat and seal it from contact with the air. Leave until the legs are cold and the fat is set, then cover with the lid. Preserved like this, the confit will keep for at least 3 months in the fridge.

When you are ready to serve the confit, preheat the oven to 230°C/Fan 210°C/Gas 8. Lift the duck legs from their container and scrape off most of the fat (save it for roasting spuds). Now lay the duck legs skin side down in a roasting tray and place in the hot oven for 5 minutes. Drain off the melted fat, turn the legs skin side up and return to the oven for 8–10 minutes until piping hot and the skin is crisp.

For a main course, serve each person a hot duck leg with warm lentils and a crunchy sharp salad. Or to serve 6–8 as a starter, shred the meat and pile over or beside lentils and salad.

Stir-up Sunday

Traditionally, the day to make your Christmas pudding, Stir-up Sunday is rooted in both the church calendar and Victorian custom. It refers to the custom of stirring the pudding mixture – from east to west to signify the journey of the Three Kings. For some years, the tradition all but disappeared and shop-bought puddings and jarred mincemeat became the norm. But recently Stir-up Sunday has had a resurgence and regained its position in the cook's calendar. The exact date changes each year but is around 22 November, falling on the last Sunday before Advent.

Stir-up Sunday is the perfect opportunity to make the Christmas angel trilogy of pudding, cake and mincemeat before the season takes over. At home we have always been a family to stir the pudding because we love an occasion. At River Cottage Stir-up activities take an entire weekend and the kitchen is filled with the intoxicating scent of spices, citrus and brandy. Hugh has created the ultimate Christmas pudding recipe for this book (overleaf).

I love Christmas pudding, and I reckon I always will. But the kind of Christmas pudding that I love best has evolved a bit down the years. These days I like something a little lighter and zestier than the classic black cannonball, and this recipe, which we like to demonstrate on one of our Stir-up Sunday Christmas courses, is fresh from my latest set of tweaks. The citrus zest and apple give it a lovely lift, and the grated roots add a natural lightness. But rest assured, it's still a gloriously fruity and boozy treat. Make it on Stir-up Sunday... or around a month before Christmas. **Hugh**

Christmas Pudding

Serves 8–10; 1 large or 2 smaller puds

For the booze-soaked fruit:

*100g pitted prunes, or unsulphured
   dried apricots, roughly chopped*
*10g dried apples or pears, roughly
   chopped*
50g currants
100g raisins
*50g natural glacé cherries, halved,
   or dried cherries*
*75g preserved stem ginger, chopped,
   plus a little of the syrup from the jar*
30g candied orange peel
15g candied lemon peel
50g whole almonds, roughly chopped
50g pumpkin seeds
100ml dry cider
*150ml cider brandy, brandy or rum,
   plus extra to 'feed' the pudding for
   longer storage, and to flame it
   for serving*

For the pudding:

*100g self-raising wholemeal flour
   (or fine wholemeal flour plus
   2 tsp baking powder)*
1 tsp ground cinnamon
1 tsp ground mixed spice
1 tsp ground ginger
½ tsp ground allspice
*150g shredded beef suet or
   grated cold butter*
75g wholemeal breadcrumbs
50g dark muscovado sugar
2 medium eggs
50g black treacle
2 pinches of sea salt
Finely grated zest of 1 orange
1 eating apple, grated
100g grated parsnip
Butter to grease the basin

You will also need:

*A 2.25 litre pudding basin
   (or 2 x 1.1 litre basins)*

To prepare the booze-soaked fruit, put all the ingredients into a large bowl, stir to combine, then cover and leave to soak overnight or, better still, for 24 hours, with a couple of good stirs.

The next day, sift the flour, baking powder if using, and spices into a large mixing bowl. Rub in the suet or butter with your fingertips, then stir in the breadcrumbs and sugar. Beat in the eggs, then add the booze-soaked fruit and all the remaining pudding ingredients and combine thoroughly. Use to fill a lightly buttered 2.25 litre pudding basin or two 1.1 litre basins.

Cover the basin with a layer of greased greaseproof paper and then a layer of foil, both pleated in the middle to allow for expansion. Tie in place with string around the rim, leaving an extra length as a handle. Lower the basin into a large saucepan (or two medium pans if you are making two puddings) and pour in enough boiling water to come halfway up the sides. Put the lid on and bring the boil, then lower the heat and simmer for 3 hours, topping up the water as necessary; do not let the pan boil dry.

Lift out the basin and set aside to allow the pudding to cool. Once cold, replace the greaseproof and foil with fresh coverings of the same. Store in a cool larder or cupboard for up to 4 weeks. If you want to keep the pudding (or one of them) for longer, you will need to 'feed' it with brandy or rum. A few days after cooking, prick the surface of the pud with a fork or skewer and pour over 3 tbsp of your chosen spirit. Re-cover the pud and leave it in a cool dark place for up to a year.

On Christmas day, you will need to steam the pudding(s) for a further 1½–2 hours, depending on size. Discard the paper and foil covers. Cut a circle of greaseproof paper to lay on top of the pudding and a second, twice the size, to go over the basin with a pleat in the middle. Cover with a piece of pleated foil, secure around the basin rim with string and then create a string handle. Steam in a covered saucepan half-filled with boiling water (as above), regularly topping up the water.

Lift out the basin and turn the pudding out onto a warmed plate. Flame with warmed brandy and serve with brandy sauce or custard. Any leftovers can be fried in butter, stirred into ice cream or added to the base of a trifle.

Lucy's brandy sauce

A classic, luxurious accompaniment to the Christmas pudding, make this on the day, or on Christmas Eve (keep the surface closely covered with baking paper to prevent a skin forming). Melt 50g butter in a saucepan over a medium heat. Stir in 50g plain flour and cook, stirring, for a couple of minutes. Slowly pour in 600ml milk and bring to the boil, stirring constantly, then lower the heat to a simmer and cook gently for 10 minutes. Stir in 30–50g sugar and 4–6 tbsp brandy. Pour into a jug to serve.

Mincemeat

One of Hugh's first festive recipes in the early days of River Cottage was mincemeat made with beef. He embraced its true origins – beef or lamb fermented with dried fruits, spices and alcohol. While it was well received, we tend to stick to the popular version nowadays – using different alcohols, dried fruits and suet or butter. Or a vegan version with no suet at all, but plumped up with grated or chopped fruit like apples, pears or plums instead. As well as mince pies, this quintessential festive preserve can be added to tarts and strudels, stuffed into baked apples or swirled through ice cream. Make it up to 6 months ahead of Christmas.

Makes 4 x 250ml jars

250g currants
250g raisins
175g dried sour cherries
75g candied orange peel
25g candied grapefruit or lemon peel
1 Bramley apple, peeled, cored
   and grated
125g beef suet or butter
50g chopped almonds

225g light muscovado sugar
½ tsp ground cinnamon
1 tsp ground mixed spice
Finely grated zest of 1 lemon
200ml cider brandy

You will also need:
4 sterilised 250ml jars

Put all the ingredients except the brandy into a saucepan and heat gently for 10 minutes. Remove from the heat and allow to cool, stirring occasionally. Once cooled, stir in the brandy.

Pack the mincemeat into sterilised jars. It will keep for at least 6 months in a cool store cupboard, if not until the next Christmas.

Individual mince pies
Grease a shallow 12-hollow individual tart tray. Prepare the sweet pastry recipe on page 300 (you'll have more than you need if you roll it thinly, so freeze the rest to make more mince pies another day). Roll the pastry out to a 5mm thickness (or thinner if you dare) and cut 12 circles, about 8cm in diameter. Use to line the tart tray and fill with mincemeat. Cut another 12 circles, 7cm in diameter, for the lids. Brush the pastry edges with a little water, then position the lids and press the edges together to seal. Cut a couple of slits in each pie, brush with beaten egg yolk and bake in the oven preheated to 180°C/Fan 160°C/Gas 4 for 20 minutes. Serve warm, dusted with icing sugar.

Quincemas Cake

In the sixteenth century, Christmas cake was served on Twelfth Night, the crowning finale to many days of feasting – until Cromwell and the Puritans banned it, and the lengthy celebrations, in disgust. Christmas Day was still an approved feast day, however, so the celebration cake moved to that day and those with money showed off and covered theirs in marzipan.

With all this in mind, I would like to make a case for not having Christmas cake on the day itself. I think it is wasted if it vies for attention with the pudding, mince pies and other sweet treats that may be lined up for the big day. Instead, I recommend making this version on an early November rainy afternoon, when apples and quince are at their finest. Well wrapped in brown paper and stored in a tin, it will just need the occasional alcohol feed before you top it with candied nuts and tuck into it from around the beginning of December. Ideal to have on standby when someone pops round, it's also great to carry a wedge in your pocket as sustenance on a long walk.

Serves 10–12

150g currants
150g sultanas
150g raisins
100g unsulphured dried apricots
50g chopped candied grapefruit peel (page 102) or mixed peel or glacé cherries
1 tbsp sloe gin (page 106) or brandy, plus extra to 'feed' the cake
Grated zest and juice of 1 lemon
125g wholemeal flour
A small pinch of salt
½ tsp ground mixed spice
½ tsp ground cinnamon
½ tsp ground ginger
125g unsalted butter, softened, plus extra to grease the tin

100g soft brown sugar
3 medium eggs
1 tbsp maple syrup
50g walnuts, roughly chopped
1 large quince (or 1 small quince and 1 small apple), cored and grated

To decorate (optional):
A few handfuls of nuts, such as walnuts, hazelnuts and almonds
3 tbsp apricot jam or crab apple jelly (or similar)

You will also need:
An 18cm round or 15cm square cake tin

Put the dried fruit and peel, alcohol, lemon zest and juice in a (heatproof) bowl and cover with foil. Either leave to soak overnight or put into a low oven, no more than 130°C/Fan 110°C/Gas ½, for 30 minutes. Take the foil off when the fruit comes out of the oven and leave to cool.

Lightly grease your cake tin and line with baking paper – cut a circle for the base and a strip to go around the side. This cake has a lengthy baking time, so to protect it from drying out, wrap a band of brown paper around the outside of the tin. It needs to be twice the depth of the tin so it extends above the rim.

Turn the oven to 160°C/Fan 140°C/Gas 3. Sift the flour, salt, mixed spice, cinnamon and ginger into a bowl and set aside.

Using an electric mixer (or by hand), beat the butter until soft, then add the sugar and beat together until creamy. Add 1 egg together with a spoonful of the flour and spice mix, and beat until just incorporated. Repeat with the remaining eggs, adding them one at a time, then beat in the maple syrup.

Fold the rest of the spiced flour into the mixture, then stir in the dried fruit mix, walnuts, grated quince (and apple if using).

Spoon the mixture into the tin, making a dip in the centre to stop the middle doming up. Loosely cover the tin with a piece of foil to protect the cake. Bake in the oven for around 2 hours. To check that the cake is ready, insert a skewer in the middle – it should come out clean.

Leave the cake to cool in the tin, then remove and peel away the lining paper. Wrap it, like a present, in baking paper and store in a tin until you are ready to decorate or serve it. It will store for at least 8 weeks before eating. In the meantime, you can feed it weekly with your chosen booze. Unwrap the cake, turn it upside down and pierce the base, using your skewer. Pour the booze onto a teaspoon and carefully drip it into the holes. Make sure the cake is tightly wrapped and returned to the tin.

This cake works without any decoration, or with marzipan or datezipan (page 167) and royal icing layers, but my favourite way to finish it is with a generous topping of glazed nuts – a handful each of walnuts, hazelnuts and almonds works well.

Put the 3 tbsp of your chosen jam or jelly in a pan with 1 tbsp or so of water. Whisk together and heat gently until you have a smooth, liquid consistency. Apply this glaze to the top of the cake using a pastry brush. Arrange the nuts (I cram them!) over the surface and then carefully and liberally paint them with the glaze and leave to set.

Cherry Vodka

Any cherry works in this recipe but the ideal varieties are the sourer or wild ones. Every year my pal Ros attempts to outsmart the birds to pick me a tray of cherries from her tree. Once you have fresh cherries it is hard not to absent-mindedly eat your way through the entire haul but I promise you this is worth the sacrifice of instant gratification. I may throw a handful of cherries into a clafoutis or an almond heavy cake but I always save enough for this recipe, which I make as soon as the cherries are ripe and ready.

The result is a stunning pink vodka that works equally as an aperitif or an after-dinner digestif. Include a cherry in the glass for extra house points, and save some to add a Danish twist to the rice pudding on page 162.

Makes about 600ml

400g ripe, fresh cherries
2 tbsp caster sugar
2 bay leaves or a few sage leaves
5 peppercorns (optional)
750ml bottle vodka

You will also need:
A sterilised 1 litre Kilner jar
A sterilised 750ml bottle
A sterilised 250ml jar

Wash the cherries and make a deep slit in each, or extract the stones. Put the cherries into your 1 litre Kilner jar with the sugar and your chosen herbs/spices and pour on the vodka. Give everything a good stir and store the jar in a cool, dark spot.

Over the next 10 days or so, check the jar and shake every few days to make sure the sugar has dissolved.

Leave to steep for at least 3 months before decanting the vodka into a bottle. Pack the cherries and bay leaves into a jar with just enough of the vodka to cover them and store in the cupboard or fridge.

Cherry syrup

For this non-alcoholic variation, de-stone the cherries and put them into a pan with 3 tbsp granulated sugar and a bay leaf. Pour in 500ml water and simmer gently until the cherries are soft. Take off the heat, remove the bay leaf and blitz. Pass the mixture through a sieve for a smoother result and then freeze in ice-cube trays. Once they are frozen, pop the cubes out of the tray and store in a marked container in the freezer ready for Christmas.

Rumtopf

The fruit-picker's perk, rumtopf, is a deliciously unusual way to capitalise on gluts of seasonal fruits. Both a compote and an alcoholic drink, it requires very little attention yet gives you a spectacular festive reward. The process follows the ripening of different fruits from the beginning of the summer, with each glut added to the pot as it matures. Inspired by Pam 'The Jam' Corbin and her collection of rumtopf pots, I begin making mine around 6 months ahead of Christmas, at the summer solstice, adding to it throughout the soft-fruit season before sharing it as part of the winter solstice celebration in December.

You can enjoy the soaked fruits with ice cream, yoghurt, pancakes or, traditionally, as a topping for baked apples. The boozy, fruity juices make a great base for cocktails or just a warming glug around the solstice fire. Avoid adding the following fruits: bananas (unsuitable texture), gooseberries (may be too sharp), apples (can develop a strange texture) and blackberries (can be too bitter and affect the colour).

You can either source traditional rumtopf jars on the internet specifically for this recipe or use a large Kilner jar (with or without a tap), which will have other uses. The container must be large enough to contain several kilos of fruit, plus at least 1 litre rum, and to keep the fruit submerged.

Makes a 1.5 litre jar
Fruit, such as strawberries, cherries,
   currants, raspberries, plums
   and pears
Granulated sugar
Rum (this is authentic, but you can
   use vodka or gin instead)
Whole spices, such as cinnamon,
   star anise or cloves (optional)

You will also need:
A large earthenware pot,
   at least 3 litre capacity, with
   a secure tight-fitting lid

All fruit that goes into a rumtopf should be washed. Don't use bruised or mouldy fruit. Remove hulls, stones, stems and leaves. Skin plums (submerge them first in boiling water and leave to dry before skinning), and peel pears. Leave small fruit such as strawberries whole, but cut larger fruit into bite-size pieces.

Start off your rumtopf with 500g of your chosen prepared fruit and 250g granulated sugar. Put these into your jar, leave to sit for an hour, then add 750ml of your chosen alcohol, making sure it covers the fruit. Put the lid on the jar and store it somewhere dark and cool to ferment. Check on it every so often to make sure the fruit is still submerged and there are no signs of mould.

Over the coming weeks and months, you can add fruit whenever you want to. With each 500g fruit add up to 125g sugar (only half the sugar of the first batch, which is larger to kick-start fermentation). You may find you only need add around 50g sugar, so give it a taste before you add. Top up with rum or your chosen spirit but do not stir.

After the final fruit addition you can tuck in some whole spices if you like. Leave the rumtopf to stand for at least 6 weeks after your final fruit layer.

When you're ready to serve, give it a good stir, making sure you combine the bottom layers. It takes a concerted effort to get to the end of this preserve over the festive season unless you are sharing it with a big group. You could decant some into sterilised jam jars as gifts. It will last for 6–12 months.

I have several blackcurrant bushes in my garden – and I look forward to their high-summer glut with anticipation each year. This home-made blackcurrant liqueur uses them in abundance. If you don't grow your own, a pick-your-own farm is a great place to get them at a good price. You can make this with defrosted frozen blackcurrants too. Serve it topped up with dry white wine to make a kir cocktail, or sparkling wine for a festive kir royale. I love to put something made from the garden in high summer into a glass on Christmas day. **Hugh**

Crème de Cassis

Makes 3 x 750ml bottles

1.5kg blackcurrants
750ml bottle fruity red wine, such as Beaujolais or Pinot Noir
About 600g granulated sugar
About 600ml vodka

You will also need:
A large jelly bag or 2 large sieves and muslin to line them
3 sterilised 750ml bottles

Put the blackcurrants and red wine into a large glass jar, or ceramic bowl or jug and leave to macerate for at least 24 hours (up to 48).

Using a blender or food processor, blitz the fruit and wine (in batches if necessary) to a rough purée. Now use a large jelly bag or line two large sieves with muslin and place each one over a large bowl. Carefully pour the blackcurrant mix into the jelly bag or muslin-lined sieves and leave to drip for several hours – ideally overnight.

Measure the strained liquor into a large saucepan. For every 100ml, add 35g sugar. Heat very gently, stirring frequently, until the sugar dissolves. You now need to cook the syrup for a couple of hours, maintaining the temperature between 70 and 80°C – use a digital probe thermometer to keep a check on it. This temperature ensures the fruit doesn't release its pectin, which could leave you with a slightly too-viscose liqueur. You might find it helpful to turn the heat off every now and again for a minute or two to keep the heat low. After about 2 hours, when the syrup is slightly reduced, take it off the heat and leave it to cool completely.

Measure the cooled blackcurrant syrup, then stir in 1 part vodka to 3 parts syrup. Decant the cassis into cold sterilised bottles. Seal, label and store in a cool, dark place for at least 3 months. Once opened, store in the fridge.

Quince Ratafia

A ratafia is a type of liqueur which differs depending on which part of the Mediterranean you are in. On drizzly, grey autumn days, I like to make a ratafia of golden sunlight to remind me of Mediterranean summers. Brandy is traditional but I stick to clear spirits like gin or vodka, so the colour of the fruit can shine through. If I lived in France, I would pick peaches or apricots from the garden and include the almondy apricot kernels too, for authenticity. Instead I go for citrus fruits, or my beloved quince, and experiment with herbs and spices.

Unlike sloe gin, this will be ready in a few months, which is excellent news for the more impatient amongst us. I make it as soon as the quince season begins, around 3 months before Christmas.

Quince ratafia works well as a long drink with tonic or soda water added, or in a cocktail, but I like it best neat, on the icy rocks, in a small vintage glass. Serve with a bowl of salted almonds to cut through the sweetness.

Makes a 750ml bottle
2 large or 3 small quince
200g granulated sugar, plus extra
  to taste if needed
2 or 3 bay leaves, 2 sprigs of lemon
  verbena, 2 cinnamon sticks or
  4 star anise, or a good thumb-sized
  piece of fresh ginger (unpeeled),
  roughly chopped
750ml bottle vodka or gin

You will also need:
A sterilised 1 litre Kilner jar
A sterilised 750ml bottle (or a few
  smaller bottles)

There is no need to peel or core the quince, just roughly chop or grate and put it into your sterilised Kilner jar. Add the sugar and herbs or spices and pour on the alcohol to cover. Give everything a good stir.

Leave to sit in a dark corner for 6 weeks or so. During this time, you can give the jar a shake when you remember to. You may also have a little taste and add 1 tbsp sugar or so if it is not sweet enough.

Strain and decant the quince ratafia, discarding the fruit. It should fill a 750ml bottle but I pour it into smaller bottles so I have a gift or two ready.

My blackberry whisky

I share Lucy's excitement for bottling the hedgerow harvest in various alcoholic guises, and my all-time favourite is one that uses probably the most abundant and easy to gather of our wild berries. I got the original recipe from the redoubtable Prue Coates, the doyenne of the farmhouse kitchen. She served me a glass of her five-year-old vintage (in her farmhouse kitchen) and I was deeply smitten.

You don't need a fancy single malt – a decent blended whisky like Famous Grouse does the job. And you can get two bottles of liqueur from one bottle of whisky by adding a hefty 2 kilos of blackberries. Ideally pick a mix of ripe, slightly under- and slightly over-ripe.

Crush the blackberries very lightly – gently squeezing a double handful at a time – as you add them to a 2 litre Kilner jar, or similar. You are not trying to make a purée, just popping a few to let the juices run, bruising a few more, but leaving most of them whole. Add 150g of sugar and that bottle of Scotch.

Keep in a dark place, and turn the jar slowly upside down and back again, once a day for the first week, once a week for the next month, and once a month for another 3 months, or so. This means a blackberry harvest from late August or early September will be ready for bottling at Christmas/New Year – a nice festive ritual. The blackberries can throw quite a bit of sediment, so it's best to strain the whole lot through a jelly bag or muslin cloth into a large jug, before pouring into 2 regular 750ml bottles. If you're a bit short, top them up with neat whisky.

As to ageing, more than any other hedgerow liqueur I've made, this one improves with keeping. The longer the better. By the time it's aged for 3 years, it tastes neither of whisky nor even, in any obvious sense, of blackberries. It simply tastes sublime! Mellow, yet complex, and deeply, richly fruity. I've tested it on friends, asking them to guess what booze, and what fruit, it's made with. And no one has ever guessed either right first time. But all have agreed that it's truly scrumptious.

Of course, it's a lovely part of the festive ritual if a previous year's batch is opened at Christmas too. And if you can make that a 3-, 4- or 5-year-old vintage, rather than just 'last year's', then you will find that the extraordinary self-restraint you have exercised in not quaffing it earlier is deeply rewarded.

These days, I am much more likely to give away my home-made sloe gin, Morello cherry cider apple brandy and crème de cassis, as Christmas presents than get stuck into them myself. But my blackberry whisky doesn't leave the house, and rarely leaves the dark corner at the back of the larder. When it does make a rare appearance, at a well-chosen moment over Christmas, everyone is poised with reverent anticipation... **Hugh**

2

Decking the Halls

DECORATING OUR HOMES at Christmas is more of an emotional activity than we may realise. As well as the practicalities of cost, space and time, we are guided by memories of Christmases past and the feelings they conjure. Yes, we have a chance to make our mark on the season with our own individual taste. But as we do so we are also paying tribute to generations past – as well as taking on board the creativity of our children and younger relatives. That can be joyful – and occasionally intense!

We are also influenced by age-old customs rooted in pagan beginnings, while many of the key decorative elements we associate most with Christmas today were established in the Victorian era, including the Christmas tree and greeting cards. In an ever-changing world it is reassuring that some traditions have endured and are just as integral to our celebrations as they were nearly 200 years ago… and earlier.

I have amassed a collection of decorations that tell the story of my Christmases from childhood, through my early independence and then to family life. Part of the joy of unwrapping these each year is to reminisce and enjoy them all over again. I don't buy new decorations any more, but there are department stores and garden centres that dedicate entire floors to them, offering everything from traditional to kitsch and exotic to extravagant themes.

Frustratingly, many bought decorations are still liberally covered in glitter, each sparkle a dot of plastic that is harmful to the environment. These tiny plastic particles too often end up in the sea – part of the 12.5 million tonnes of plastic that are estimated to enter our oceans every year. Nobody likes a lecture, least of all at Christmas, but it's depressing to think that our seasonal celebration is adding unnecessarily to this grim statistic. Thankfully retailers have started to pick up on the glitter issue and some are banning unsuitable products and switching to biodegradable options.

Sourcing second-hand decorations, like the vintage glass baubles that occasionally surface in junk shops, charity shops and car boot sales, can take a little patience but is so rewarding. And so is making decorations by hand. Many of us will remember our first Christmas craft experience of making paper chains, a tradition I repeated with my own children. As they've got older we still set time aside for Christmas projects, not just for practical purposes but to get us into the festive spirit too.

At River Cottage we turn to the natural world for our festive decorations, which can set the scene as evocatively as any tinsel, bauble or plastic reindeer. As well as foraging for ingredients to use in the kitchen, we responsibly pick some of what grows around us to create our Christmas displays. Your local hedgerows, woodland and coastline should be great sources of material, but so too will be your back garden or local park. It is amazing how much foliage – both evergreen and dried – as well as berries, pine cones and seed heads can be discovered once you start looking. Think about what you plan to make and gather accordingly, whether it's for a wreath, garland or arrangement. The forager's rules apply, so make sure you do not over-cut from one patch or prune incorrectly, damaging the plant. I am a big re-purposer of windfall foliage too. Always check that you are not trespassing and have permission to be where you are and take what you take.

Many of the recipes in the first three chapters of this book can be given as gifts and in this chapter we include some of our favourites made from the hedgerows as well as treats that may be less seasonally sensitive. There is also a focus on how to transform these bottles and jars into gifts with sustainable wrapping of brown paper, fabric, twine and herb posies.

One of the most important elements of the festive home is creating areas to celebrate and relax in, whether as a large group or in cosy solitude. The River Cottage barn is a communal space filled to the rafters with celebration and carousing, but there are also small intimate areas to enjoy. Some of my favourite moments on the farm have been sitting around a blazing fire in the yurt with a spicy apple aperitif, drinking coffee on the sun-warmed stone farmhouse doorstep, or enjoying a mug of lunchtime soup on the wobbly old bench in the kitchen garden.

Of course, this cosy customisation of our surroundings has become all the rage with the recent popularising of the Danish concept of 'hygge'. It amused us all at River Cottage that Meik Wiking's best-selling *Little Book of Hygge* mentions River Cottage as the best British example of a hygge approach to life and entertaining. But it didn't surprise us. Cosy comfort has always been a focus at River Cottage, and never more so than at Christmas.

We have a huge Christmas fir tree in the courtyard at River Cottage, simply decorated with fairy lights. It can be seen from the farmhouse, the cookery school and the eighteenth-century barn and stands as a reminder of the season we are in. The wood-fired braziers at the entrance of the farm and outside the barn are lit every afternoon as we begin to lose the light. They create a circle of welcome, warmth and conviviality for our guests (9 out of 10 on the hygge scale) as we pass around mulled cider and watch steam rising from the cups.

At home, with much less room, I still endeavour to create flexible spaces to relax in throughout winter with warmth and light. So a fire, beeswax candles, a pile of blankets and a steaming mug of something are all beacons – inside and out.

Outside I replicate River Cottage in a smaller way, with outdoor fairy lights, little baubles of bird feed hanging from the apple tree and a fire bowl: my way of bringing light into the darkness. Others choose to do the same with extravagant, joyful flashing displays complete with Santa, sleigh and reindeer on the roof. Each to their own – and it certainly brightens up the evening dog walk – but for me, the greatest pleasure from other people's decorations is found at dusk, before the curtains are closed, when I catch glimpses of glowing Christmas trees through windows.

The Christmas tree

We have Queen Victoria's husband, Prince Albert, to thank for the popularity of the Christmas tree in the UK. Originally a German custom, which was then adopted in the USA, it is said that Albert insisted on a tree at Buckingham Palace. When a newspaper of the time published a sketch of the royal family gathered around a huge evergreen, bedecked in decorations and brightly lit by real candles, it captured the hearts of the nation. A new tradition was born and has happily endured. The tree is now one of the central symbols of Christmas and takes pride of place in households and city squares across the country.

In the past I have replaced the traditional tree with a bare branch strung with decorations, a tree made of driftwood and a verdant bay tree perfect for the tiny city flat I was living in at the time. These are all valid, recommended options but once I had children they clamoured for a real tree.

In recent years debate has been growing around the most sustainable option. There is an argument in favour of artificial trees as, although they are made from plastic, they can be reused every year. However, it takes at least a decade to ensure the environmental impact of an artificial tree is less than that of a real tree.

Alternatively, you can buy a growing tree and move it into your home for the Christmas period before returning it to the garden. There are obvious challenges with this, including potentially shocking the tree with the change in temperature, the size it will grow to and the risk of it simply dying – but it's by far the most sustainable option if you can make it work.

To find a reputable Christmas tree farm near you, offering FSC-certified trees and sustainable replanting, contact the British Christmas Tree Growers Association. Or investigate the recent trend for renting a tree in a pot. You may even get the same tree the following year.

Of the different species available, Nordmann Fir is one of the most popular, more expensive choices in the UK. It holds onto its needles well and has an evocative pine fragrance. The Norway Spruce is the most affordable but it doesn't generally last as long. The Fraser Fir, a compact non-drop variety, is the favourite tree in the USA; it is less well known here but becoming more popular. The Blue Spruce is good for making garlands.

At the end of the tree's life, do not be tempted to break it up and burn it in your fire or log burner because the smoke from the unseasoned wood is a pollutant and the resin in the tree could create issues in your flue, with the potential for a chimney fire. Check with your local council, as many will collect Christmas trees and recycle them. Otherwise, they can be turned into wood chips, mulch or chopped up and put on the compost.

Decorating the tree

I am not an early tree decorator who springs into action on the first day of December, although I have no problem with others doing it. I don't like to peak too soon or spend the main days of Christmas with a withering, apologetic tree, but I can see how tempting it is to embrace the sparkle as soon as possible. There is nothing like strings of fairy lights to set a festive heart aflutter.

Real candles are sublime but carry the obvious risks of fire and dripping wax. One Christmas, my mother decided we would try them and then spent the entire time on tenterhooks, constantly instructing us to 'stand back!' She didn't repeat it again. I know friends who add candles to their tree on Christmas Eve and light them once, when they return from the Crib service. This sounds magical to me.

At home I hang a mix of old baubles, vintage treasures and past things made by little fingers – all beloved pieces that are joyfully unwrapped from their storage boxes each year. It is lovely to make something new to add to the display too. At River Cottage the decorations are ephemeral or recyclable – such as paper cut-outs, dried apple and orange slices, seed heads, gingerbread biscuits and strings of foraged things. A brisk walk around the farm and a rummage in the kitchen is often enough to inspire an afternoon of crafting.

Foliage

Decking the halls with boughs of holly is a festive custom which began in a time long before Christmas. It can be traced back as far as the Roman festival of Saturnalia and pagan midwinter celebrations, with greenery being cut down and brought into living areas. As well as being decorative it was said to protect against evil spirits and signified the promise of spring during a dormant time. The tradition continues today with Christmas trees, wreaths, garlands and arrangements.

Everything you to need to create a wreath or display can be foraged for. Start in your garden (this activity can double up as a little welcome pruning) and think about texture, longevity, practicality and pops of colour. Think ahead for next year too, and plant things that will look great in your garden through the summer, knowing they will also have a second life in a Christmas arrangement. That's the sort of organisation I dream of.

As I have mentioned before (on page 22), foraging beyond your own boundary requires a responsible attitude to gathering. Armed with that knowledge, explore further afield to see what can be garnered from your local area. Some of the useful plants you may find are described on the following pages.

Holly If any plant signifies the season, it is this one. Its festive history stretches back to the Druids who believed it had magical properties and symbolised fertility. Holly is easy to find but prickly to pick. Don't be tempted to take too many of the stems with berries as these are a good source of winter food for birds. It works best used as sprigs rather than boughs.

Mistletoe After holly, this is probably the most iconic plant of the festive season and is firmly rooted in pagan folklore. It grows predominantly on apple trees, as well as blackthorn, crab apple and hawthorn, but is hard to find or reach in the wild so go to your local farm shop, florist or market. Originally cut down on the winter solstice and brought into the house to protect the occupants from storms, this plant's significance has shifted over time. Now it is a romantic adornment, a bunch hung overhead for people to kiss under. Folklore states that for each kiss a berry is plucked from the plant until there are none left and the kissing must cease. I always keep a single sprig after Christmas and hang it somewhere discreet for the rest of the year as my grandmother used to do. This is supposed to bring wealth to the household. It hasn't worked yet but I am too superstitious not to do it.

Ivy This classic festive evergreen is a prolific climber, in its constant search for light, so cutting some back to use for decorations is likely to be mutually beneficial for both you and your garden. The berried ivy makes the perfect addition to wreaths and garlands; most varieties are incredibly flexible and don't dry out too quickly. It also adds a festive flourish if trailed over picture frames, down the middle of a dining table or simply strewn along a mantelpiece.

Evergreen herbs Rosemary, bay and sage, in particular, will add texture to any arrangement; they also smell divine. Every year I make a small herb-only wreath to hang in the kitchen and then use the herbs, once dried, for January cooking.

Twisted willow Also known as the corkscrew willow, Salix matsudana 'Tortuosa' offers the perfect branches and backdrop for hanging decorations.

Evergreen trees Specifically fir, spruce and pine, these have branches that make a great base for wreaths and garlands. You may have a tree in your garden or in local woodland – where there may be an occasional tree thinning and a forest floor of strewn branches. Christmas tree sellers often have offcuts to give or sell you. And if your own tree needs a trim to look just how you want it, then you've also garnered some greenery that can be deployed elsewhere in your decorative plans.

Eucalyptus Native to Australia, these trees are now being grown across Europe and in significant numbers in the UK. The leaves have a festive silvery blue tinge to them and a fresh, clean scent. If you are considering planting one, bear in mind that they are fast growers with shallow roots.

Shrubby dogwoods Grown for their bright red stems, species such as Cornus alba 'Sibirica' and Cornus sericea (Red Osier) look as dramatic in a vase as they do in the garden.

Moss This makes a natural base for wreath-making as it holds moisture and creates a lovely green backdrop. It also means the wreath can be soaked in a tray of water or given a regular spritz to keep it fresh. When foraging for moss, only take a small percentage of each patch and be careful not to damage any bark it sits on.

Dried foliage

There is something both spectacular and sensible about dried foliage arrangements. It means you can gather ahead of time, although you do need somewhere dry to store your bounty in the months leading up to Christmas. Here are some beautiful decorative plants to grow or keep an eye out for:

Honesty A cottage garden favourite and all-year joy, this plant is worth finding a moist, partly shaded spot for. From the white or lilac flowers in spring and early summer to the unmissable papery seed pods in the winter, it adds interest to the garden. Honesty's Latin name Lunaria means moon-like and describes the shape of the pods. They look great dried in arrangements; they're also to easy to harvest and present as a gift.

Alliums Striking species such as Christophii, Purple Sensation and Schubertii look magnificent in winter arrangements or as bauble decorations, bringing a memory of summer with them. They can be cut as they begin to dry out and then hung somewhere cool and dry until needed.

Angelica The attractive rosette-shaped flowers of this plant can be dried and used in the same way as alliums (above).

Wild carrot I grow this cow-parsley-like plant (Daucus carota) in my garden because its tall stems are as elegant dried and displayed indoors as they are swaying gently outside my kitchen window. Alternatively, you can pick cow parsley as it begins to dry out in June, creating starburst seed heads, and hang the stems somewhere out of the way.

Hydrangea The dried blooms of this popular shrub look fabulous in a wreath. Cut the flower heads as they begin to dry out and the petals take on a papery look and feel. They do not need to be hung up but it helps protect their fragility if you do. Keeping their original colour is impossible without chemical intervention but their second beauty is in the subtler, ageing tones.

Poppy The seed heads of this distinctive flower look fantastic dried on their stems, used as individual heads on a wreath or threaded together to make a garland. Cut them down once they are dried and leave them somewhere warm to lose any residual moisture.

Pampas grass Popular in the 1970s, this robust grass (Cortaderia selloana) fell out of favour, mainly because it is invasive. It also had a strange association with wife-swapping! It is regaining popularity, not least because it looks fabulous dried in an arrangement. It is, however, hellish to harvest because the foliage is sharp, so wear protective gloves and clothing. Handle with care!

Sea kale Often found along the coastline, this plant dries out with small bauble-like seed pods in winter. Don't always discount those plants that look dead as they may bring a structural value to your creation – as this one does.

Finishing touches Fir cones, hips, berries, broken branches, golden beech leaves, acorns and various seed heads will all add colour and natural beauty to your decorations. Also consider culinary elements like dried chillies, crab apples, star anise and cinnamon sticks.

Flowers

If you prefer local, seasonal blooms then fresh floral arrangements are hard to achieve in winter. Cut flowers, transported from overseas, are an expensive alternative and not a very sustainable one. However, if like me, you love flowers on the kitchen table or by your bed there are ways to achieve it in winter.

Think about bulbs that will grow into pretty blooms, often with a heady scent and a longevity far beyond a bunch of roses. Of course, these can be bought already in flower from your local florist or garden centre just before Christmas if you prefer, but it's well worth nurturing your own and, of course, it will save you money.

Bulbs

I would recommend growing hyacinths and scented narcissi (paperwhites are a classic Christmas variety). They are quite easy to look after and pretty dependable for festive flowering. Potted-up and just in bud they make fabulous gifts. Pots of white hellebores, also known as Christmas roses, and red cyclamen, also work well indoors and can be planted outside after Christmas.

I collect pots for my Christmas bulbs throughout the year. It's a good excuse for regular visits to the local junk and charity shops. I keep an eye out for vintage bowls, chipped tureens (much cheaper if the lid is missing), jelly moulds, earthenware mugs, copper pots, colanders, baskets and trugs.

When buying bulbs for this purpose make sure they are the 'forcing' type rather than the garden variety. It means they have already been stored at a low temperature and are ready to be planted up. Depending on the variety, you will need to plant them in September or October. The bulbs will like a moist, good-draining soil or a multi-purpose compost, with a layer of grit at the bottom. If you are planting them in vessels without drainage then choose a bulb-fibre compost. Plant them with the tip facing upwards but do check the specific planting information for each variety as the instructions may vary.

Once your bulbs are planted up you can slow the growing process by keeping them in a dark, cool, dry spot – a shed or garage is ideal. They will need to be taken indoors when the shoots are around 5cm high and after a month or so you should have flowers. As a final aesthetic flourish, cover the soil with moss and tuck it around the stems. Some plants, narcissi in particular, can grow tall with stems that may start to lean and look unstable. Collect twigs from the garden to create an architectural structure that will support the arrangement and add to the overall look. I keep a few pots for myself and give the rest away as gifts, once the plants are well established.

Fruitful giving

I think there's something to be said for giving the same presents you love to receive, and on that basis one present I particularly enjoy giving is trees. Unsurprisingly, the trees I most like to receive (and therefore give) are trees that bear edible fruit. I could just say 'fruit trees', but I use the more elliptical phrase to include trees that bear the fruits we call nuts, and trees that bear fruits that are, realistically, more likely to get eaten by the birds, than by me and my family.

I've bought and planted a lot of such trees down the years, so I'm not an easy person to give fruit-bearing trees to. We are fortunate to have a nuttery as well as an orchard, and a bunch of trees (including rowans, crab apples, damsons and unusual varieties of hawthorn) that have been shoehorned into the hedges. So, there's the risk of presenting me with a tree I have already considered, and passed over. But whether it's a tree I've never thought of, or one I thought I didn't need, the fact that it was chosen for me by someone else gives it special status.

One of the trees I'm most thrilled to own still hasn't produced fruit – not at all unusual, as it's only about 3 years old. It was a present from my mum a couple of years ago. It's called a Plumcot and yes, it is a cross between a plum and an apricot. I am incredibly impatient to see and sample

its fruit – apricots and plums are two of my favourites and their lovechild could turn out to be better than either. It's a brilliant example of a gift from someone who knows me better than I know myself.

Another of my favourite tree gifts is a trio of almond trees – a fortieth birthday present from my wife. I didn't originally choose any almonds for our nuttery because they are not really native and my research suggested they wouldn't be productive. That's not the sort of technical consideration to bother my wife, who is French, and loves almond trees, and almond blossom, and indeed eating almonds. The trees have thrived. All blossom beautifully, but only one of them produces much fruit.

The little green unripe nuts can be picked in late May or June and sliced and eaten raw in salads. And by late August the proper nuts can be harvested. Eating them is a kind of nutty roulette: most are pleasantly sweet but the odd one has that intense, bittersweet, aromatic flavour associated with almond extract and frangipane sweetmeats. It's quite challenging in a freshly picked almond, but I actually quite like it.

I can only assume that I'm not alone in developing an involved intimacy with trees I have been gifted, which I forever associate with the dear ones who gave them to me. And so, dishing them out also feels like a worthwhile endeavour. I love giving fruit trees to friends who have just moved house, as something that can take root and prosper. (Although a tree that has established in a pot is a flexible option for small gardens and urban spaces, and of course hedges one's bets on the possibility of future moves.)

For a novice grower, a classic and productive eating apple like James Grieve, Ida Red or Falstaff, or the all-time great 'collapsing cooker' Bramley Seedling, will be cherished and enjoyed for years – with luck, decades. But if you want to give a 'character fruit tree', something a bit more unexpected, here are few good candidates, with the briefest of notes to help you match tree to giftee:

Greengage Literally my favourite fruit, and hardly anyone grows them. Choose a classic sweet, nectary variety like Old Greenage or Cambridge Gage.

Fig The lovers' fruit, and therefore a good choice for a lifelong partner. Best up against a sunny wall... To grow and ripen successfully in the UK, Brown Turkey is the best variety to choose.

Damson The opposite end of the plum spectrum from the gages – complex, tannic and bittersweet – damsons make wonderful jam and amazing ice cream. Merryweather is really a plum with damson tendencies, Farleigh the true mouth-puckerer.

Quince Everyone who is into preserving should have a quince tree, so they can make the incomparable (and very gift-able) membrillo (aka quince cheese). A grated quince in a Bramley compote is also fantastic. Quince trees can be temperamental, if not suicidal. The Serbian Gold variety is more stable and more productive than many.

Medlar This is the tree for 'next level' preserving: when you've 'been there and done that' with quinces. You will need to learn to 'blet'. I won't tell you what that is – like I said, you'll need to learn!

Hawthorn These are great fruit trees for people who, when it comes down to it, are quite happy to let the birds take the harvest. Ornamental varieties include some trees with amazing pink and red blossoms and others with extra-large fruit.   **Hugh**

Decorating the table

Table decorations are tricky because there isn't always enough space on the dining table for food, let alone a huge arrangement. My sister-in-law, Ali, the clever crafter of our family, has an ingenious solution to this – which I have, of course, copied. At the beginning of December, she goes out foraging for a large broken branch, which she drags home and leaves to dry out in the shed, giving insects a chance to relocate. It is then hung above the table and decorated with trailing ivy, paper cut-outs and fairy lights. The result is both stunning and practical, creating an 'indoor winter al fresco' feeling, without encroaching on useful table space.

Before trying this at home, do check you can suspend a branch safely and forage for the size and weight accordingly, as well as choosing something that has the odd small branch to suspend things from. It needs to be light enough not to bring the ceiling down and high enough to avoid people hitting their heads or poking an eye out. You will need strong twine to hang the branch, and florist's wire can be helpful for securing greenery and decorations.

I make sure there is enough table space for beeswax candles, whether they are fat pillars, tall wands, tapers, votives or a mix of all to cast different levels of light. Include something green or floral, maybe pots of bulbs, Christmas roses (Hellebores) or strands of trailing ivy. 'Paper' napkins are not always recyclable – many actually contain plastic fibres – so be sure to choose a properly eco version if you decide to go down this route. For me, linen napkins are so much nicer to use. They don't need to match and you can pick them up cheaply in charity and junk shops.

It is a good idea to make personalised napkin rings so that you are not washing napkins after every meal. The rings can be simple tied ribbon with a name tag, or you could find second-hand wooden versions and paint names onto them. If you want to make a crafty session out of customising napkin rings, then those large wooden curtain rings are a cheap and cheerful (and natural) way to go. Personalised napkin rings can also double up as place markers too.

I don't like Christmas crackers, for several reasons. Most importantly, unless they are sustainable, their contents of foil, glitter and plastic items will end up in landfill. Secondly, they take up valuable table space. Thirdly, the time to pull them seems to be when the hot roast lunch is ready. As the cook, that's the moment when you want everyone to '*Eat before it goes cold, for goodness sake*'. What I do like about them is the communal action, uniting the table, all the guests wearing paper hats at a jaunty angle. If you love a cracker, do have a go at making your own (you can still order the 'cracks' to go in them) – or, as an alternative, make an envelope for each guest and include a tiny gift such as a packet of seeds, a (home-made) paper hat or sweet treat. A handwritten joke or quirky factoid also goes down well.

Reducing plastic at Christmas

There's no doubt that, as Lucy points out, Christmas provides a worrying opportunity for an extra flood of single-use (and simply use*less*) plastic to enter our homes, and leave them again pretty promptly, without the reassurance that they are going to be disposed of in a way that will not cause further problems for the environment. While so much of the foods we eat (at any time of year) and the goods we buy continue to be wrapped in disposable plastic, a plastic-free Christmas is going to be a stretch for most of us. But, with a New Year fast approaching, the run-up to Christmas seems to be a good time to make a few early resolutions, if you haven't already, to reduce your plastic footprint.

First up is what I call the 'no-brainer' don't-leave-home-without it shopping trip kit. The items are even more vital when you are Christmas shopping, as you will be even more acquisitive than usual – and Christmas shopping is thirsty work.

So, take with you: a refillable (and full!) water bottle, a reusable 'keep cup' for hot drinks, and a bunch of reusable shopping bags. The string bags that scrunch up small are particularly useful: you can get several in a coat pocket. Best to avoid the so-called 'bag for life' that supermarkets are giving away – research shows they are often treated as disposable.

Try and do as much of your 'food and essentials' Christmas shopping (and all your shopping hereafter!) as you can at 'refill' or 'zero packaging' shops – or in the 'refill' sections of the supermarket (still at the 'trial stage' for most big retailers). Many independent refill shops are happy for you to bring your own reusable containers – so that's worth embracing too.

If you can also make the switch to plastic-free bathroom essentials, even better. For me these days, one lovely-smelling bar, that comes in a tastefully wholemeal-coloured, fully recyclable cardboard box, does it all – shower, shave and shampoo. And it really does all three jobs quite well enough to keep me sweet-smelling, tender of cheek, and free of dandruff.

I'm not quite so enamoured of the toothpaste in jar, but that's because I have a bad habit of leaving the lid off – and it dries out to the point where I need to excavate a portion with the handle of the toothbrush. But, as my wife insists (optimistically, perhaps), I can learn.

If you don't know already, find out when your local markets are. There tend to be more at this time of year,

and they offer a great opportunity to support local, independent farmers and artisan food producers. And if the home-made edibles and crafts that Lucy champions are outside your comfort zone, then locally made delights are another good option.

Both food markets and craft markets are usually pretty switched on to the plastic-free approach to Christmas shopping, but it's never a bad plan to have a few extra containers on hand. In the kitchen, reduce your use of cling film – and ideally foil too. The festive leftovers can go into a lidded container or jar, rather than a bowl with a single-use cling-film lid. If you do want to cover a bowl or wrap a lump of cheese then a beeswax or soy wax wrap can do the job over and over again.

You can, of course, extrapolate from the above a number of environmentally oriented Christmas gifts to gently nudge the plastic-avoiding habits of your loved ones: the water bottle, keep cup, beeswax wrap – all make good pressies. But best not to give them to those who are likely to be well laden with such eco-cred items already. Personally, I am happy to own two water bottles. I think having a 'spare' is reasonable and improves the chances of me laying my hands on one when leaving in a hurry. But I don't need a third (just in case you were thinking of sending me one). However, feel free to give me as many three-in-one shower/shave/shampoo bars as you like, as long as they smell nice... **Hugh**

Gift wrapping and cards

At the risk of sounding even more like Scrooge after my cracker revelation, I confess to being a haphazard Christmas card sender. Perhaps I am suffering from card-writing fatigue after many years of sending them but it can feel like one chore too many. And there is a broader issue of the growing concern, which I share, around unnecessary waste and recycling.

One response to this has been a rise in the sending of email 'e-cards' with senders often donating the amount of cash they would have spent on cards to charity. It is an interesting development though it does lack the festive feel of a pile of colourful envelopes landing on your doormat.

If sitting down with a glass of sloe gin and your favourite pen to write a pile of cards is a treasured tradition, I think you should continue to enjoy it. Hand-making your cards from recycled paper and natural materials is one way to make them more sustainable – and please add me to your recipient list because handmade greetings are my favourite to receive and send. I have included an idea later in this chapter (see page 91).

If a domestic production line of crafting is a prep step too far, consider charity Christmas cards, of which there are always hundreds to choose from, with a percentage of the profit going to worthwhile causes. Choose from those that aren't covered with glitter or foil and you will at least know they are recyclable or, even better, can be cut up and used as gift tags the following year.

There are even more concerning sustainability issues with wrapping paper. That's because most of it these days – and certainly anything that is at all shiny, glittery or metallic looking – is not in fact paper at all, but plastic. And of course, it's designed to be used just once, and thrown away.

These days I prefer to wrap presents in brown parcel paper that can be recycled, and use a biodegradable paper tape instead of the plastic versions. Brown paper may look dull after years of foil, metallic shine and iconic Christmas images but there is beauty in its simplicity. It acts as the perfect backdrop to further decoration, although do bear in mind that painted paper may be harder to recycle. But you can make even plain brown paper look elegantly festive with decorations like coloured string, second-hand ribbon and herb posies. If the paper does get ripped or crumpled beyond the possibility of recycling, then at least it's still paper. It can be put straight into the recycling or twisted into small knots and used to light the fire.

Fabric wrapping is another lovely idea, particularly for adult recipients. In the past, I have wrapped gifts in material remnants, napkins and even tea towels which works brilliantly, particularly if the person you are giving it to also loves fabric. The ancient Japanese art of fabric wrapping – furoshiki – is enjoying a renaissance too.

It promotes the use of one square of cloth that can be continually reused for different purposes. Craftspeople are even hand dyeing their own versions, which fills me with the desperate desire to collect them in every shape and colour. The only problem with this is being able to let my favourite furoshikis go – and giving a gift where the packaging is arguably more valuable than the content! But with any luck this charmingly 'wabi-sabi' way to wrap a present will catch on, so that eventually what goes around, comes around.

Whatever you choose to do it with, I would recommend present wrapping early. You could do this in one session but it can turn into a monumental chore so better to do a few parcels a day. It is worth setting up a gift-wrapping station or 'kit box'. This sounds much more glamorous than it really is, simply meaning that you have everything you need to hand in one place: wrapping paper (ideally the kind that really is paper, whether brown or otherwise), paper tape, labels, string, butcher's twine and scissors that can live in a quiet corner for a couple of weeks, or be whipped out and put on the table at opportune moments – or taken into another room for any secret wrapping requirements.

Hoard useful envelopes, boxes, ribbon, tissue paper and packaging, even those old Christmas cards to cut up and use as labels. That way your 'wrapping kit' is bursting with colourful items in the months prior so you have items ready to reuse and up-cycle.

If you focus on a few gifts each time, you can make the wrapping more creative and avoid the last-minute frenzy of paper and string on Christmas Eve that tends to lead to wrapping fatigue (unless this happens to be a treasured tradition of yours). It gives me palpitations just to think about the stress induced when I realise, too late, I have forgotten someone.

Totes amazing

A word on the ubiquitous tote bag and the seasonal opportunities it presents. These cotton, jute or sisal bags are the go-to give-away for companies and brands who are keen to show us just how much they care about the planet. It's good that we should have a few to take shopping, it's good that they are eminently reusable, and it's good that they are not plastic. When they do finally give up the ghost (of Christmas shopping trips past) they will rot away naturally and without causing harm (but beware the tote bag with plastic lining – yes, they really do exist!)

They may be biodegradable, but tote bags have a carbon footprint of their own. And some people – including me – have somehow acquired far too many of them. So, for a few years now we have been re-purposing our tote bags – as Christmas gift wrap. Almost every present that leaves our house en route to another will do so in a pre-loved tote bag.

Sometimes (and especially if my youngest daughter is involved in the giving) the tote bag will be customised with festive designs in paint or fabric pens, and/or graffitied with messages of love and season's greetings. I always dare to hope that these decorative additions (which often clash somewhat with the pre-existing messages and logos) will make the recipient more, and not less, inclined to resurrect the bag, post-Christmas, for its original intended use of holding shopping. But it's hard to be sure.

It appears to be a good way of redistributing tote bag wealth in an equitable way. Although it seems ours is not the only household to have drawn this conclusion or to be over-endowed with ethically sourced, branded, reusable shopping carriers. Quite a few of the gifts we received last Christmas came in second-hand tote bags... and I think I had previously encountered one or two of them. **Hugh**

Making gifts

Aspiring to the spirit of Louisa May Alcott's classic, *Little Women*, I believe that it truly can be better to give than to receive – or at least the pleasures can be pretty equal. Having said that, I can't quite imagine giving away an entire Christmas feast, as those four fictional sisters did. Still, as the story tells it, it was only their breakfast...

It is those truly thoughtful gifts, presents from the heart, that can have the most positive impact on both giver and receiver. That's why I think there is a welcome shift away from high-street consumerism and expensive gifting. People are becoming more considered about their Christmas shopping and, while cost plays a big part, there is also growing concern around waste, including excessive packaging, single-use plastic and throwaway goods. Many of us are seeking out artisan producers and makers, and shopping from them directly or through local independent stores.

More of us are making our own gifts too, and these are often the ones that bring the greatest pleasure to both the maker/giver, and the lucky recipient, who knows there is real love in the package. Home-made edible presents are some of the most fun to make and to get, so too those inspired by nature, including wreaths. Hugh and I are delighted to share some of our firm favourites in the recipes that follow.

If you do not have the time to create presents, there are other ways to do your Christmas shopping. Second-hand and vintage books are a winner. In the past I have bought them from charity shops and given them to the family on Christmas Eve, echoing the Icelandic custom Jolabokaflod, which means 'Christmas book flood'. It's a little treat before the day and a distraction for excited children.

Board games and jigsaw puzzles are ever-popular at Christmas and one or two new ones can be something to cheer the winter months ahead. So are packets of seeds, either bought or dried from your own garden, gifting the promise of warmth and spring. For bigger gifts, look at purchasing experiences to create memories.

Or consider a new approach to present giving. If you have a big family you could make a collective decision to buy for small children only and donate the adult buying budget to a charity instead, or towards the Christmas lunch. Or adopt the Secret Santa method, set a budget and pull a name out of a hat to decide who gets a present for whom. You cannot fail with a thoughtful, home-made present.

At the River Cottage Christmas party, we have delighted in Secret Santa for many years. I get misty eyed when I remember the year I was given a perfectly baked Dundee cake decorated with toasted almonds, or the Polish-inspired hamper of rye crackers and potent vodka. Our rule is to stick to a budget of £10 or under, choosing something second-hand or home-made. Offerings of hedgerow booze are among the most coveted – so coveted in fact that they are quite often consumed before the party is over. Each year the team become more inventive and competitive...

Making a Christmas wreath

An abundant festive wreath on the front door gives a lovely welcome. You can buy one from your local garden centre, florist or farm shop but they are simple and cheap to make. There are several options for the base of the wreath: a copper or wire ring, a bought wicker ring, or you could weave your own using willow branches. The equipment is easy to source and the greenery is free (see page 64).

Once you have everything ready, clear as much workspace as possible. You will need a table to construct the wreath on, floorspace to lay out your foliage and a hook (or person) to hold the wreath up during the assembly. This is the loveliest activity to do with family or friends, from the collecting of greenery to the making of the wreaths. It's an annual ritual for me, with or without company.

If you can, create several wreaths – up to 3 weeks ahead of Christmas – as they make such great presents.

Willow- or hazel-based wreath

You will need:

*Around 10–15 long willow or hazel
   stems, thin enough to bend easily*
Garden twine
*Garden gloves (to handle
   thorny foliage)*

Secateurs
Greenery (ivy, holly, fir etc)
Additional foliage (herbs, berries)
*Decorations (pine cones, seed heads,
   cinnamon sticks, ribbon etc)*

Strip the leaves off the willow (or hazel) stems and select three of similar length and width. If they are dry and difficult to handle you may want to soak them in water overnight. Weave them together as you would a braid, or plait, but do not worry if they are a little loose and ragged. As you weave, bend the stems so they create a circle.

Weave the two ends together. If they spring apart you can help them by tying a little string to hold them. You should be able to cut this string off once the ring is finished.

Now weave the rest of the stems into the structure. Add each stem a third around the circle from where you joined the last one so you are not starting or ending at the same spot. Make sure that any weak spot is strengthened by threading another reed into it.

Now your wreath is ready to decorate. You can poke individual stems of foliage into the base and build up. Choose a section of the wreath to decorate rather than the entire thing as part of its beauty is seeing the twisted base. Remember to choose the top point of the wreath and make a loop of twine or florist wire to attach ready to hang it from.

It's now time to choose and apply the final decorations and secure them to the wreath with twine or wire.

Moss-based wreath

You will need:

35cm diameter wire, copper or
  wicker ring
Garden twine
Garden gloves (to handle
  thorny foliage)
Foraged moss (to generously
  cover both sides of the ring)

Floristry wire
Secateurs
Greenery for the base (ivy, holly, fir etc)
Additional foliage (herbs, berries etc)
Decorations (pine cones, seed heads,
  cinnamon sticks etc)

Liberally cover both sides of your wreath ring with mossy handfuls, securing it by tightly winding the twine around the moss. Take your time – make sure there are no gaps and the wreath base is compact.

Make small bunches of your base greenery, choosing three varieties, and repeat the bunches until you have between eight and ten, depending on the size of the bunch. You need them to be big enough to cover the wreath base, but not encroach too much into its middle or extend too far over the edge. Work in a clockwise direction, with the leafy end pointing anti-clockwise and the stems clockwise. Fasten each bunch to the wreath with wire, making sure they overlap slightly and are evenly laid out as you work your way round.

It is a good idea to step back at this point and look at the wreath to check for gaps or loose stems. Ideally hang it or ask someone to hold it up so you can see the overall shape.

Now select extra foliage like bay, rosemary and berries and poke into the wreath, ideally tucking into the existing wire. This is a good way to use any foliage that may need replacing so you can refresh your wreath and it will last for as long as you need it. Also consider bringing colour into it with silvery eucalyptus leaves, burnished beech or Old Man's Beard.

Now for the final touches. Consider the weight of the final wreath and where you will be hanging it before you load it with additional decorative detail. It will definitely need a few pine cones or seed heads though!

Hold up your wreath and move it around until you are happy with where the top should be. Tie twine or twist wire through the back of the wreath, securing it to the frame and making a loop to hang it from.

Making tree decorations

Hand-crafted decorations are a lovely alternative or addition to baubles and other bought tree ornaments. You can make these up to 8 weeks ahead for Christmas.

Dried orange and apple slices

We hang these on the tree at River Cottage, making a fresh batch to replace any from previous years that are looking a little ragged. They are easy if a little time-consuming to make and look fabulous on a tree, garland or centrepiece.

Cut oranges into 1cm thick slices. Pat dry to remove excess moisture and place in a single layer on an oven rack or baking sheet lined with baking paper. Place in the oven on a very low setting (about 120°C/Fan 100°C/Gas ½) for 3 hours, keeping a relaxed eye on them, and turn the slices every 30 minutes or so to stop them curling up too much. Once cooled, thread twine or ribbon through if you want to hang them.

Core apples, then slice them vertically or horizontally into 5mm thick slices and immediately immerse in a bowl of cold water with the juice of 1 lemon and 1 tbsp salt added to prevent discoloration. After 10 minutes, drain the apple slices and pat dry. Place on a rack in a single layer in a low oven to dry out, as for oranges (above).

Decorative strings

In the absence of tinsel, I still like to do a bit of swathing and festooning. Whether it's on the Christmas tree, along the mantelpiece, around lampshades or at the windows, strings of dried berries, rose hips, seed pods or dried chillies are eye-catching and easy to use. The berries and hips can then be put out for the birds in January. You just need a needle with an eye wide enough to take the thread you are going to use – an upholstery needle is ideal.

Alternatively, consider treasures like old brass buttons or vintage counters from board games and create a string that will endure for Christmases to come. The counters will need a carefully drilled hole in each before threading. Take a length of waxed cotton and tie a jewellery finding (small ring) into each knot, approximately 5–10cm apart. Attach findings in the drilled holes of the treasures you will be hanging and then join each ring to one on the string. These decorative strings make thoughtful presents too.

Decorative treats for garden wildlife

Winter is a tough time for wildlife. Food is scarce so they need all the help they can get – maybe even their very own Christmas tree with edible decorations of birdseed balls and strings of popcorn or dried berries. Choose a tree or spot where you have a good vantage point from your window, which is also safe from predators, decorate and then sit back and watch the birds arrive.

Birdseed baubles

You may already have the ingredients to make these special treats for our feathered friends. You'll need one part suet or lard (no other fat is suitable) to two parts oats, currants or breadcrumbs (or a mix) and a spoonful of peanut butter. Heat the fat in a pan and then combine it with the dry ingredients and peanut butter. Shape into balls or flatten and use festive biscuit cutters to cut out shapes before threading string through each. Put them in the fridge overnight to firm up. Hang them out the following day.

Popcorn

This needs to be the sort you make yourself – without any salty or savoury additions. Follow the usual instructions to cook the corn, using vegetable or coconut oil, then leave it to cool. To create the strings, thread a needle with cotton and poke it through the kernels. Secure each end of the strings onto the branches and leave for the birds and squirrels. If you want to add dried berries, first check that they are suitable for wildlife. Don't forget to untie the empty strings from the branches.

Alternatively, you can dry whole cobs of corn. Place the ears of corn on a baking sheet on the bottom rack of the oven at around 175°C/Fan 155°C/Gas 2½ for 8 hours to shrivel the kernels. (You could bake items on the shelves above at the same time.) I would suggest using the dried cobs as an indoor decoration and then hanging them outside in January for the wildlife to enjoy.

Crafting for Christmas

Wrapping presents in brown paper, as I have suggested, may sound a little austere but it is a practical, sustainable solution to non-recyclable gift wrap and sticky tape. And the paper is just the start: there are many ways to embellish your packages with posies of evergreen herbs, twine and handmade gift tags. Here are some other simple and effective festive craft ideas.

Pressed flower gift tags/cards

This is a project that needs to be tackled earlier in the year. In fact, it is the sort of thing I do throughout the year and use for all types of greeting cards and tags. Experiment with anything from pretty weeds that grow through the cracks in the pavement to your favourite herbs or your prize roses. Steer clear of anything too big and blousy and opt for the flatter styles, as they press well. Some, like sweet peas, give fragile, papery results that look beautiful against vintage paper.

A flower press makes the job easier, but I have also done it with newspaper and a pile of cookbooks. Simply choose your blooms, lay them carefully sandwiched between two sheets of paper and apply weight evenly. A pile of books will do it but make sure they do not become dislodged or moved. Leave for at least a week and then check your presses.

Carefully glue or tape onto pieces of card with a hole punched in each for string to go through if you are making tags. On a corner of the card include the name of the plant and when and where it was picked.

Longshore makers, Melanie and Julia of Molesworth & Bird, go one step further and press seaweed – a coastal pursuit once popular with Victorian women. It is a more complicated process than flower pressing and easier to tackle small projects like gift tags or cards.

Fill a roasting tray with about a 5cm depth of fresh tap water and slip a piece of watercolour paper in. Place your snippet of seaweed above it and float into position. Lift the paper out with the seaweed sitting on top, giving the fronds a tweak to make sure they are displayed as you would like them. Carefully wrap in a tea towel to remove the excess moisture and then place in your wooden press, using a sheet of greaseproof paper and then cardboard. Alternatively, you can place it under a pile of books. You will need to change the paper every day until the seaweed is dry.

Seed purses

My daughter, Hebe, has been blessed with more patience and creative flair than me and can spend all day crafting. One of her missions was to replace crackers for the Christmas table with a sustainable alternative. Inspired by an age-old craft and the artist Eleanor Percival, she settled on puzzle purses, which include a joke, fact or quote and a tiny gift – such as a packet of seeds. These envelopes can be personalised and while they don't make a loud bang, they do create a lovely moment. They don't just have to be for the Christmas table either and can be themed to tie in with the seed you are giving.

To make a seed purse:

- Cut a square of paper: 21 x 21cm is a good size. Measure each side into thirds and mark with a pencil at 7cm and 14cm.

- Fold the bottom edge of the paper up to the second pencil mark, to create a crease a third of the way up.

- Turn the paper 90° and repeat to the remaining sides.

- Open out the paper. You should have a creased grid of 9 squares.

- Take the bottom-right corner to the top left corner and fold.

- Open out the paper and take the bottom-left corner to the top-right corner.

- Open out the paper and place as a square in front of you.

- Turn the paper over so you are working on the reverse. You now need to fold each corner of the square to each corner of the creased square in the centre of your paper.

- Take the bottom-right corner to the top-left corner of the creased square and fold.

- Unfold the paper and take the bottom-left corner of the paper square into the top-right corner of the creased square.

- Turn the paper 180° and repeat with the remaining two corners.

- Flip the paper back over to the original side and pinch each of the corners. The creased central square will create a base.

- Take two diagonally opposite corners and begin to twist gently. You are creating a pinwheel effect so follow the creases to fold the paper. It will take a little time to pop into place but the creases will flatten into triangles that create a star shape.

- Now fold each triangle over the next one, turning the square 90° each time and tuck the final triangle under the first.

Twig trivets

There is a tiny stone-and-slate cottage I know. Off grid, impossible to find and out of this world, it sits wedged into the far corner of an almost inaccessible field. Each time we turn up I expect it to have vanished, possibly never to have been there at all. The cottage is an eccentric mix of etiquette and roughing it, full of home-made answers to modern living that have been created over the years by grateful guests. One of them is a wooden trivet, made using twigs foraged from the forest of beech, sweet chestnut and rowan trees.

At home I made my own version of this twig trivet with hazel offcuts from a stint of amateur hedge-laying and a ball of thick garden twine, using the 'clove hitch' knot that my husband Steve taught me from his youth. (He is also an excellent Martini maker but I doubt he learnt that from his Boy Scout days.)

Collect the twigs from your garden or local walks. They should be at least pencil thickness, ideally fatter, but it is up to you how big you go. Just remember the function of the final piece is to keep your table top protected from a hot pan or pot. You will need between 12 and 16 sticks to make a medium-sized trivet. They should all be a similar length but do not have to be uniform. You can, of course, find longer sticks and cut them down to size; a garden hand saw is good for this.

To make a twig trivet:

- Line your 12–16 sticks up in the order you think works.

- Take your ball of thick garden twine and, leaving a good 10cm of twine, make a clove hitch knot. Push the stick through the middle of the knot and pull tightly. This creates a cross of string on the twig facing you.

- Continuing to use the twine, attach the next sticks in the same way, making sure you pull each knot tightly before you move on to the next twig.

- At the end of the row, leave a good 10cm of twine before cutting.

- Do not turn the twigs over but repeat the process at the other end, so both ends are woven securely with twine.

- Once you have finished, turn the trivet over and you will have neat 'stitching' along both edges. You can tweak the sticks into place and tighten the knots. Once you are happy, tie each of the twine tails into a loop to secure the end twigs and then cut off the excess twine.

Hanging cards

My pal Katy Shields is often distracted from everyday life by creative pursuits. Her passion for cooking, gardening and making is infectious so I am glad I can share one of her projects. This craft is both a card and a hanging decoration, easy to make and so effective whether singular or in a row.

Do try out your own designs too – maybe a small boat being guided by the moon, or a hare running under a pink winter sun.

To make a festive house card:

- Draw and cut out a simple house shape on a piece of medium weight card – you could draw the silhouette of your own house to make it more personal. Place this shape on a second piece of card, draw around it and then cut out – this second shape will form the reverse of the card.

- Decide on the position and shape of a window and draw this on the first piece of card. Paint the window golden yellow.

- Paint the rest of the house, including the second cut-out, in various shades of inky blue.

- Cut a perfectly imperfect star shape from a piece of medium card. Place this star on another piece of card, draw around it and cut out to create a second star that will form the back.

- Paint the stars golden yellow or cover in gold foil or even gold leaf.

- Choose a cord, string or ribbon the length you require, and attach it to the house with glue. Back the house with the second cut-out and glue the two pieces together. Attach the star in the same manner.

Preserves are a lovely home-made gift and it's great to have one up your sleeve that isn't laden with sugar. Few are easier to make than this as there's no cooking required – just a bit of slicing and salting. Prepare them well ahead. After a month or so, the lemons will have transformed into a tangy preserve with a unique sour-salty flavour. Leave them for 6 months until they have turned tawny brown, and they'll taste even better.

Preserved lemons are found in dishes, hot and cold, across the Levant and North Africa and I find myself adding them to all kinds of on-the-hoof stews, soups, salads, dressings and dips at home. They are great for zhuzhing up festive leftovers. Most recipes call for just the tender rind (peel and pith) of the fruit to be used, with the flesh scraped away and discarded. But I think that's a bit of a waste. The fleshy pulp has a similar but milder flavour and you can use it almost anywhere you'd use the peel itself. Don't eat the pips though! **Hugh**

Preserved Lemons

Makes 3 x 750ml jars

20–30 unwaxed lemons
  (the smaller the better)
About 250g coarse sea salt
12–15 bay leaves

You will also need:
3 sterilised 750ml Kilner or
  Le Parfait jars

Cut half of the lemons from top to bottom almost into quarters, i.e. without going right through so that the lemon is still joined at one end. Push sea salt into these deep cuts – 2 scant level tsp (about 10g) for each lemon.

With very clean hands, squash the salt-packed lemons into the sterilised preserving jars. You can cut 1 or 2 lemons fully in half or into quarters so they fit into any smaller gaps. Tuck a few bay leaves into each jar with the lemons. Seal the jars and leave for a couple of days.

The salt will draw out a lot of juice, which you'll see in the jars. Add enough juice squeezed from the remaining lemons to completely submerge the fruit in each jar. (Those miscreant wedges in the jar on the left will need to be covered!) Seal the jars again and store for at least 1 month before using, turning the jars upside down and back every now and then.

Once opened, keep each jar of lemons in the fridge. As long as the fruit is completely covered by the salty liquid, they should keep well for at least a year. They will slowly change colour, from yellow to a rich dark brown.

Pink Grapefruit & Bay Curd

Citrus fruits take centre stage in the winter. A big bowl of organic, unwaxed lemons in the kitchen, a wooden crate of leafy clementines to pluck from, or an orange in the toe of your Christmas stocking, they sing through the heavy richness of the season. For me, pink grapefruit feels like the ultimate festive fruit and each year I find ways to incorporate it into the celebration. My younger son, Jesse, votes for this curd every time and swirls it through his breakfast yoghurt. It's a little less mouth-puckery than the traditional lemon version but it is also the softest, most exquisite shade of shell pink. The sort of colour that looks good in sunsets and socks, and makes a pretty gift. Make one jar to keep and one to give away, up to 4 weeks ahead for Christmas.

Makes 2 x 250ml jars
100g butter
150g caster sugar
Juice from 2 pink grapefruit
   (you need 200ml)
2 bay leaves
4 large eggs

You will also need:
2 sterilised 250ml jars

Melt the butter slowly in a heavy-based saucepan over a low heat (or in a bain-marie or heatproof bowl set over a pan of barely simmering water) and then stir in the sugar until it begins to dissolve. Add the grapefruit juice and bay leaves and continue to stir for a couple of minutes. Take the pan off the heat and leave to cool for a few minutes.

In a separate bowl, whisk the eggs until smooth. Set a sieve over the pan (or bowl) of melted butter and pour the egg into it. Hold the sieve up a bit and, as the egg drips through into the butter, stir the mixture with a wooden spoon. Use the back of the spoon to press through any egg left in the sieve; don't be tempted to tip it into the pan as it could form a solid eggy mass.

Put the pan back over the very low heat (or the bowl back over simmering water) and stir regularly until the curd thickens; this should take about 10 minutes. Take out the bay leaves. Occasionally, if the mixture is too hot, the egg forms white threads through the curd. Don't panic if this happens – use a hand blender to give it a little blitz and the strands should disappear, leaving you with a silky smooth curd. Pour the curd into sterilised jars and seal immediately. Once opened, store in the fridge and use within 2 weeks.

Candied Grapefruit Peel

This is a brilliant way to use the leftover peel from your curd making, or transform the leftover flesh and juice from this recipe to make curd! Whichever way you approach these grapefruit recipes it is so satisfying to use the whole fruit. Candying peel is a time-consuming process and not one that I tackle at any other time of year, but give it a go and it may well become a treasured tradition for you too. There are several recipes in this book that would welcome this grapefruit peel, including mincemeat (page 44), stollen (page 165) and quincemas cake (page 47).

Alternatively, you can give the candied pieces a light sugar dusting or dip them in chocolate and leave to set for a sweet after-dinner treat with a kick of sour. Prepare up to 6 weeks before Christmas.

Makes a 300ml jar

2 pink grapefruit
  (only the peel is needed)
200g caster sugar

You will also need:
A sterilised 300ml jar

Wash the fruit and cut it into quarters, peeling the skin off the flesh. With a sharp knife, carefully scrape or cut away the remaining thick white pith without cutting into the skin. (If using the grapefruit peel from the curd recipe, then halve to create quarters and cut the pith away from the peel.)

Slice the peel segments into narrow strips and place them in a pan. Cover with cold water and bring to the boil. Allow the peel to boil for a minute or so then drain and repeat, using fresh, cold water. Repeat the process twice more, to soften the peel.

Once you have drained the water after the third boil, put the peel to one side. Pour 250ml water into the pan, add the sugar and bring to the boil to dissolve the sugar. Add the peel and simmer for around 30 minutes until it has absorbed all the sugar and is translucent. Drain the syrup and leave the peel until it is cool enough to handle.

Take any stringy pith off the peel strips with a sharp knife and discard. Lay the pieces out on a wire rack and leave to dry for at least 24 hours until they feel dry to the touch. The candied peel is then ready to use in baking.

Note: For sugared peel, roll the candied pieces in a little granulated sugar before drying them out. If you want them dipped in chocolate then you can do this once they are dry. Store in an airtight jar.

I discovered a few years ago just how easy it is to ferment vegetables at home, and I've never looked back. Turning endless different veg combos into crunchy, savoury, delicious versions of sauerkraut is fun, creative and a great way to minimise food waste, while the resulting ferments are teeming with the friendly live bacteria that we know are incredibly good for us.

Following the same basic steps, you can ferment almost any veg – though cabbages and root veg are particularly simple and successful – and you can add your favourite aromatics and spices too. This recipe is a variation on a classic sauerkraut, gloriously coloured from red cabbage and beetroot, and given a Christmas twist with warming spices. Make it at least a week ahead and serve with cheese, in sandwiches, with hummus or other dips, and with all manner of wintry leftovers. **Hugh**

Christmas Kraut

Makes at least 10 servings

40g fine sea salt
½ medium red cabbage
1 medium beetroot, 200g, scrubbed
2 large or 3 medium eating apples
A thumb-sized piece of fresh ginger,
   about 25g, finely grated

½–1 tsp dried chilli flakes, to taste
4 cloves
½ cinnamon stick

You will also need:
A sterilised 2 litre Kilner jar

Remove the rubber seal from the lid of your preserving jar (to allow gas to escape as the veg ferments). Dissolve the salt in 1 litre cold water to make a brine.

Remove any dirty outer leaves from the cabbage; rinse the outside well. Set aside a large leaf. Cut the rest of the cabbage into 2 or 3 wedges and grate coarsely, leaving the fibrous base of the stem. Thinly slice any larger bits that fall off as you're grating. Put the shredded cabbage into a large bowl. Trim any stalky bits off the beetroot and scrub it, then coarsely grate it into the bowl with the cabbage. Wash the apples (no need to peel) and coarsely grate them, down to the cores, into the bowl too.

Add the ginger and spices to the bowl and toss everything together well. Pack the mixture into the prepared preserving jar, pressing the veg down and leaving at least a 5cm gap at the top. Pour the brine slowly into the jar, so it filters down through the veg. Keep going until there is enough brine in the jar to come about 3cm above the veg when you press them down with your hand (the veg will want to float). Keep any leftover brine for now. Tip the jar this way and that a few times to help release any air bubbles.

Put the reserved cabbage leaf over the top of the shredded veg and push it down so that it traps all the veg underneath it and keeps them submerged. Make sure the leaf itself is submerged too. Veg that is exposed to air above the brine tends to go mouldy and this can spoil the whole jar. You can top up the jar with more brine if you need to, and use a non-metal weight such as a clean pebble or small jar of water, if that helps.

Close the jar and stand it on a plate. Leave at cool room temperature for 1 week. Have a look at it every day – you should be able to see bubbles of carbon dioxide forming inside. Every couple of days, open the lid, to let any excess gas escape, then close it again. It's not unusual for a little brine to escape the jar – hence the plate.

After a week, taste the kraut. It should be pleasantly sour and tangy, which means it's ready to eat. If it doesn't have that tang yet, or it seems 'fizzy', leave it another day or two. Otherwise, transfer it to the fridge. It will keep for weeks, as long as the veg stays submerged in brine. If your kraut does go mouldy or develops a bad or really 'off' smell or taste, discard it.

Sloe Gin

The hedgerows bordering River Cottage are thick with spiky, lichen-crusted blackthorn bushes that produce sloe berries throughout autumn. Sloes have a similar colour and powdery blush to a damson but are much smaller and very sour. Be sure you have identified them correctly before picking to avoid collecting berries that are not edible. There is debate and folklore around whether you should wait until after the first frost to pick, as this can split the fruits and make it easier for them to release their juice. You can mimic this by putting them in the freezer overnight, or prick the berries instead. I am including this recipe as much for the other drinks you can make with the sloes after they have outgrown their initial usefulness for the sloe gin. Ideally, you need to start at least a year ahead for Christmas.

Makes a 750ml bottle

*300g sloes, washed, stalks and
   leaves discarded*
150g caster sugar
700ml gin or vodka

You will also need:
*A sterilised large (1 or 1.5 litre)
   Kilner jar*
A sterilised 750ml bottle

Prick the sloes with a skewer or needle and put them into a large Kilner jar with the sugar and alcohol. Give everything a good stir then seal and tuck away in a cool, dark spot. Shake the jar several times over the first few days to make sure the sugar has dissolved then leave for a good 3 months.

Strain the liquor into a bottle but don't throw the sloes away if you want to tackle the slider and port. Store the bottled liquor for another 6 months at least but preferably for a full year to allow a good level of maturation. This can be left for several years without the berries and makes a lovely discovery at the back of a cupboard.

Note: It is possible to make sloe gin without the addition of sugar. You may want to add spices, like star anise or cinnamon, and the jar still needs to be shaken. It will take longer to mature to acquire the full, fruity flavour.

Boozy variations

Slider Put the 300g drained alcohol-steeped sloes into a sterilised 1 litre Kilner jar. Pour dry cider (not sparkling) on top and leave to sit for 2 weeks (no longer or the sloes may make the cider ferment further and could cause the jar to explode). Decant the liquid into a sterilised bottle and store in the fridge. Warning: it is much more potent than a normal cider!

Sloe port Put the 300g drained alcohol-steeped sloes into a sterilised 1 litre Kilner jar. Pour half a bottle of red wine on top. Add 50g caster sugar, give everything a good stir, seal and tuck away in a dark corner, shaking it occasionally for the first few days to help dissolve the sugar.

After a month, decant the liquor and add a shot or two of brandy (according to your taste) and the resulting sloe port is ready to drink. Do not be tempted to get anything further from those sloes now. Thank them for their sterling service and put them in the compost.

Sloe Sin Sauce

As the bitter bedfellow of the plump, fruity blackberry, the sloe offers limited options beyond hedgerow jams and jellies and the booze-steeping favourites on the previous pages. Gelf Alderson, head chef at River Cottage, is always looking for new ways to use these foraged beauties and this umami-style ketchup, with a nod to hoisin sauce, was inspired by him. Wonderful as a glaze or a sauce for roast goose and duck, it also makes the most marvellous addition to stir-fries and an excellent dip for pork ribs and tempura vegetables. I would go as far as to say that if I only had a small crop of sloes this is the recipe I would assign them too. And steep something else in my gin. Make it ahead for Christmas – as soon as the sloes are ripe.

Makes about 500ml

250g sloes

150ml fruity red wine

2 star anise

1 small onion, roughly chopped

250g plums, halved and stoned

1 garlic clove, roughly chopped

¼ small hot chilli, chopped, or a good
   pinch of dried chilli flakes

1 tbsp dark muscovado sugar

125ml soy sauce

100ml cider vinegar

1 tbsp Chinese five-spice powder

Sea salt

You will also need:

A sterilised 500ml jar
   (or 2–3 smaller jars)

Rinse the sloes well and put them in a pan with the red wine and star anise. Bring to the boil, then lower the heat and simmer for around 20 minutes until the berries have broken down and released their stones.

While the sloes are cooking, put the onion and plums into a large saucepan and add the garlic, chilli, sugar, soy sauce, cider vinegar and five-spice. Bring to a low simmer and cook until the plums are soft.

Take the pan of sloes off the heat and push the contents through a sieve, leaving the stones behind. Pour the resulting sloe syrup into the pan of plums, then take off the heat. Tip into a blender and blitz until smooth.

Return the sauce to the pan, add a pinch of salt and simmer for a few minutes. If it is too runny, cook for around 15 minutes to reduce down. Leave to cool slightly – the silky sauce will thicken as it cools.

Pour the sauce into sterilised jar(s), seal and store in a cool, dark place. It will keep for 6 months. Once opened, refrigerate and eat within 2 weeks.

This wonderful stuff – a toasty, spicy, seed-and-nut sprinkle – is a kitchen staple for me all year round. At Christmas, I particularly like the way it works magic with leftovers, being the perfect finishing touch on everything from bubble and squeak and veggie soups to Boxing Day salads. A jam jar of dukka also makes a lovely present, especially for a stressed festive chef. Make it a week ahead. **Hugh**

Dukka

Makes a 400ml jar (20 servings)

50g whole, skin-on almonds, hazelnuts or walnuts, roughly chopped or bashed

50g cashew nuts or peanuts, roughly chopped or bashed

75g pumpkin, sesame and/or sunflower seeds (or your favourite ready-made seed mix)

2 tsp cumin or caraway seeds

2 tsp coriander seeds

1 tsp fennel seeds (optional)

A good pinch of flaky salt

A few twists of black pepper

A good pinch of dried chilli flakes

You will also need:

A 400ml jar (or 2 smaller jars)

Put a heavy-based frying pan over a medium-high heat. Add the nuts and seeds (not the spice seeds yet) and toast them for 2–3 minutes, shaking the pan regularly so they colour a little bit all over.

Meanwhile, lightly crush all the spice seeds using a pestle and mortar – they don't need to be finely ground; a few whole seeds in the mix is fine. Add these to the nuts and seeds, along with the salt, pepper and chilli flakes. Continue to heat for 2–3 minutes, moving or turning the mix now and then, until everything looks toasted, but not burnt – do keep a close eye!

When done, tip the mixture onto a plate and set aside to cool. You can use the dukka immediately, or store it in lidded jars for a week or so.

Variations

There are plenty of things you can add to your dukka just before serving: finely grated orange or lemon zest is lovely, especially if your dukka is going on a salad, or try some finely chopped preserved lemon (see page 98) for a hint of sour. Chopped thyme or rosemary makes dukka particularly roasted-veg-friendly, or you can up the quantity of dried chilli if you want a little more heat in the mix (particularly good on hummus).

I've long been a fan of a fruit fumble – a cross between a crisp-topped crumble and a creamy fool. Part of the fumble's appeal is that you can make the fruit and crumble elements separately, then bring them together, with a spoonful of something creamy, whenever it's time for pud. It's the concept for my 'fumble station' (see page 186).

Fumbles can be served hot or cold, and the fruit element is endlessly variable. Here, I've given a classic compote of Bramley apples a fragrant spin with dried lemon verbena. If you haven't any verbena, try the citrusy variation. **Hugh**

A Festive Fumble

6 servings

For the 'independent' crumble:
50g butter, diced (or use 50ml
  vegetable oil, for a vegan crumble)
75g light wholemeal cake flour or
  wholegrain spelt flour
50g porridge oats or fine oatmeal
50g ground almonds or hazelnuts
100g almonds, hazelnuts or walnuts,
  roughly bashed or chopped, or
  100g cooked chestnuts, crumbled
30g sugar (soft brown, golden
  granulated or demerara)
A pinch of salt

For the Bramley and verbena compote:
Juice of 1 lemon
1kg Bramley or other cooking apples
12 dried lemon verbena leaves
  (see page 24)
50–100g caster sugar

To serve:
Plain yoghurt, lightly whipped cream
  (or a mixture of both)

For the crumble, preheat the oven to 190°C/Fan 170°C/Gas 5 and have ready a large baking tray. Either rub the butter into the flour in a large bowl to get a coarse breadcrumb texture then stir in the other ingredients, or soften the butter first and mix everything together in one go with your hands (which is the best approach if you've used oil).

Either way, break the mix into crumbs with a few chunky clumps and spread out on the baking tray. Bake for 15–20 minutes, stirring at least once, until golden brown. Leave to cool completely. If you're not using it straight away, store the crumble in a jar or sealed tin, for up to a week.

To make the compote, put the lemon juice into a large pan. Peel, core and thinly slice the apples into the pan, tossing them with the juice as you go so they don't brown. Add the dried lemon verbena leaves, 50g sugar and

2 tbsp water. Cook gently, stirring often to help the apples break down, for about 20 minutes until you have a slowly bubbling, slightly chunky purée. Taste and add more sugar if you like – but keep the compote nicely tart because it will be paired with the sweet crumble. You can either serve your compote straight away or let it cool then chill it.

To assemble, divide the apple compote between serving glasses. Add a generous dollop of yoghurt, whipped cream or a mix of the two. Top with a layer of crumble mix, and tuck in – swirling your fumble as you eat.

Variation
Citrusy Bramley compote Instead of lemon verbena, use the finely grated zest and juice of 1 orange; also include the grated zest of the lemon used in the recipe. Add all this to the lemon juice in the pan as you start the apple compote and proceed as above, but don't add the 2 tbsp water.

3
Advent

THE RELIGIOUS SEASON of Advent begins in late November, five Sundays before Christmas Day and continues until Easter. However, the 1–24 December is the most celebrated part of Advent, with a countdown of calendars and candles. These are also the busiest days of preparation and anticipation for what is ahead.

Now is the time to make lists, stock the larder with essentials and treats, tackle last-minute recipes, buy presents, shop for fresh produce – but also to celebrate with family and friends. Advent is a hive of activity at River Cottage, the culmination of 12 months of growing, harvesting, cooking, teaching and feasting. We celebrate our ingredients and their provenance throughout the year but we revel in the festive richness the season brings.

Of course, there is never enough time. Every day seems to go twice as quickly in fun-filled December as it does in bleak January. So, I always start the month writing several lists that become the cornerstone of my planning and sanity. At the top of the list is the kitchen larder, the nucleus of Operation Christmas, split into four parts: preserves, essentials, dry goods and festive treats. If all else fails in the countdown to Christmas, my pantry at least will uphold my good name.

One of the things that the experience of lockdown taught me was to keep a good selection of adaptable ingredients in store. I am absolutely not encouraging you to stockpile but simply reminding you how helpful an extra bag of flour, tin of tomatoes or packet of rice can be. These days you may well be able to go out on Christmas Day to get more butter – but do you really want to? Organised sourcing and moderate stocking now will save a lot of time later and it will help with costs. Spreading your shopping out over several weeks will lessen the financial blow and should prevent last-minute panic purchases.

The Advent countdown can be crammed with events like parties, early evening drinks, intimate dinners, vibrant Christmas markets, pantomimes and rousing carol concerts, if we are lucky. Of all the significant dates and moments to be shared and celebrated, the winter solstice (on or around 21 December) has a special place in my heart and the River Cottage calendar. An acknowledgement of the darkest point of the year before the light slowly returns, we always mark it in some way. This also signals the end of Christmas preparations and the beginning of the main days of celebration from Christmas Eve onwards.

One important note before I launch into this chapter... I hope that what follows will fill you with inspiration, ideas and confidence. What I emphatically do not want is to increase the pre-Christmas pressure or inflate the expectations you have of yourself.

When my father was a child, my grandmother worked in a successful florist opposite Harrods. December was always her busiest month and she would work until late on Christmas Eve. Arriving home that night, she would burst into exhausted tears, wishing that Christmas would disappear. I think of her every year because there is always a point when I feel myself tipping towards that. None of us want to be wailing the night before Christmas. We want to be feet up, presents wrapped, veg prep done, brandy in hand with a second poured for Father Christmas. That is to say, remember you do not have to do everything, or indeed very much at all. Take what you need from this chapter and do what you can; most importantly, enjoy the things you choose to do.

Advent calendars

Do you remember the joy of Advent calendars as a child, prising open a window each morning, excited by the picture it revealed and the knowledge you were another day closer to Christmas?! These simple printed calendars originated in Germany in the early 1900s and were redesigned to incorporate little windows 20 years later.

Since then the calendar has adapted and developed and, while the pictorial style is still popular, it has been overshadowed by the 'filled' versions offering chocolate, toiletries, toys or gifts. The 'gifty' ones can be safely avoided, I feel; but it seems the chocolate versions are now 'standard traditional' for young children.

At home, as well as the traditional pictorial calendar, we have an Advent candle marked with the days of December. We light it each day, to signify the passing of time and the darkest hours before solstice (and try to remember to snuff it out before we blaze through the next 3 days of Advent…)

There are other, charming ideas to make this countdown your own by creating a personal Advent calendar for your family. Some of my favourites include filling 24 small envelopes or boxes with notes of affirmation, coins, jokes or forfeits – and yes, something chocolatey or sweet. Or baking a gingerbread house with 24 biscuit people to eat.

A friend made a fabric calendar out of an old sheet with 24 pockets and decorated it with fabric pens. It still comes out over a decade later but the treats are now real coins instead of chocolate (good on her) so her teenage children can put it towards an item they would like. Christmas Eve always includes a packet of 'reindeer food'.

Recently there has been a welcome trend towards the 'reverse Advent calendar' – giving something back each day instead (or as well as) receiving, either with a good deed or donation, or filling a box with produce for the local food bank. This feels like one of the best ways to mark the counting down of the days.

Advent tasks and reminders

Start December with a list. Mine is a big list with subsections for food, drink, gifts, decorations, events, date reminders and memory joggers. This is a personal endeavour and may not be your preferred method, but I have included pointers in case it is useful. At the very least it can act as a good reminder or reference point. I'm a jotter and pencil person but, of course, you can make a dedicated file for this on your phone or laptop.

Dates
- Events you are invited to
- Event(s) you are hosting
- Delivery dates for orders
- Last post for cards and gifts

Food
- A loose menu plan for the main days of Christmas
- A menu plan for any event you are hosting
- Additional handmade endeavours for gifts/store cupboard
- Book an early date for supermarket/ veg box/farm shop delivery
- Stocktake and tidy the larder
- Clean and clear out the fridge and freezer to make space (a week of 'freezer clear out cooking' in early December can be useful)
- Full list of food preparation
- A larder shopping list
- A fresh grocery shopping list
- Any produce that needs to be ordered with cut-off dates
- Things to make for the freezer

Drink
- Stocktake of the drinks cabinet
- Check and decant home-steeped booze
- A shopping list of spirits and mixers (ideally decreasing annually!)
- A wine plan (perhaps including a tasting with a local wine seller)
- Beer (order from the local brewery/ maker)
- Keep an eye out for any deals/offers
- Non-alcoholic selection (order River Cottage kombucha!)
- Stock up on ice cubes – fill trays, freeze and pop out into a freezer bag

Gifts
- List of those to buy for
- 'Blue Sky' ideas for presents
- Home-made gifts – those made and still to make
- Shop-bought gifts
- Order online deliveries before cut-off
- Matching gifts to people
- Write Christmas cards
- Wrap presents

Decorations

- Home-made decorations
- Get existing decorations down from the attic
- Check the tree lights
- Christmas tree collection
- Walk(s) to cut and gather greenery
- Make a wreath and garlands

Miscellaneous

- Buy candles
- Buy brown wrapping paper, biodegradable tape, string

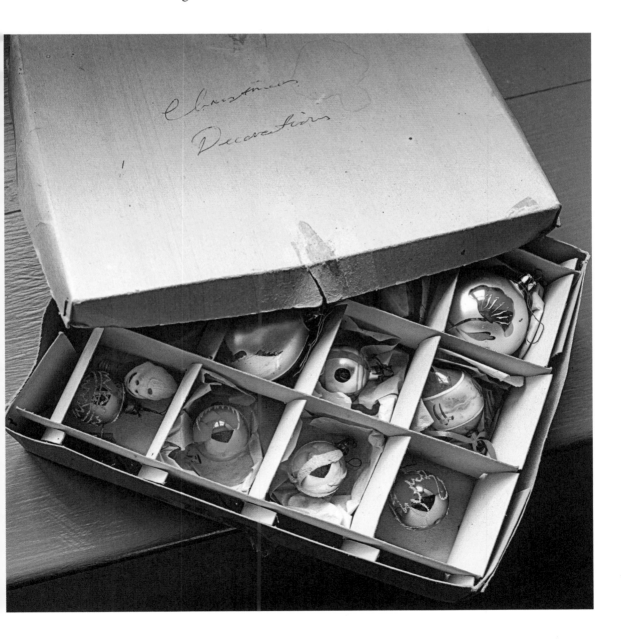

The Christmas larder

The arrival of Advent marks a shift in preparations. You may congratulate your summer self for the planting, preserving, pickling, fermenting and pudding-making of previous months but there is still work to be done. One of the more important jobs is to sort out the store cupboard(s), freezer and fridge in readiness for what is ahead. Tackle these chores now before the kitchen is full of people and activity. I value these quiet times alone, even if I'm knee-deep in tasks – it's an opportunity to listen to a podcast or audio book as I work.

Whether you have a larder, old-fashioned pantry, store cupboard(s), or a couple of shelves, clearing a space for what comes next is time well spent. I also check use-by dates and winkle out jars that have been pushed to the dark recesses. It is a good point in the year to do a full stocktake and note what needs to be finished, topped up and replaced.

Go through recipes you want to make and begin to put a shopping list together. This is less about creating a strict menu plan – we all need a level of spontaneity – and more about making sure you have the right ingredients to hand to avoid last-minute panics. However, let us not fall into those traps of excess or buying unfamiliar ingredients that are likely to sit there until the following Christmas. Considered purchasing will avoid waste and expense.

Think of your store cupboard in four parts:

1 Preserves

Those spirit-lifting jars of goodies. You may have a little store already after a late summer/autumn harvest, perhaps including jams, pickles, chutney, booze, preserved veg and/or fruit. Rediscovering things you made earlier, ready to eat, is a particular type of pleasure. To complete your store of preserved treats, find a local WI market or farm shop, who will stock the best local products. Honey is a great example of this. Seeing the name of a village you know on the label makes you feel like you're eating it straight from the hive with a spoon.

2 Essentials

Your essentials may not be mine, but this is a useful checklist for your store cupboard at any time of year:

- Flours (strong bread, spelt, rye, wholemeal, plain and self-raising)
- Oats
- Baking powder and bicarbonate of soda
- Sugars (granulated, light and dark brown, caster, icing)
- Salts (flaky sea salt, fine, flavoured)
- Peppercorns (black and a mixed bag of black, green and red)
- Dried herbs (most importantly oregano, thyme, bay)
- Nuts (almonds, walnuts, hazelnuts, peanuts, pistachios)
- Seeds (linseed, sesame, sunflower, pumpkin)
- Dried fruits (raisins, sultanas, currants, apricots, dates, figs, cherries, cranberries)
- Spices (including cloves, cinnamon, cumin, coriander, star anise, chilli powder, dried chilli flakes, turmeric)
- Mustard
- Soy sauce (tamari or shoyu, or both!)
- Capers
- Olives
- Oils (olive, rapeseed, hemp)
- Vinegars (cider, white and red wine)
- Organic stock cubes or bouillon

3 Dry goods

The foundation of so many meals:

- Pasta
- Rice
- Noodles
- Pearled spelt and barley
- Quinoa
- Dry pulses (lentils, chickpeas, beans)
- Tinned pulses (chickpeas, cannellini beans, kidney beans)
- Tinned tomatoes
- Tinned fish: sardines, anchovies, mackerel, tuna (look for the 'blue tick' MSC logo signifying sustainably caught)
- Coconut milk

4 Treats

The little things that make Christmas:

- Sourdough crackers, oatcakes, digestives and any other favourite biscuits to go with cheese
- Roasted nuts and crisps
- Dark chocolate
- Stem ginger in syrup
- Turkish Delight and/or other sweets

The fridge

Your final shopping trip before Christmas will be for perishables that fill the fridge: dairy (butter, cheese, milk, cream), eggs, salad, vegetables, fruit, poultry, meat and fish. For those items you haven't already ordered, head to the independents on your local high street or the nearest farm shop if you can. Some veg box schemes will include additional items at this time of year which makes shopping easier.

If you are struggling for cold space in the final few days then you can store veg and fruit outside or in a shed or garage, out of the weather and, if necessary, in rodent-proof containers. If you are entertaining a crowd then it helps to have a second fridge but don't buy one especially! A cool box with regularly refreshed ice packs should help you get through the run-up to the event and may be helpful for storing leftovers too.

The freezer

Once you have tackled the dry goods, think about what you plan to make in advance and freeze. Early December is a good time to do some batch cooking, focusing on recipes that freeze well. In this category, I include quick bites like sausage rolls and scones, lunch fail-safes like bread and soups, evening meals of casseroles and curries, and mince pies, crumbles and ice cream for pudding. I am not suggesting you make all of these for the freezer but you will be glad if there are at least a couple of loaves and a batch of mince pies in.

Every freezer should have a big bag of peas and a full ice-cube tray, as well as any produce you were inundated with over the summer, like broad beans and soft fruit. If your freezer space is limited then choose a few items, such as savoury and sweet pastry and a pot each of chicken and veg stock, that can be turned into a quick soup – anything that will help you at a future point when you really do not want to be in the kitchen.

Where appropriate, I have included a note about freezing individual recipes. I don't tend to pre-cook and freeze elements of the Christmas lunch but I know this is a practical solution some choose, to save time and sanity on the day. It works particularly well with things like stuffing, stock for the gravy and cheese sauce.

Herbs and spices

What would our cooking be without the crucial additions of herbs and spices? We know how much they elevate a dish yet we don't always pay enough attention to these hard-working flavour bombs. Many herbs are evergreen and incredibly easy to grow, giving you a constant supply of fresh flavour through the winter. These include rosemary, sage, thyme, winter savory and parsley (if you keep it under cover or indoors from early autumn). They are all versatile and transformative.

One herb that deserves more recognition is chervil. It suits a large pot in a sheltered position and responds well to regular cutting. The leaves carry an enjoyable burst of aniseed and boost winter salads, vegetables, mayonnaise and sauces. However, if I was only allowed one herb, it would have to be the fragrant bay. I add the leaves to my cooking daily, almost subconsciously, as well as using it in infusions and to add texture and scent to wreaths.

While there is a vast array of dried herbs available, it's very pleasing to preserve some of your own at the end of the summer. There are various ways you can do this: drying or freezing them, or in butter, which can also be frozen. It is better to freeze parsley, tarragon and chives either by popping them into a sealed tub or mashing them through softened butter and then freezing them. Alternatively, chop them and put into ice-cube trays, top up with water and place carefully in the freezer.

Herbs that respond well to being dried and keep their flavour include thyme, rosemary, sage, bay, lemon verbena, oregano, marjoram and fennel seed. A couple of herbs I always want through the winter months are lemon verbena, which makes the best early morning and late evening tea (Hugh waxes lyrical about this herb too, see page 24), and oregano for the stews, bolognaise and pizzas.

The best way to dry herbs is to hang them in the airing cupboard or a warm, dark corner where they can dry slowly and completely. Alternatively, you can put them on a baking rack or tray in a cool oven (120°C/Fan 100°/Gas ½) with the door slightly ajar to keep the air flowing; they will take at least 3 hours to dry in the oven and you will need to keep an eye and turn the herbs every so often. To check there is no moisture left, place a couple of leaves in a glass jar with the lid on to see if they create condensation. Once you are sure they are dry they can be stored in glass jars with tight-fitting lids.

Warming, fragrant spices like cinnamon, cloves, ginger, nutmeg, allspice and star anise take centre stage at Christmas. Stock up on these before Christmas as they will be integral to many winter recipes – as are cumin, cardamom, coriander, chilli flakes, turmeric, smoked paprika, juniper and fennel, mustard and onion seeds. Evocative, exotic and often with layers of heat, these spices transform curries, vegetables and bakes. Some are also essential in mulled wine or cider.

Bay: the other Christmas tree

Bay leaves produce one of my favourite smells. We have two bay trees in our garden and when I pass either of them I often grab a leaf and scrunch it and sniff it. Sometimes the leaf ends up in my pocket – where I may well be pleased to find it later in the day, for another quick aromatherapeutic hit.

This behaviour is not confined to my own garden. It happens to other people's bay trees, including those belonging to complete strangers whose front gardens I happen to be walking past. So, it's not unusual for me to find random bay leaves in varying states of desiccation and disintegration in the pockets of jackets and trousers. And it's certainly not unheard of for these remnants to find their way into my cooking.

Because I use bay A LOT. Almost every stew, soup and sauce – whether it's meaty, fishy or veggie – gets a twisted (to release the aroma) bay leaf or two. And almost every roast (again, animal, vegetable or marine) has a few tucked in or under. Its gift to these dishes is subtle, almost mystical. And in all honesty, I couldn't promise you that I can always clearly discern the flavour of bay in a stew, or indeed tell you if it was missing from a sauce. I just know that it's good when it's there.

Yet there are times when the intensely scented note of bay comes at you in spades – and it's invariably when a leaf has had contact with the exterior of some food that's been roasted or grilled to crispness, and the heat has both charred and fused the leaf to the food. When that happens – on the crisped skin of a roast chicken or barbecued fish for example – it's insanely good.

As is perhaps becoming clear, my love for bay is bordering on obsessive. By way of a clincher, perhaps I should mention that my youngest daughter's middle name is Bay. And I once owned a boat called Jane Bay, which some people assumed referred to 'bay' in the nautical sense. More fool them...

I may be nuts about bay, but I'm not grasping when it comes to these leaves (except literally). In fact, I'm very keen to spread the bay love – far and wide. I think everyone who likes to cook, and has even a minimum of outdoor space, should own a bay tree. It will be quite happy in a pot provided you keep it watered in dry weather.

So, I highly recommend a potted bay tree as a Christmas present for anyone whose life in the kitchen you want to enhance (or whose pockets you think could smell nicer).

There's a hitch. Bay is a slow-growing evergreen. This, plus the tradition of pruning bay trees into either pyramids or lollipops, makes a tree thus-shaped, and of any size, eye-wateringly expensive. In fact, if you've never stopped in a garden centre to look at the price of a bay tree that greets you at eye level with pom-pom clipped foliage about the same size as your head, then brace yourself. It's likely to cost over a hundred quid.

But if you already have a bay tree of your own, then you can give a piece of it for free... If you are green-fingered you may know that you can take cuttings from bay trees which often propagate very successfully. But slowly! It will take a couple of years for a single-stem 15cm cutting with half a dozen leaves at the tip to have 3 or 4 stems and a few dozen leaves. There's no denying that such a lovingly nurtured bay-ling comes from the heart. So, it's really a gift for someone who will fully take that on board – and is in it for the long haul.

A small shrubby plant from a garden centre will be a couple of years on from that – and more reasonably priced than anything sculpted. There's a lot to be said for choosing such a specimen to give – it will grow on vigorously in a self-willed free-form manner, and produce plenty of leaves. And this, of course, is what you must tell the lucky recipient of your thriftily chosen, slightly shabby, entirely un-topiarised bay. Feel free to pin it on me. **Hugh**

Fresh produce in season

At Christmas there is an abundance of earthy roots, frost-resistant greens and hardy brassicas available. These are the hearty stars of winter which will feature in veg boxes and veg patches across the country. Good old dependables like potatoes, beetroot, parsnips, celeriac, swede and turnips alongside the less common but worth it Jerusalem artichokes, kohlrabi and salsify. Onions, shallots and leeks are in fine supply too and most Christmas feasts will not be complete without cauliflower and Brussels sprouts. Kale, kalettes and chard inject any meal with much-needed greenery and celery and chicory create fresh, crunchy salads.

Fruit options are limited to apples and pears, but what fruits they are! Two of the most versatile that work just as well with savoury as sweet. Don't forget nuts too – hazelnuts, walnuts and chestnuts, which are pure Christmas.

Food orders

Sustainability and provenance are at the heart of everything we do at River Cottage. What we cannot grow or nurture ourselves we find from sources we trust. This means we are dealing directly with local farms, growers and artisan producers so we know where our produce has come from and the story behind it. Many of these small businesses take orders and organise direct deliveries to individuals too, especially at Christmas.

If these direct food deliveries are something you have not considered before, do look into it. Not only will you be buying the very best, most delicious produce but you will be championing the passionate, committed suppliers behind them. You will need to be organised and check delivery deadlines but you should be able to order anything from organic meat, fish and shellfish, charcuterie, cheese and vegetables to chocolate and booze.

You can also support local independent businesses by ordering through your nearest farm shop, veg box scheme, butcher, greengrocer and wine shop. The milkman may also be able to provide more than milk. Not only are we able to get milk in nostalgic glass bottles but also yoghurt too, and some will deliver other stuff in returnable, reusable packaging.

I still use supermarkets, as almost everybody does (except Hugh!), but I aim to limit my spend to domestic items rather than fresh produce.

Festive fish and shellfish

We love to have a fishy feast at least once over the Christmas holiday, and if we can land it on Christmas Eve, then so much the better. It usually takes the form of a starter of oysters, and a more variable fin-fishy main course.

The exact date, and the final menu, will depend on whether the weather has permitted a pre-Christmas fishing trip, and if it has, what – if anything – we have caught. The plan is invariably hatched with my best fishing buddy, and River Cottage Fish Book co-author, Nick Fisher. We usually aim to go out on the 21, 22 or 23 December – a date we'll optimistically stick in the diary sometime in November.

We are always hoping for one of those crisp, pure, blue-sky December days without a breath of wind. It might start frosty, but once the sun's up (or as up as it's going to be on what's almost the shortest day of the year), then you can feel its warmth through your several jumpers. Even so, the gloves probably only come off for tying fishing knots and, with luck, when there's a fish to be landed. As often as not the trip gets bumped to the post-Christmas window. No matter. We'll make it a New Year fishy feast instead.

Occasionally we have even managed to bag a sea bass or two within a few days of Christmas, in which case a whole fish, baked on a bed of winter veg (leeks, celeriac and parsnips), lemon zest, and plenty of parsley and bay, will grace the table on Christmas Eve. Fish suppers don't get much smugger than that.

It's more likely, though, that bass will have eluded us. But there's still a very good chance we will have consoled ourselves with a decent haul of whiting and pouting, and maybe a hefty pollack or two. In either of these cases, two time-honoured preparations are very likely to come into play.

Catch night, whenever it falls, will be celebrated with fillets of catch-of-the-day, given the flour-egg-and-breadcrumb treatment, fried until crispy, and served with a River Cottage classic – cheaty tartare sauce. This is made by 'pimping' mayonnaise (ideally home-made, but it has been known to come out of a jar) with chopped hard-boiled eggs, capers, gherkins, a dab of mustard and a squeeze of lemon.

The other dish is one whose festive associations grow on me by the year: brandade. Classically this is made with dried salt cod which has been soaked in several changes of fresh water for at least 24 hours before being cooked and blended with stale bread, olive oil, garlic and cream.

Our version uses the fresh fillets of our just-caught cod relatives, only lightly salted, and some lovely floury spuds, with the bready element switched up to a crispy breadcrumb topping. It's just lovely, and so I'm sharing the full recipe with you on page 146. And sometimes I make this with fish that's been smoked as well as salted – so sustainably sourced smoked haddock from your local fishmonger would do the job very nicely.

Preceded by a plate of oysters (see page 138 for my festive twist), and served up with a side of winter greens (kale or sprout tops, and leeks) the 'F-W house brandade' absolutely cuts it as a Christmas Eve main course. If it does get bumped by a whole baked bass, then no one's complaining – we are just slightly adjusting the festive meal plan. The lightly salted fillets will keep for 5 days (or freeze brilliantly), so it will definitely have its day before Twelfth Night is out. **Hugh**

Winter solstice

There is one date which often gets overlooked in the rush to get to the main days of Christmas: the winter solstice. An important point on the pagan calendar, it was also known as 'midwinter' or 'mother night', an apt name for the shortest day. It marked the arrival of winter and was celebrated in ancient cultures with a final feast before the cold, hungry months set in. Bonfires were lit, livestock killed and eaten, fermented alcohol uncorked and greenery brought inside as a symbol of life and renewal. Many of the winter solstice rituals have merged into the Christmas celebrations we have now. Today it occurs around the 21 December in the Northern Hemisphere and often coincides with the end of the school term and the beginning of the Christmas holiday for many of us.

The winter solstice feels more significant than New Year's Day for me and I always acknowledge it. It is a turning point in the natural world, a moment to consider the year as it draws to a close and think about what comes next. I am lucky to live near the coast and swim most mornings with friends. We celebrate every solstice with a sunrise swim, followed by a beach fire and a breakfast picnic of bacon and marmalade sandwiches or a generous slice of stollen as we watch the light shift. Later in the day as the sun sets, I light a fire and take a spoon to the rumtopf that has been steeping since the summer solstice to give to family and friends, a symbolic sharing of the year's fruitful produce.

If you are keen to commemorate this point of the year, you do not have to go to such great lengths or take your sleeping bag to Stonehenge. One age-old tradition is to head to the highest point near you, somewhere that has far-reaching views of the landscape and the horizon, and wait for the sun to rise. Contrary to what you might imagine, that doesn't mean setting your alarm clock for the wee small hours, as sunrise on 21 Dec is actually around 8 a.m. But if that doesn't work for you, then lighting a fire bowl (or the barbecue!) in the garden, or simply a candle on your windowsill, are both fine ways to mark the ritual of light.

You could invite others to join you and celebrate together, or take time out of the festive frenzy for yourself. Some people like to use this as an opportunity to write about things they have struggled with over the year, stuff they want to let go of, before burning the notes on the fire. Whatever way you may choose to acknowledge it, I hope you do. Now, more than ever, it is important to appreciate, connect with, and immerse ourselves in the natural world around us.

Little Christmas Eve

For most younger children, the very thought of Christmas Eve still evokes fizzing excitement and the day itself is spent in breath-taking anticipation of what is to come. As grown-ups, the magical thrill is easy to remember but considerably harder to recapture. However, it is still possible to summon up a little youthful delight, not just vicariously through your own or others' children but also by making the day joyful for yourself.

The trick is not to lose those hours to last-minute panics about food, presents or house organisation. And this is why in our house, we have Christmas Eve Eve – a day designated for bustle, busyness and final tasks, relieving the pressure on 'the real' Christmas Eve.

In Denmark, 23 December is known as Little Christmas Eve, a concept we now fully embrace at home. As part of the celebration, they serve a hot rice pudding, making enough to have cold with a hot cherry sauce on the 24 December (it's not a bad breakfast). I have incorporated this warmly into our family traditions and I include the recipe for you on page 162.

Christmas Eve

When I lived in London, and before I had kids, Christmas Eve meant an early morning trip to the butcher to collect the turkey, happily queuing with lots of other jolly people, followed by a quick stop for a coffee in a little café with steamy windows. Then home via the local Italian deli for slices of wafer-cut Parma ham, fennel- or peppercorn-edged salami, a doorstop wedge of Parmesan and a sweet treat, maybe some marrons glacés or a beautifully packaged panettone – all the things I would wish to receive in my Christmas stocking if I had one now.

It was a treasured part of the Christmas build-up and I still make a point of popping out, even if just for a coffee and a last look at the Christmas lights. These small moments are where I find the festive thrill.

While it feels like many of us are sharing more or less the same rituals of feasting and present-giving on Christmas Day, Christmas Eve is much less defined. Some may still be at work, have family commitments or be swept up in last-minute shopping missions. However, one thing is certain: it is almost impossible to avoid the kitchen. But I would not want to: it can be a joyous place on Christmas Eve, whether you are cooking a splendid dinner for the evening, prepping for the feast the following day or just knocking up a batch of sausage rolls while you listen to *Carols from King's* on the radio.

In many countries, particularly those with a strong Catholic tradition, Christmas Eve is just as important as Christmas Day. Presents are exchanged, feasts shared and Midnight Mass attended, even by the smallest members of the family. Each country has its own culinary traditions for this special evening and it is fascinating to see how these shift between regions.

In Italy, fish takes centre stage – spaghetti vongole in Naples, eel in Rome and salted cod in Sicily. In France, oysters, scallops, truffles and aïoli garni (garlic mayonnaise with crudités, see page 140) are all popular elements of the Christmas Eve feast, depending where you are. Provence boasts an additional tradition of 13 desserts on Christmas Eve, symbolising Jesus Christ and his 12 disciples (even though they weren't much in evidence at the first Christmas). The popular smörgåsbord in Sweden becomes a julbord for the night, full of hot and cold dishes including fish, charcuterie, cheese and bread.

In Mexico, they make a beetroot, orange and peanut salad called nochebuena, which is the word for Christmas Eve in Spanish. And in the Caribbean the first slice may be cut of the black cake – a rum-laden cross between a Christmas cake and a Christmas pud.

In the UK, we do not have a national or regional dish for Christmas Eve and with so much global and local inspiration it is hard to know what to cook. Keep it simple if you are also in charge of cooking Christmas lunch the following day. Consider the structure of your Christmas Eve: the number of people you may be feeding and any additional arrangements, such as drinks with neighbours or Midnight Mass.

If you are busy, this may be the time to slice your Christmas ham and throw a winter slaw together (like Hugh's lovely recipe on page 221), or whip up a garlic mayonnaise and platter of vegetables. Alternatively, if you are in for the evening, you can turn the meal into a group activity and involve all the family with pizza making. The dough can be made in the morning and left to prove until you are ready to roll it out.

Before you go to bed to dream of sugar plum fairies, you might want to take your Christmas bird out of the fridge (if you are cooking it for lunch rather than dinner, so it will slowly come up to room temperature overnight). But do make sure it is safe from curious pets. And of course, don't forget to leave a snack out for Father Christmas – I have heard he is rather fond of a glass of sloe port and a couple of pumpkin seed biscotti. Luckily you now have those recipes to hand…

Roasted Nuts & Seeds

Too good for the reindeer, this seed and nut mix is a bowl of umami heaven. It has been a huge hit ever since its debut on my first River Cottage Christmas course. Stored in a lidded jar, it will last at least a couple of weeks but the truth is it's likely to disappear in one sitting. Make this batch and you will have enough to give a jar (or two) away... or store in the larder as a chef's perk when you are knee-deep in potato peeling. Prepare up to 2 weeks ahead of Christmas.

Makes 3 x 250ml jars

200g mix of whole skin-on almonds, hazelnuts, walnuts
200g pumpkin seeds
100ml tamari
50ml olive oil
About 4 sprigs of rosemary (optional, but worth it)
About 4 sprigs of sage (optional)

You will also need:
A 750ml Kilner jar or 3 x 250ml jars

Preheat the oven to 200°C/Fan 180°C/Gas 6.

Put the nuts and seeds into a bowl and douse generously with the tamari and olive oil. Toss to mix.

If using, spread your herbs out on a baking tray. Scatter the nut and seed mix over them and roast in the oven for 5 minutes.

Take the tray out, give everything a good stir and shake, then return it to the oven for another 5 minutes, keeping a close eye as the nuts and seeds burn easily. Repeat this a final time by which time everything should be nicely toasted. If not, return to the oven for a couple more minutes.

Leave the seed and nut mix on the tray to cool down and crisp up before transferring to a jar. You can discard the herbs if you've used them but I like to crush them and toss through the mix.

Oysters are my favourite first course for Christmas Eve. I like estuary-grown oysters best, as they are less salty, and I buy mine (ordered well in advance for Christmas) from local oyster farms in either Teignmouth or Yealm. They always taste fantastic when enhanced with something a little bit sharp and piquant. Shallot vinegar and Tabasco sauce are classics but the spicy, slightly salty liquor from a batch of kimchi is the key to my new favourite dressing, delivering maximum, umami-rich flavour when paired with the shellfish. That kimchi 'juice' is full of beneficial live bacteria too, which is just one more good reason to try this... **Hugh**

Oysters with Apple & Kimchi Dressing

Serves 4 as a starter

16–24 fresh live oysters
1 tbsp kimchi, drained
2–3 tbsp kimchi juice (from the jar)

1 medium eating apple, such as Cox's
*   or Discovery*
½ lemon

Use an oyster knife with a finger guard to open the oysters. Hold an oyster firmly inside a tea towel (which will protect your hand) on a steady surface, with the flatter half of the shell uppermost and the hinge pointing towards you. Insert the knife just to the left or right of the hinge and work it between the two halves of the shell. Twist and lever the shell open, trying not to spill any of the oyster's delicious juices.

Once the shell is open, discard the flatter top half. Now run the tip of the knife gently under the oyster itself, severing it from the shell but leaving it sitting in the rounded half-shell in its juices. Repeat this process with the remaining oysters.

Arrange the oysters in their half-shells on a tray or large plate. Laying them on crushed ice is traditional, though not essential – but you should certainly keep them very cold until a few minutes before serving. Put them in the fridge if needed.

To prepare the dressing, chop the kimchi fairly fine and put it into a small bowl with the juice. Peel, quarter and core the apple, then dice into tiny 2–3mm cubes, and add to the kimchi mix. Add a squeeze of lemon juice, a twist or two of black pepper, and mix well. Bring the oysters to the table with the dressing and, if you like, some brown bread and butter. Tip a small spoonful of dressing over each oyster before eating.

Aïoli Garni

This dish of garlicky mayonnaise with delicious things to dip into it is a Christmas Eve tradition in Provence. It also reminds me of the Swedish smörgåsbord. I cannot think of an easier, more versatile and delicious platter. It can be prepared for as few or as many people as you like, kept restrained as a starter or served generously as a main course, and can be adapted for all dietary needs. It is fast becoming a year-round favourite for me, as I like to make it with the first new veg of each season.

I've suggested some of the seasonal ingredients that work alongside the aïoli but feel free to do your own thing. It is all about personal preference and how much you can squeeze onto the platter. I keep to veg and fish on Christmas Eve as a rule, but if I want more of a smörgåsbord then I'll include slices of cured or cold roast meat.

Serves 4–6

For the aïoli:

2 garlic cloves, crushed
2 egg yolks
1 tbsp Dijon mustard
150ml light rapeseed oil
150ml extra virgin olive oil
Lemon juice, to taste
Sea salt and black pepper

For the garni:

Raw veg, such as carrot, pepper and
*   celery batons, and radicchio wedges*
Blanched veg, such as purple sprouting
*   broccoli and cauliflower, cut into florets*
Roasted potato wedges, served hot
Fish, such as poached salt cod or smoked
*   pollack, served hot or cold*
Shellfish, such as sautéed scallops,
*   boiled lobster and/or large prawns*
Meat, such as rare roast beef, cold
*   chicken or cured meats*
Extras, such as olives and pickles

To make the aïoli, put the garlic, egg yolks and mustard into a small blender or food processor and blitz briefly to combine. With the motor running, add the oils a few drops at a time to begin with, then in a steady trickle. (If your mayonnaise 'splits', either beat in 1 tsp boiling water or beat a fresh egg yolk in a clean bowl and slowly whisk into the mayonnaise to re-emulsify.)

If your aïoli is too thick, whisk in a spoonful of warm water. Season it with lemon juice, salt and pepper to taste. Transfer to a serving bowl and refrigerate until needed; use within 24 hours.

When you are ready to serve, assemble your chosen garni ingredients on a large platter (or several plates) and accompany with the aïoli.

Red Cabbage & Beetroot Pickle

Red cabbage is a familiar element of Christmas lunch. It is often braised, which makes it an easy dish to cook ahead of time, freeze and then reheat at the last minute. I think it is always good to have at least one vegetable you can get on the table with the minimum of fuss but I prefer my cabbage crunchy. This recipe is exactly that, injecting a fresh zing into the Christmas feast and the days that follow. I usually make mine several weeks in advance. You don't even need to decant it from its glass jar – just plonk it straight on the table. Make sure you save enough for your Boxing Day buffet too.

Makes a 1.5 litre jar

200g beetroot, peeled and grated
500g red cabbage, sliced
Finely grated zest of 2 oranges
10g cumin seeds, toasted and bashed
5g caraway seeds, toasted and bashed
5 juniper berries, lightly crushed

For the pickling liquor:
700ml cider vinegar
20g coriander seeds, toasted
20g fennel seeds, toasted
10g black peppercorns
20g salt
1 dried red chilli (optional)

You will also need:
A sterilised 1.5 litre Kilner jar

First, prepare the pickling liquor. Put all the ingredients into a saucepan, pour on 200ml water and slowly bring to the boil. Remove from the heat and set aside to infuse for an hour.

Meanwhile, put the beetroot, red cabbage, orange zest, toasted spices and crushed juniper berries into a bowl and toss to mix.

Bring the infused pickling liquor back to the boil, then pour it through a sieve straight over the veg mix. Stir to combine.

This pickle is nice to eat as soon as it cools, but ideally should be packed into a sterilised 1.5 litre Kilner jar, sealed and left for a couple of weeks. It will keep in a cool, dark cupboard for up to 6 months; once opened, it needs to be stored in the fridge.

Sausage Rolls

Sausage rolls can be whatever you want them to be – big and chunky for hefty snacks or lunchboxes, or small, neat, single-mouthful canapés, which are perfect for parties. I always have at least one batch in the freezer ready to bake – prepared up to 6 weeks ahead of Christmas. Anyone who believes they can't make pastry should try this recipe, which is more about patience than skill.

Makes about 25

For the rough puff pastry:

400g plain flour, plus extra to dust

200g fridge-cold butter or lard, cut into walnut-sized pieces

1 medium egg, beaten, to glaze before baking

Sea salt

For the sausagemeat:

500g pork mince (at least 20% fat)

A big pinch of ground white pepper

A good grinding of black pepper

A generous pinch of ground mace

A generous pinch of dried oregano

1 tbsp chopped sage

To make the pastry, in a bowl, mix the flour with a pinch of salt, add the butter or lard pieces and toss to coat in the flour. Add just enough iced water to bring the dough together with your hands (up to 4 tbsp); you want a medium-firm dough that is not too sticky, with pieces of fat still intact.

On a well-floured surface, shape the dough into a fat rectangle and roll out using a well-floured rolling pin, in one direction, away from you, keeping the shape, to a 2cm thickness (or less). Fold the furthest third towards you and then fold the nearest third back over that, to create a rectangle a third of the size and three times as thick. Give the pastry a quarter turn (90°) to the right and roll it out again, away from you, into another long rectangle.

Repeat this folding and turning at least 4 times (ideally 6 or 7); you will need to keep dusting with flour. If the dough becomes too soft, chill it for an hour or so, then dust with more flour and resume rolling. After the final folding, wrap the pastry and refrigerate for at least an hour before use.

Meanwhile, prepare the sausagemeat. Combine the pork mince, pepper, spice, herbs and a generous pinch of salt in a bowl and mix thoroughly.

Roll out the pastry on a lightly floured surface to a long rectangle. Form the sausagemeat into a long sausage and lay it along the left-hand side of the pastry, placing it 3cm in from the edge. Brush the pastry margin with water then fold the other side of the pastry over the sausagemeat and press the edges together to join. Trim away any excess pastry. Crimp the edges to seal then cut into 5cm lengths. If you are freezing the sausage rolls do so now, otherwise place in the fridge to rest for 10 minutes while you preheat the oven to 200°C/Fan 180°C/Gas 6. Line a baking sheet with baking paper.

Brush the tops of the sausage rolls with beaten egg and make a couple of slits in the top of each one. Place on the lined baking sheet and bake in the oven for 20 minutes. Transfer the sausage rolls to a wire rack to cool. Serve while still warm or leave until cold, wrap in greaseproof paper and store in a tin. They will keep for several days in a tin in the fridge.

A slightly cheaty, but super-delicious version of the Provençal classic, this is fantastic, fish-based comfort food. We often have it at home on Christmas Eve with a dish of leeks and winter greens. It also makes a good starter, and can even be adapted into a hand-around canapé, by piling it on little toasts trickled with olive oil.

You can make the brandade earlier in the day and bake it with its breadcrumb topping just before serving – just give it a little longer if it is fridge-cold when you start. **Hugh**

Brandade with Breadcrumbs

Serves 4–6 as a main, 8–10 as a starter

About 500g fillets of sustainably caught white fish, such as whiting, pouting, pollack, cod or haddock

About 400g floury potatoes, such as King Edward, peeled and cut into even-sized chunks

50g unsalted butter

1 large garlic clove, chopped

150ml milk

4 tbsp extra virgin olive oil

75g coarse breadcrumbs

Flaky sea salt and black pepper

First, lightly salt the fish: slice the fillets off their skins and check for any remaining bones. Sprinkle a thin, even layer of salt on a board, lay the fish fillets on top, then sprinkle over a further light covering of salt. Leave for just 15–20 minutes, then rinse off the salt under a cold tap. Pat the fish dry with kitchen paper. While the fish is salting, cook the potatoes in boiling water for 15–20 minutes until tender; drain and return to the hot pan.

Melt the butter in a large pan over a low heat, add the garlic and sweat gently for a couple of minutes. Add the salted fish to the pan and pour over the milk. Bring slowly to a simmer, cover and cook very gently for another couple of minutes or until the fish is cooked through. Scoop the fish out of the pan with a slotted spoon onto a plate, leaving the hot milk behind.

Add 3 tbsp of the extra virgin olive oil and a few grinds of pepper to the hot milk in the pan, then tip in the hot potatoes and mash well, but don't overwork. Break the fish into flakes and mash roughly with a fork then add to the potato mash and stir in. Taste and add more pepper if you like.

Preheat the oven to 190°C/Fan 170°C/Gas 5. Spoon the brandade into a shallow ovenproof dish. Mix the coarse breadcrumbs with the remaining 1 tbsp olive oil and scatter over the surface of the brandade. Bake in the oven for 15–20 minutes until golden and piping hot.

Quick Kedgeree

Whether you serve it for supper on Christmas Eve, brunch on Christmas morning or during the quiet, last days of December, kedgeree is a festive classic. I like this relatively speedy version, based on a favourite method of Hugh's – it's very useful in a time of multi-tasking. It is also incredibly adaptable, incorporating any leftovers you may have. You can leave the fish out completely and make it totally veggie or shred leftover duck or goose through for something meatier. Take the time to crisp up some kale too and you won't regret it for the flavour and texture it brings.

Serves 4

200g kale (optional but worth it)
2 tbsp olive oil (if using kale)
100g butter
2 onions, thinly sliced
A thumb-sized piece of fresh ginger, grated
2 garlic cloves, finely chopped
1 tbsp curry powder or paste

A handful of sultanas
250g brown rice, cooked (500g cooked weight)
A handful of cooked peas
250g leftover cooked fish, such as pollack or undyed smoked haddock
4 medium eggs
Sea salt and black pepper

If using kale, preheat the oven to 220°C/Fan 200°C/Gas 7 and cut the leaves from the stalks; set the stalks aside. Put the leaves into a roasting tray, trickle over the olive oil and add a big pinch of salt. Mix well with your hands. Place in the oven for about 10 minutes while you cook the kedgeree, remembering to shake the kale around several times so it crisps evenly.

Melt 50g of the butter in a large frying pan or sauté pan over a low heat. Add the onions and fry slowly for a good 15 minutes or so until soft and translucent. Put a pan of water on to boil (for the eggs).

Add the ginger and garlic to the onions and cook for a few more minutes. Then add the curry powder, sultanas and kale stalks, if using, and stir well. Add the rice with the remaining 50g butter and stir gently. Now add the peas and fish and gently move the ingredients around in the pan for 5 minutes. Season with salt and pepper to taste.

Meanwhile, add the eggs to the pan of boiling water and time for 5 minutes, then transfer to a bowl of cold water. When cool enough to handle, lift out and carefully peel the eggs (the whites will be set but the yolk still runny). Halve the eggs and arrange on the kedgeree. Serve on warmed plates, with the crispy kale (if including).

Christmas Eve Pizzas

This is a crowd-pleaser of an idea and a brilliant communal activity. Admittedly there is some prep involved – most notably to make and prove the dough earlier in the day and get the toppings ready – but once you've done this, the pizzas will be ready to assemble when you are. I particularly love the freedom of everyone choosing their own toppings and sharing the oven duty. After supper, wrap any leftover slices of pizza in greaseproof paper and store in the fridge for a late-night or dog-walk snack.

Makes 4 or 5

For the dough:

*500g strong white bread flour, plus
extra for shaping and cooking*

5g active dry or fast-action dried yeast

10g fine sea salt

*2 tbsp rapeseed or olive oil, plus extra
to finish*

For the tomato sauce:

2 tbsp rapeseed or olive oil

1 garlic clove, finely sliced

*2 x 400g tins chopped tomatoes
(or 1 tin plus a 400g jar passata)*

A pinch of sugar

Sea salt and black pepper

For the topping (choose from):

Grated Cheddar or other hard cheese

Crumbled goat's cheese or blue cheese

Torn mozzarella

Shredded ham

Sliced chorizo

Sliced or chopped cooked bacon

Cooked thinly sliced onions

Anchovies

Capers

Olives

*Thin slices of cooked beetroot
or roasted squash*

Strips of roasted pepper

Sliced sautéed mushrooms

Torn sage, thyme, oregano or rosemary

*Extra virgin olive or rapeseed oil,
to finish*

To make the dough, combine the flour and yeast in a large bowl. Stir in the salt then add 350ml tepid water and the oil and mix to a rough dough. Turn out onto a lightly floured surface and knead for about 10 minutes, until silky and elastic. Don't be tempted to add too much extra flour, even if the dough seems sticky – it will become less so as you knead. Alternatively, use a food mixer fitted with the dough hook on a fairly high setting for 5 minutes.

Put the dough into a lightly oiled bowl, turning it so it gets a coating of oil and then cover and leave to rise in a warm place until doubled in size; this should take at least an hour.

In the meantime, make the tomato sauce. Heat the oil in a frying pan over a low heat. Add the garlic and sizzle gently for a couple of minutes. As the garlic begins to colour, add the tomatoes. Give everything a stir and simmer gently, for 15 minutes, stirring regularly until you have a thick sauce. Transfer to a jug or bowl and purée with a hand-held stick blender or crush the chunks of tomato in the pan with a fork or a potato masher until you have a reasonably smooth sauce. Add the sugar and season with salt and pepper to taste.

Preheat the oven to 250°C/Fan 230°C/Gas 10 and put a couple of baking sheets inside to heat up.

Tip the risen dough out of the bowl onto a floured surface and punch down with your hands. Cut into 4 or 5 pieces depending on the number and size of pizzas required. Use a rolling pin or your hands (or both), to roll and stretch one piece into a thin circle or square. It should be no more than 5mm thick, the thinner the better.

Carefully take a hot baking sheet from the oven, scatter it with a little flour or, if you have it, some cornmeal, polenta or semolina, and lay the pizza base on it. Thinly spread a little tomato sauce (about 2 tbsp) over the dough. Now add the toppings of your choice with a sprinkle of salt and a grind of pepper.

Bake the pizza for 10–12 minutes, until the base is crisp and golden brown at the edges. While it is cooking, roll out the next piece of dough, and prepare the next pizza in the same way. Continue until they are all cooked. Serve hot, trickled with a little extra virgin oil.

A big platter of beautiful baked fish and aromatic winter veg makes a perfect Christmas Eve supper: understated yet still celebratory, and full of goodness to boot. My favourite for the festive feast would be a whole line-caught bass (ideally self-caught!), a day-netted turbot or brill, or perhaps a good-sized gurnard. If you've more than six to feed, by all means scale the recipe up – using two separate roasting trays if necessary. **Hugh**

Whole Baked Fish

Serves 6

1 large fish (see above), 1.2–1.5kg, or
*   2 medium fish, about 750g, gutted*
*   and descaled (at room temperature)*
6 bay leaves
A knob of butter
2 tbsp vegetable or olive oil
2 onions, thickly sliced
2 medium leeks, cut into 1cm slices
300g celeriac, cut into 2cm chunks

2 large parsnips, cut into 5mm slices
2 large carrots, cut into 5mm slices
A couple of sprigs of thyme
6 garlic cloves, peeled and bashed
A few strips of lemon zest (optional)
A glass of dry white wine
Sea salt and black pepper
Flat-leaf parsley, roughly chopped,
*   to finish*

Preheat the oven to 190°C/Fan 170°C/Gas 5. Season the whole fish (or both smaller fish) inside and out, and tuck a bay leaf into the cavity.

Heat a large frying pan or stockpot over a medium heat and add the butter and oil. When melted and bubbling, add all the veg, season with salt and pepper and stir well. Allow to sweat, stirring occasionally for 8–10 minutes, until the root veg are starting to soften. Transfer to a large roasting dish.

Add the fish (or two), nestling them down into the veg, and piling some of the veg over the top, too. Tuck the rest of the bay leaves and the thyme and garlic around the fish, along with the lemon zest, if using. Trickle the wine over the veg and sprinkle over a glass of water too.

Cover the dish loosely with lightly oiled foil or baking paper. Bake for 25–35 minutes, depending on the size of the fish. To check it is cooked, insert a knife into the thickest part – the flesh should be opaque and come easily away from the bone. Scatter chopped parsley all over the veg.

If you're serving one large fish, it's nice to bring the whole dish to the table. You don't really need an accompaniment, although a dish of wilted kale is good with all those lovely roots. Mash can be a welcome addition too.

Yule Ham

One of the best things about picking up a generously sized joint of gammon is how it can sustain you through the twelve days of Christmas. It is the gift that keeps on giving, straight from the fridge. I like to serve it freshly cooked with parsley sauce a few days before Christmas, then sliced cold as part of the Boxing Day spread (with a celeriac slaw), before shredding the last of it into a creamy, rib-sticking pasta, or enjoying it with lazy breakfast eggs in the blurry time before New Year. You can choose smoked or unsmoked ham, on or off the bone – just make sure it's free-range or organic. Once cooked, it will keep well wrapped in the fridge for up to a week.

Serves 8 with plenty of leftovers

4kg skin-on uncooked gammon joint
1 onion, halved
1 carrot, halved
2 leeks, halved
10 black peppercorns
2 bay leaves

For the glaze:
1 tsp coriander seeds, crushed
1 tsp grated orange zest
3 tbsp demerara sugar
3 tbsp light muscovado sugar
2–3 tbsp English mustard powder
100g runny honey
A handful of cloves

Put the gammon joint into a large pan, cover with cold water and leave to soak for 12 hours to remove excess salt, changing the water at least once.

Drain off the water then pour enough fresh cold water over the gammon to cover and add the onion, carrot, leeks, peppercorns and bay leaves. Slowly bring to the boil, put the lid on and turn the heat down to a gentle simmer. Cook over a low heat, allowing 20 minutes per 500g. (If you are serving the ham hot, make the parsley sauce towards the end of the cooking time.)

Preheat the oven to 220°C/Fan 200°C/Gas 7. Let the ham cool in the pan for several minutes before lifting it out onto a board. Strain the cooking water through a sieve into a jug; discard the contents of the sieve. This liquor can be kept in the fridge for several days and used as stock.

Using a sharp knife, carefully cut the skin from the meat but leave on a generous layer of fat. Score the fat layer in a criss-cross fashion, to create a diamond pattern. For the glaze, put all the ingredients, except the cloves, into a bowl and mix together. Rub the glaze all over the ham then push a clove into each diamond. Put the ham on a rack in a roasting tray.

To protect the exposed face of the ham, cut a foil cover and secure it in place with cocktail sticks or skewers. Bake for 15–20 minutes until the glaze crisps and colours nicely. Serve hot, carved into generous slices, with parsley sauce and veg of your choice, or cold with salads and condiments.

Parsley sauce
Melt 40g butter in a saucepan and stir in 40g plain flour. Cook, stirring, for 2 minutes, then gradually stir in 600ml milk. Simmer gently for 8 minutes. Season with salt and pepper and stir through 4 tbsp finely chopped parsley.

Kale with Anchovy Cream

I am always drawn to a recipe that includes anchovy and cream as a base – Jansson's Temptation with its winning layering of potato, onion, anchovy and cream, for example. This is a lighter dish and one you can swap around the veg with. It makes a great partner to many festive meals, including the Yule ham, but I like it best as a lunch or light supper, with a hunk of sourdough on the side.

Serves 4 as a side dish

500g kale

2 tbsp olive oil

50g anchovies in olive oil

3–4 tbsp double cream

1 tbsp tomato purée

Black pepper

To prepare the kale, cut off and discard the tough ends of the stalks, then chop the tender stems and leaves. Heat the olive oil in a wide pan, add the kale and fry gently for 10 minutes until the leaves are cooked but crispy at the edges. Transfer to a warmed serving dish.

In a small saucepan over a low heat, warm the anchovies in their oil for a few minutes, breaking them up with a wooden spoon. Add the cream and tomato purée and stir well over the heat; don't let the sauce boil.

Transfer the kale to a warmed serving dish or individual plates and spoon the anchovy cream on top. Add a good grinding of pepper but no salt (the anchovies provide enough). Serve straight away.

Variations

• The anchovy cream also works well with Brussels sprouts – roughly slice and sauté as above.

• Or, for a gratin, put the al-dente-cooked veg into an oven dish, toss with a fried finely chopped onion, then top with the anchovy cream. Finish with a generous scattering of breadcrumbs and bake in the oven at 180°C/ Fan 160°C/Gas 4 for 20 minutes.

Beetroot, Orange & Pumpkin Salad

This rooty, citrus salad is inspired by the Mexican dish nochebuena (meaning Christmas Eve). The authentic recipe is full of gorgeous exotic fruits, which are definitely not a seasonal blessing in the UK, as well as jicama, which is quite like kohlrabi. I've changed some of the traditional ingredients but hopefully retained the essence of the dish. It is a delight alongside the Yule ham (page 154) and other cold meats, or heaped in a pile on your plate and eaten on its own.

Serves 6–8

A couple of handfuls of pumpkin
  seeds
A dash of tamari or soy sauce
2 oranges
2 medium beetroot
1 kohlrabi
2 eating apples, such as Cox's
  or Discovery

A few handfuls of winter salad leaves,
  such as chicory and radicchio, torn
A small bunch of coriander or
  parsley, roughly chopped
2 tbsp cider vinegar or white wine
  vinegar
A squeeze of lemon juice
Sea salt and black pepper

Heat a frying pan over a medium heat, add the pumpkin seeds and dry-fry for a few minutes, shaking the pan constantly, until the seeds are golden and release their aroma. Remove from the heat, add a dash of tamari, stir and set aside.

Peel the oranges, removing all the pith, and cut into slices. Place in a large bowl. Peel the raw beetroot and kohlrabi, cut into matchsticks and add to the bowl. Core and thinly slice the apples and add these too. Add the salad leaves and chopped herbs and toss to combine.

Trickle the vinegar over the salad, add a squeeze of lemon and season with salt and pepper to taste. Toss lightly. Just before serving, scatter over the toasted pumpkin seeds.

Chestnut & Sage Loaf

This is a festive riff on the River Cottage farmhouse loaf and a stand-out adaptation. It plays an excellent second fiddle to soups, cold meats and cheeses but also proudly stands alone, thickly buttered. Make a loaf in advance and pop it in the freezer. Or find a window between Christmas and New Year to bake this beauty, using any leftover chestnuts and the onion at the bottom of the veg bowl.

Makes 1 loaf

350g strong white bread flour, plus
   extra to dust
150g wholemeal flour
5g fast-action dried yeast
10g salt

1 red onion, finely diced
150g peeled, cooked chestnuts,
   cut into quarters
8 sage leaves, chopped
A little oil, for oiling

In a large bowl, combine the flours, yeast and salt with 325ml tepid water to form a rough, sticky dough.

Tip the dough onto a clean surface and knead by stretching it away from you, using the heel of your hand, and then folding it back over itself before stretching it out again. This develops the gluten in the flour and incorporates air into the dough. Continue to knead for 10 minutes until you have a smooth, stretchy, slightly shiny dough.

Press the dough into a rough square and scatter the raw onion, chestnuts and sage over it. Fold the dough over to enclose, then knead for a minute or so to fully incorporate the added ingredients. Finally, fold the dough in half about 4 times, working round from the top, flipping it over each time and forming it into a round. This helps build structure within the dough.

Now pop your dough into a lightly oiled bowl and cover with a damp tea towel or cloth. Leave to rise at room temperature for 1–1½ hours, or for 2–4 hours in the fridge, until roughly doubled in size.

Tip the dough onto a lightly floured surface. Grab a corner and fold it into the middle. Repeat this stretching and folding inwards, working around the dough, until it is in a rough round. Tip the dough over so that the folds are on the bottom. Put your hands on either side of the round and move them into the middle until they meet, so you start to seal up the seams created from the folding. Repeat this action for 30 seconds or so, rotating the dough as you do so to form a smooth, tight, round shape.

If you have a proving basket, flour it, put your dough seam side up in it and cover with a cloth. Otherwise, simply place your dough on a heavily floured cloth on your work surface and cover with another cloth. Leave to prove for 45 minutes–1 hour.

Preheat the oven to 240°C/Fan 220°C/Gas 9. Put a baking tray on the middle oven shelf to heat up, and set a roasting pan on the bottom of the oven.

Take the tray from the oven. Uncover your dough and gently tip it onto the tray. Using a bread knife or Stanley knife, make slashes, no more than 1cm deep, on top of the dough. Quickly put the tray back in the oven; also, carefully pour about 200ml water into the roasting pan to create steam.

Bake the loaf for 20 minutes, then turn the oven down to 210°C/Fan 190°C/Gas 7 and bake for a further 15–20 minutes (or a little longer if you want a crustier loaf). Transfer to a wire rack and leave to cool down. Wait for at least 30 minutes before tucking in.

Rice Pudding

In Denmark, celebrations begin in earnest on 23 December – Little Christmas Eve. A traditional rice pudding is served with a hot cherry sauce and the leftover pudding is then revamped as a risalamande on Christmas Eve, with cream, chopped almonds and the rest of the sauce. One almond is left whole and hidden in the dessert. Whoever is the lucky recipient wins a prize. Sound familiar?! Here I have jumped straight to the risalamande stage.

You can serve the pudding with a few of the cherries from the vodka that might be sitting in a jar in your cupboard (see page 49) or a tablespoonful of sugar mixed with a generous pinch of cinnamon for a sweet spiced sprinkling. Either way, this works particularly well as a substantial dessert after a light lunch of soup or salad.

Serves 4–6

100g pudding rice
1 litre whole milk
1 vanilla pod, split
2 tbsp caster sugar

To serve:
200ml double cream, whipped
150g blanched or peeled almonds,
  chopped
Boozy cherries (page 49) or
  cinnamon sugar (see above)

Put the rice and milk into a large saucepan and heat gently to the boil, stirring all the while. Scrape the seeds out of the vanilla pod and add them to the pan, along with the pod. Stir in the sugar.

Leave the pudding to simmer for 30 minutes, stirring often to prevent it catching on the bottom of the pan. Take out the vanilla pod.

The pudding can be served warm at this point, simply as it is, or if you want to take it to the next stage, leave it to cool and then refrigerate.

Just before you are ready to serve, carefully stir the whipped cream and chopped almonds into the cold rice. Spoon into small bowls, top with a few boozy cherries or a sprinkling of cinnamon sugar and serve.

Prune & Apricot Stollen

Stollen is a luxurious enriched-dough loaf said to symbolise the nativity because it looks a little like a swaddled new born babe. Or as I often think, a plump, warm puppy. A classic in Germany, it appeals to those who aren't fussed about a heavy fruit cake but still want festive flavours. I love the fact that this recipe makes two loaves, one to keep and one to give away. It makes a great solstice beach breakfast too. Once past its best, it's excellent toasted.

Instead of the traditional marzipan, you could try our River Cottage created version, datezipan, which is light on the sugar and heavy on the amazing nutty, fruity flavours.

Makes 2 loaves (18 slices each)

200g chopped prunes
100g unsulphured dried apricots,
  chopped
100g mixed chopped peel (or the
  candied grapefruit peel on page 102)
Finely grated zest of 1 large orange
50g flaked almonds
½ tsp ground cardamom
½ tsp ground ginger
½ tsp ground nutmeg
1 tsp ground mixed spice
50ml brandy
100g unsalted butter
175ml milk
15g active dry yeast

125g caster sugar
500g strong white bread flour,
  plus extra to dust
½ tsp salt
2 large eggs, beaten
A little rapeseed or vegetable oil,
  for oiling

For the filling:
250–300g marzipan or datezipan
  (page 167)

To finish:
25g unsalted butter, melted
Icing sugar, for dredging

Place the prunes, apricots, peel, orange zest, almonds, spices and brandy in a bowl and toss to mix. Leave to soak overnight.

To make the stollen dough, melt the butter in a small pan over a low heat, then leave to cool down. In a separate pan, warm the milk until tepid (not hot), then take off the heat, add the yeast and sugar and stir until dissolved. Set aside until the mixture has started to froth.

Put the flour and salt into a large bowl. Make a well in the centre and pour in the yeast mixture, melted butter and beaten eggs. Mix first with a wooden spoon to combine, then with your hands to form a dough that comes away cleanly from the bowl.

Turn the dough out onto a floured surface and knead until it is soft, elastic and no longer sticking to the surface. Alternatively, use a free-standing electric mixer fitted with the dough hook to bring the dough to this stage. Lightly oil a large bowl, add the dough and turn it so that it is coated all over with a thin layer of oil. Cover the bowl and leave in a warm place for 2 hours or until the dough has doubled in size.

Turn the dough out onto a lightly floured surface and knock back. Flatten the dough with the palm of your hand and scatter over the brandy-soaked spiced fruit. Mix in, by first folding the dough over the fruit, then lightly kneading until the fruit is evenly distributed and any residual brandy has been worked in.

Divide the dough into two equal pieces. Flatten each piece to a rectangle, about 25 x 15cm. Split the marzipan (or datezipan) in two and roll each portion into a sausage shape, the same length as the dough. Position one of these along each dough rectangle, slightly off-centre. Fold the dough over the filling to make two long, loose loaves.

Place the loaves, seam side down, on a floured baking sheet. Cover loosely with a tea towel and leave to prove in a warm place for about an hour until the stollen has almost doubled in size. Preheat the oven to 180°C/ Fan 160°C/Gas 4.

Bake the loaves in the middle of the oven for about 20 minutes, checking them after 10 minutes – if they are colouring too quickly, cover loosely with foil. Once the 20 minutes is up, turn the oven setting down to 150°C/ Fan 130°C/Gas 2 and bake for a further 20 minutes, until the tops of the stollen are firm and a lovely golden brown colour.

As you take the loaves from the oven, immediately brush with the melted butter, then transfer to a wire rack to cool. Once cold, dust liberally with icing sugar. Wrap the stollen in greaseproof paper, store in an airtight tin and eat within a day or two.

Can you see what I've done here?! It's a River Cottage marzipan but with dates instead of sugar. And it's delicious! You can use it in the stollen recipe on page 164, or put a layer in the middle of the quincemas cake on page 47 before baking. In fact, you can swap it for traditional marzipan in any recipe. The datezipan makes lovely festive petits fours, too (see below). **Hugh**

Datezipan

Makes about 1kg
150g hazelnuts, toasted
500g pitted dates
350g ground almonds
75ml apple juice, cider brandy or rum

Put the toasted hazelnuts into a food processor and blitz until finely ground. Tip into a bowl and set aside.

Put the dates into the food processor and blitz to a smooth paste – it will form a ball. Break this up and return it to the food processor, along with the ground hazelnuts and almonds. Blitz until you have a loose crumbly mixture, then add your chosen liquid and blend to a smooth ball. Wrap in greaseproof paper and place in the fridge until needed.

When you are ready to use your datezipan, take it out of the fridge and let it come to room temperature. If it is a little sticky as you roll it out or shape it, use a light dusting of icing sugar.

Variation
Chocolate datezipan sweets Whether you're using this recipe for a stollen or to cover a Christmas cake, there may well be enough left over to make these treats. Roll small balls of datezipan and flatten into bite-size circles; set aside. Melt a small knob of butter in a pan over a very low heat. Once it is melted, add 100g chocolate, in pieces, and melt very gently, stirring constantly. Take the pan off the heat. One at a time, partially dip the datezipan discs into the melted chocolate to coat one half and then place on a tray lined with baking paper. Use the cherries from your cherry vodka (page 49), chopped stem ginger or whole nuts to top each one – or ring the changes. Place in the fridge to harden the chocolate.

Pumpkin Seed Biscotti

Around Christmas, when indulgent treats tend to dominate, I find my tastebuds searching for a different kind of biscuit from the rich ones on offer. These biscotti do the job – they are healthier, vegan and just as moreish. So, a week or so before Christmas, I bake biscotti for my biscuit barrel, plus several batches to give away.

In the months leading up to Christmas I keep an eye out for old tins or save any from my kitchen, ready to fill with biscotti and hand out as gifts. Occasionally the tin is returned in the New Year with something delicious inside… I think this is what is meant by a win win.

Makes 10–12

250g plain flour (or 125g plain and 125g wholemeal), plus extra to dust
130g caster sugar
5g baking powder
60g dried cranberries or raisins

70g pumpkin seeds, toasted and roughly chopped
40g coconut oil
90ml oat milk
Finely grated zest of 2 oranges

Preheat the oven to 190°C/Fan 170°C/Gas 5. In a large bowl, mix the flour(s), sugar, baking powder, dried fruit and pumpkin seeds together; set aside.

Melt the coconut oil in a pan over a low heat then take off the heat and whisk in the oat milk and orange zest. Pour this onto the dry mix and knead quickly with your hands to bring it together as a dough; do not overwork but make sure everything is combined.

On a lightly floured surface, roll out the dough into a log, about 25cm long. Your finished biscuits will be slices of this, so the width of the log determines the size of your biscotti. Lay the log on a baking tray and bake in the oven for 30–35 minutes until firm. Leave to cool on the baking tray for about 20 minutes.

Using a sharp, serrated knife, cut the log into 1cm thick slices and place the slices on a baking tray lined with baking paper. Bake for 15 minutes until crisp and pale brown, then turn the biscotti over and bake them for a further 10 minutes, but keep an eye on them.

Transfer the biscotti to a wire rack to cool. Once cooled, store them in an airtight container for up to a week (though I have kept these biscotti successfully for an extra week).

Lebkuchen

Originally made in the thirteenth century by monks in Germany, these lightly spiced biscuits have become a festive favourite. Whether you ice them, dip them in melted chocolate or eat them plain, they can transport you to somewhere snowy and alpine, possibly with a delightful outdoor Christmas market. I make a couple of batches and stack them in a large glass jar or tin. They are also a sweet treat alternative for those, like my niece Kitty, who doesn't eat the dried-fruit-heavy mince pies and cake but who likes Christmas spices. Serve with my fiery hot chocolate (on page 283) or mulled cider (on page 197) for a double spicing.

Makes 24
85ml honey
115g dark brown sugar
30g butter
225g plain flour
1 tsp ground cinnamon
1 tsp ground ginger
½ tsp ground nutmeg
¼ tsp bicarbonate of soda

1 egg
50g ground almonds

For the icing glaze:
25g icing sugar, sifted

You will also need:
Small biscuit cutters (ideally festive)

Put the honey, sugar and butter into a large pan (it does need to be big as you will be making the dough in it). Place over a low heat until the butter and sugar have melted. Remove from the heat.

Sift together the flour, ground spices and bicarbonate of soda. Beat the egg in a separate small bowl. Add half the flour mixture and half the beaten egg to the melted mixture in the pan and mix well. Repeat to incorporaste the remaining flour mix and egg. Finally add the ground almonds and mix until thoroughly combined.

The very sticky dough now needs to be chilled, so wrap it in greaseproof paper and refrigerate overnight, or for up to 3 days – to develop the flavours.

When ready to bake, preheat the oven to 180°C/Fan 160°C/Gas 4 and line a baking tray with baking paper. Take the dough from the fridge and roll it out between two sheets of greaseproof paper to about a 5mm thickness. Cut out shapes using festive cutters (ideally small) if you have them. Transfer the shapes to a baking tray, spacing them well apart to allow room for spreading. Bake in the oven for 7–9 minutes until golden brown.

Leave the biscuits to cool on the tray for 5 minutes to firm up a little, then carefully transfer them to a wire rack to finish cooling.

For the glaze, mix the icing sugar with 2 tsp water to make a watery icing. Lay the biscuits on a wire rack with a sheet of greaseproof paper underneath (to make cleaning up easier). Using a pastry brush, apply a thin layer of icing. Add a second coat and leave until the glaze is dry.

The lebkuchen will keep for up to 3 weeks in an airtight container, but they are unlikely to last that long!

4
Feeding a Crowd

WE ARE FAMOUS FOR OUR FEASTS at River Cottage, and that is a lovely thing to be known for. Park Farm is a buzzing hub throughout the year, but the final month brings with it an extra special rush of excitement and celebration. From small intimate dinners to long table lunches and merry groups of revellers, our seventeenth-century farmhouse and eighteenth-century threshing barn have played host to many visitors over the years.

Indeed, after the first phase of renovation at Park Farm 15 years ago, we threw a raucous barn warming for the team which has set the tone for the goodwill and feasting that has followed. In big ways and small, River Cottage has been a marvellous place of enjoyment and relaxation.

Feeding large groups of people can be a daunting prospect, even if you are accustomed to it. It takes planning, effort and energy – all things you may be low on as you get closer to Christmas – but the warmth and generosity of spirit it engenders among family and friends is priceless. Whether it is a small affair or a big bash, it's worth the organisation: spontaneity can be fun but often the best celebrations are those that appear effortless because someone has worked hard to make sure everything comes together perfectly.

The term 'dinner party' feels like it should belong in a cookbook from the 1980s and is in danger of insisting on a rigid formula of aperitif, starter, main course, pudding and cheese. It's not that we don't have people over to eat now but it's likely to be a more informal invitation and, thankfully, a more laid-back approach to the menu. It's also rarer to sit in a dining room since the fashion for open plan conversions took hold and urged us all to create one big living space. These days, for most of us, the kitchen table is where it's at.

I can seat eight comfortably around my kitchen table, although it isn't technically mine. It is the one loaned to the River Cottage farmhouse, originally, and temporarily, for purposes of filming, although it took up residence there for over a decade. Then, following renovations, it was loaned to me. The sanded pine top is slightly warped, there are old burn marks from pans, a side drawer (for children to surreptitiously hide sprouts in) and many memories of Hugh cooking for countless TV programmes and photoshoots. Now it has a further life under my watch until one day it will return to my friend Jessamy, its rightful owner.

It's lovely to have a table with a bit of history, however quirky. Now, looking at a bunch of animated candlelit faces around that table, bowls being passed over heads, impromptu toasts being made along with demands for seconds, fills me with a deep contentment and quiet joy. Feeding family and friends, whether it's a few or many, is a pleasure at any time of year, and a real highlight of my Christmas calendar.

Recently it has been a lot harder to party. I can't write this chapter without acknowledging the sad lack of gatherings with family and friends during the

pandemic. If we needed a reminder of how important celebrating with our loved ones is then this was surely it. What was refreshing was learning to adapt to a world where much of our social interaction had to take place out-of-doors and discovering just how enjoyable that could be, regardless of the weather. It has shown us there are other ways to gather, even in the winter months.

At this time of year there are still going to be plenty of opportunities to get outside for a companionable dog walk, family hike or big group meet-up. Making food and drink an element of such gatherings is always going to raise the spirits and help foster the festive camaraderie. You can elevate a chilly, grey day just by unscrewing the Thermos or lighting a fire in your garden and passing around mugs of mulled cider to warm the cockles.

The food

The creativity and risk involved in my cooking reduces somewhat as the number of people I am feeding increases. I'm not remotely apologetic for that, and I suspect it's the case for many of us who are not professional chefs. It makes perfect sense to me.

When the guest list hits double figures, it feels like I have a gathering on my hands and I shift my menu accordingly. Now is not the time to make soufflés or cook steaks to order, and instead I'll think about focusing on doing a few elements well rather than providing a full multi-course feast.

A plentiful pile of one or two things feels more generous than too many dishes of not quite enough. So, I might put together a small selection of chunky canapés; or a pile of sausages served with seedy buns and home-made ketchup; or sometimes just a monumental cheeseboard with plenty of good bread, biscuits and chutney. And, of course, there's always the option of taking a leaf out of Hugh's book and going for a huge and heart-warming pot of stew.

We love communal cooking at River Cottage where everyone pitches in and takes a role in the final feast. There is a particular kind of pleasure in prepping and cooking together as a group and sharing the result, around the table or fire. This approach works brilliantly at home too, with the added bonus of taking some pressure off the host/head chef.

Pizza-making sounds labour-intensive but it's easier than you might think and a great way to get children involved. Make the dough earlier in the day to allow time for proving, or prepare ahead of time and freeze it. Make lashings of thick tomato sauce. Assemble a range of grated and sliced cheeses and plenty of different toppings so that everyone can fix their own creation (and in our house, share it around too, in a mildly competitive spirit).

I hate to brag but our village is pretty good at spontaneous gatherings. It could be as simple as tea and cake. Or it could be my neighbour Dan and his old, French iron waffle press – the kind you normally heat up over a gas ring. He makes a vat load of batter and sits the waffle iron in the outdoor fire bowl, serving waffles hot off the press (I know, sorry). Guests bring their favourite accompaniments: jars of poached autumn quince, home-made mincemeat ice cream or the rumtopf compote (my own dependable contribution) are popular toppings. Then there's the farm at the end of our lane and the seasonal invitations to join them. One New Year's Eve we all trooped down to help with orchard planting followed by a pokey mulled cider reward and a kitchen table groaning under the weight of everyone's Christmas leftovers. Mass catering does not have to mean a monumental headache… leave that for the hangover.

Most shellfish is in season in December and a special treat if you are not feeding the five thousand. Head to your local, reputable fishmonger to find out what is fresh and sustainably sourced (the Marine Stewardship Council website msc.org will also help with this). Festive as they are, I'm going to leave the oysters to Hugh, as there are so many other fishy treats I would prefer to eat. I do, however, love to cook a big bowl of clams or cockles to stir through spaghetti; or steam them open, like mussels, and dish up in deep bowls with sourdough to mop up the garlicky wine juices.

Or lay the table with sheets of newspaper, line up a few simply-boiled cold lobsters (bought pre-cooked if you like), a couple of hammers or large pebbles, and a nutcracker or two, and tell everyone to roll up their sleeves and get cracking. A tray of roast potatoes/oven chips, a green salad and a bowl of aïoli are all the accompaniment you need.

Hand-dived scallops still in their shells are great for the outdoor grill. This can be an interactive activity as long as the shells are prepared in advance, because a tipsy guest attempting a bit of shucking with a sharp knife is inadvisable. Line up the plump, pearly scallops, sitting in their half shell, which acts like a miniature frying pan. Guests can add their own butter or olive oil, fresh herbs, garlic, crumbled chorizo or black pudding, maybe a few cooked peas and a squeeze of lemon. Each shell goes on the hot coals to bubble and pop for just a few minutes. Give it a moment for the shell to cool and dive in with fork or fingers as soon as the sizzling stops. Knock back the exceptional cooking juices straight from the shell.

Huge stews

I can get very excited about stews, especially at Christmas. It's a racing certainty that at some point over the holiday I will serve up a big hearty stew to a table of ten or more family and friends – and it might be double that.

I rarely look at a recipe. I love the process of 'building a stew' from scratch, and feeling my way with the ingredients I have to hand. The process usually starts by taking a piece of meat, or several, out of the freezer. It might be a shin of beef and a smaller piece of pork belly; or a couple of home-reared chickens; or a shoulder of lamb or a few shanks and some spicy lamb sausages.

These, respectively, might give me a pretty classic beef stew in the 'bourguignon' tradition; something in the 'coq au vin' ball park; a tagine, of sorts. Or the same cuts might produce, if the mood takes me (or the family consensus sways me): a fiery beef chilli with lots of winter veg; a mushroomy 'chicken chasseur' finished with a dash of cream; or a lamby beany hotch potch.

Whatever destination I'm travelling towards, I make sure I'm not in a rush. I sometimes cook a stew in the morning, for the evening. More likely, I'll cook it in the evening, for the next day or the day after that. And more often than not, unless there is a crowd to be fed, at least half of it will go in the freezer.

The meat usually gets cut up. I favour chunkier pieces of beef and lamb – three or four pieces should feel like a handful, and a portion. If the fat on the meat is excessive, it might get trimmed a bit, but not too much. It's going to be the source of flavour and tenderness. If I'm looking at a prepped pile that's about 10–15 per cent fat to meat, I'm happy. On a lean cut like shin, I love to add pork belly or bacon, or even a bit of diced beef fat (trimmed from another cut).

I will assemble a pile of veg that's at least as big as the pile of meat. These days, as I'm always looking to up the veg, it's more likely to be twice as big. Invariably I'll use plenty of onions and carrots. Other veg that are welcome at this time of year are parsnips, swede, turnips, celery and celeriac. Again, I cut them chunky – medium onions into quarter-wedges, for example.

I always brown the meat. Putting a deep colour and caramel on it creates fantastic extra flavour that will percolate around the stew as it cooks. So, I fry fast and hot in a large heavy pan. And I fry in batches, so the meat doesn't crowd the pan. The fattier cuts (or the pork and bacon, or even the trimmed fat) go in first, to render some of their fat into the pan, and create a good sizzle for the next batch. The outside of the meat should be dark brown like a well-seared steak (or the skin of the chicken like it's been roasted) and this is why I cut big pieces – they can take plenty of colour without drying up. The sizzle without the shrivel.

I rarely flour the meat – it gets in the way of the browning, and I'm more concerned with the flavour of the liquor than its viscosity. A little shake of flour at the end of the browning is an option, followed by a few more flips of the meat, to cook the flour a bit, if you like your liquor to have a 'gravy' character.

The browned meat goes into a plenty big enough casserole. The veg gets batch-browned too – colour is where the flavour is. I deglaze the browning pan, ideally with a large glass of wine or beer, but stock or water will do – scrape and stir, then add it all to the casserole.

Just a few more decisions now – to add layers of subtlety and delight to the stew. The liquor needs a top-up to (only just) cover the meat and veg. A splash more wine or beer – but not too much or you will pickle the meat. Tomato purée if you like. No shame at all in water, just to get the level up. Herbs and spices, yes. Bay leaf is a given, and fresh thyme too, if you've got it. Pepper, and just ½ tsp of salt for now (none if you've used bacon). Something a little left-field, but thoughtful, will add an unexpected dimension: a star anise perhaps, and the merest pinch of ginger. It is Christmas, after all.

Bring all to the slowest trembling of simmers. Never let it get fierce or fast. Two hours may be enough, or it might need three. It's your teeth and tongue that will tell you, not me. When it's right, cool fast (outside works well). Then, ideally, leave overnight for all to marry and mingle.

Next day, you can lift any hard-set fat off the top, as its work is done. Then a gentle reheat, back to the point of simmer, and no more. A taste and a tweak of seasoning, which can include a final splash of the chosen booze, and your stew is ready. **Hugh**

Canapés

I adore canapés – individual mouthfuls of carefully crafted deliciousness – and often I would prefer an evening of these to a big dinner. At River Cottage our nibbles are sometimes a little heftier, requiring several bites and a napkin to catch the overflow, which is quite nice as you need fewer of them. Bear in mind though that, for the cook, finger food is not necessarily an easier, quicker option than cooking a three-course dinner; but it is totally worth the work.

One approach I like is to make a couple of generous canapés (perhaps alongside a few lighter nibbles, nuts, olives etc) to kick off an evening, with a celebratory cocktail. This sets a wonderful tone for the rest of the celebration, and guests are then more than happy to tuck into a hearty main without the formality of a fancy first course.

I could write a book of canapé recipes and it would be big enough to prop a door open with, press flowers in, or use as a step to reach a high shelf. That's how many possible nibble and snack recipes there are to choose from. What you decide upon depends on the numbers you are hosting and the time you have available to prepare them. They rank from the 'straight out of the packet and into the bowl' variety, to the 'lovingly crafted over hours using many ingredients' sort. Here are a few favourites of mine, Hugh's and River Cottage's.

Something simple

Raw veg crudités Often these are served with hummus, aïoli or a favourite dip, or you could offer them 'straight up' – for a clean, palate-cleansing crunch and contrast. My favourite way to serve them is with a French-style olive oil, wine vinegar and mustard dressing. And I like to include less obvious seasonal options like celeriac, radicchio and chicory.

Marinated olives Buy these already marinated or make your own quick dressing if you prefer. Also, if you fancy, stuffed olives, which I always do. Green olives – plump with blanched almonds or anchovies – are best.

Caper berries The big fat ones with their stalks on, these are the gourmet's pickled onions. Though, if you like pickled onions, knock yourself out.

Crisps I think the plain salted option is far preferable to any of the wacky flavours we are bombarded with these days. Let your home-made canapés do the talking on that score.

Nuts You might want a fancier selection of roasted, salted nuts than the standby dry-roasted peanuts. Best of all though is to roast (and spice) your own (see below).

Salami It's well worth sourcing some of the increasing range of salamis and other charcuterie produced in the UK, especially those made with free-range, rare-breed pork. If you haven't already made best friends with your local deli then check it out too. These cured meats are wonderful all year round but spectacular in the lead up to Christmas. Of course, you could always get hold of *The River Cottage Smoking and Curing Handbook,* and make your own.

Pre-made canapés

Festive nuts My go-to recipe is the roasted nuts and seeds with tamari and rosemary on page 137. Prepare a few days before the event and store in an airtight jar. Give them a shake and an extra sprinkle of sea salt and fill several small bowls. These can be dotted around the sitting room and kitchen.

Hummus The classic River Cottage hummuses are usually made with English split peas rather than chickpeas, always include distinctive spicing, and often some roasted roots such as beetroot, carrots or parsnips too. See Hugh's adaptable recipe on page 288.

Dips Everyone has a favourite family dip recipe and if yours just happens to be made from cream cheese whipped with Worcestershire sauce, Tabasco and ketchup then I won't tell on you (and will happily dip into it myself). If you want something a bit different, try the curried hummus.

Aïoli More of an accompaniment than a dip, this is a lovely thing to have with crudités or roast potato/root wedges. See the recipe on page 140.

Grissini These are easy to make and store well for a few days. They can be sprinkled with sea salt, herbs and spices before baking, and make a great partner to dips, soups and cheeseboards. See the recipe on page 201.

Sourdough crackers A great way to use excess sourdough starter, these can be topped with whatever combinations work for you.

Spelt digestives These are a River Cottage classic and, of course, it's brilliant to have something home-made on the cheeseboard. See the recipe on page 225.

Showstoppers

Buckwheat blinis A lovely finger food, these are classically served with smoked salmon or fish eggs, but given the sustainability concerns around those, I prefer a veggie topping – such as labneh and quick pickled celery (see page 205).

Cheese straws These will disappear the *moment* they come out of the oven! Finely grate 100g Cheddar and 50g Parmesan or hard goat's cheese into a large bowl. Add 100g plain flour and a good grind of black pepper. Rub in 100g cubed butter until the mix resembles breadcrumbs. Mix in an egg yolk and bring the dough together with your hands. Roll out on a lightly floured surface to a square, 5mm thick. Cut into strips and lay slightly apart on a lined baking sheet. Bake in a preheated oven at 220°C/Fan 200°C/Gas 7 for 8 minutes or until golden brown (check after 5 minutes). Leave on the baking sheet for 5 minutes before transferring to a wire rack to cool.

Devils-on-horseback An absolute classic; at their simplest, these are just prunes wrapped in bacon and roasted. Over the last few years I have been playing around with these and I have included one of my favourite twists on page 202. If you love a devil on a horseback then I think you will approve.

Rarebits A properly made, béchamel-based Welsh rarebit on top-notch sourdough or wholegrain toast makes a lovely substantial canapé and is ripe for customisation.

The buffet

Buffets have got a bad name over the years, with images of lukewarm carveries, all-you-can-eat restaurants or a table full of uninspiring beige food. It transports some of us straight back to the cheese and pineapple hedgehogs of the 1970s.

At River Cottage we favour 'sharing plates' where the food is put on communal tables and guests help themselves – and each other. This takes the pressure off the kitchen and creates a sociable, convivial atmosphere. It may backfire if you are sat next to someone with a large appetite. But then it is also likely to be of benefit if your neighbour doesn't want their pork crackling (a rare occurrence, admittedly, unless you are sitting next to my nephew Dodge).

Much as I love the sharing plate approach, it only really works for a seated table. At Christmas parties where people are wandering about, and settling where they will, I see no reason why we can't still offer up an old-school buffet, if we populate it with dishes that are colourful, imaginative and truly celebratory.

I love the generosity of a good buffet, the ability to manage what is on my plate and the communal atmosphere it encourages. It can take more work in the prep stages but will leave you freer once your guests have arrived. All you need do is signal that the buffet table is 'open' and leave everyone to help themselves. It is also a great opportunity to encourage others to bring dishes to add to the selection. The BYO buffet is a particularly good way to throw a last-minute party and/or entertain a number of guests that is beyond your catering capacity (or energy levels).

A cold buffet often has a centrepiece – a ham, poached or cured fish, cold roast chicken, a nice side of beef or several rooty vegetable tarts. Just a couple of these is enough. Serve alongside several hearty winter salads of grains and pulses, and slaws. Maybe a couple of chestnut and sage loaves (page 160), too. Whether you are catering for vegetarians and vegans or not, it's a good idea to provide at least one main plant-based dish and make sure all the salads are suitable or can be adapted.

A few generous dishes, made using the best ingredients, is all you need. Holding back some of what you have made (in the larder or another cool place, out of sight of guests) is a useful tactic which allows you to stretch to unexpected extra guests or late-night returns to the table.

A hot buffet is an entirely different beast but it comes into its own in the winter. It does require timely attention from your guests so bear this in mind when you are considering recipes and numbers – stews, trays of roasted veg, hot pies or curries with help-yourself ladles and big bowls of rice and/or a pile of flatbreads, or perhaps baked spuds, are all winners.

One year I made several cottage pies (three beef, one vegan) in advance and popped them in the oven to reheat as the party started. I served them with bowls of peas, pickled red cabbage and a simple dressed green salad. It was exactly the food everyone wanted on a cold, early December night.

Sweet and cheesy

I may dream about a sweet trolley laden with different trifles (pear and amaretti, black forest, classic sherry…) but my dessert reality is much more straightforward. I tend not to make puddings (other than *the* pudding) at Christmas and rely instead on the tins of biscotti, tiffin and mince pies I have squirrelled away. These are easier to serve at the end of a meal or a party and can satisfy the festive fondness for a little sweet something without increasing the washing up too much.

Having said that, Hugh has come up with an ingenious solution to my dessert conundrum. I love his creation of a festive pudding station that encourages guests to make their own combination of treats, and doubles up as a neat party piece too.

Alternatively, or in addition, there is the cheeseboard, which over Christmas becomes another member of the household (and one of the most helpful ones!). I like to have a selection of cheeses, re-wrapped in greaseproof paper, tucked away ready to put out with a stack of spelt digestives (page 225), a pile of oatcakes and a jar of Christmas glutney (page 32).

Drinks

First impressions count. When your guests arrive, whether there are six or sixty of them, offering a ready-made welcome drink – mulled cider perhaps, a cocktail if you like – is a wise move. It makes people feel instantly welcome, rapidly relaxed and eases any awkwardness.

Prep all the components beforehand so the cocktail is ready to be mixed with as little fuss as possible (avoid shaker-based cocktails for larger groups). One of the simplest and most pleasing of welcome drinks, which shouldn't floor anyone too soon, is kir royale, where a dash of cassis, or some other fruity liqueur, is topped up with icy cold sparkling wine. You can have a tray of glasses already dosed with the liqueur standing by, ready to be topped up and handed to each guest as they arrive. For a gin-based tipple, try adding my ginger and honey switchel (page 192) to a shot of gin. Or, for a non-alcoholic cocktail, Hugh's bucha fizz on page 194 is ideal.

Some might see this as an opportunity to share some of the home-steeped alcohol that's been stored, by using it instead of cassis in such a cocktail. Feel free to do so but remember how long you have waited for this reward and how many you may have to share it with…

If you've laid on a welcome drink I would say you can feel pretty relaxed about shifting to self-service mode for the rest of the evening. Show guests where you have set the bar up and encourage them to help themselves. This could be a dedicated table or a section of the kitchen worktop but make sure there is also enough space for people to gather and pour drinks without forming a disorderly queue.

If you are providing spirits then remember the mixers, citrus slices and plenty of ice. Keep sparkling wine, white wine, beer and cider in the fridge or, even better, fill a big trough with ice and leave it outside the back door. When I lived in a flat I would fill the bath with ice for a party and store bottles there. Happy days. A plastic gardening trug or cooler box is just as useful. And don't forget the non-drinkers. They deserve special treatment, either a non-alcoholic cocktail or a fruity cordial or the switchel (on page 192) that can be mixed with tonic, soda or fizzy water.

It is wonderfully generous to supply all the booze – but few guests expect this so do not feel remotely uncomfortable about asking people to bring a bottle.

Festive fruits and fumble stations

With all that rich food flying around, I think it's important to put a few antidotes on the festive table from time to time, including some fresh and zesty winter salads and slaws, like the one I've given on page 221 (with a bunch of variations).

The other thing that's great for cutting that fat of course, is fruit. At Christmas, we tend to encounter our fruits mostly dried – in mince pies, puddings and cakes. I'm all for them, but in this concentrated form – and the pudding/cake context – let's face it, they are not really cutting it as fat-cutters. Although they are brilliant booze-soakers!

There is a danger that fresh fruit – apart from the odd clementine or easy peeler – gets forgotten almost completely over Christmas. But I'm not going to let that happen in my house. You might say the fact that no home-grown fruits are in season at Christmas doesn't really help the mission. But, actually, it isn't quite the case. Both apples and pears store pretty well through the winter and are therefore, in my book, very much in season over Christmas. So, I use them a lot in salads, both savoury and sweet. But not too sweet...

Add to the roster the non-native but very much available citrus fruits, and expand from the clems to include oranges, grapefruit, lemons and limes (all of which are increasingly widely available organically grown) and you have got a great fruity repertoire to work with.

Much as I love my Christmas pud, one of my favourite festive dessert memories is my mum's caramelised orange and chestnut salad: knife-peeled oranges (so no pith) sliced into rounds, in a very sweet syrupy caramel flavoured with orange juice, served chilled and topped with crumbled marrons glacés. While the tang of fresh oranges was still present, there was definitely a sugar rush to be had.

These days I have a version which is tarter and simpler, drawing all the sweetness it needs from dried apricots. You just peel and slice half a dozen oranges (and a few clems too if you fancy). Then juice a couple more (of each), and add to the sliced fruit. Snip a couple of dozen unsulphured dried apricots into a few pieces and stir in. Leave covered in a cool larder or the fridge for at least 24 hours (48 is better). By then, the apricots will have given up much of their considerable sweetness to the liquor, and taken on a pleasing tartness from the juice.

It's a great exchange, the fresh fruit sweetening naturally and the dried fruit zesting up a notch. Sometimes the chestnuts still get a look in too – but they don't have to be sugar-saturated marrons glacés. Some slices of cooked chestnut, steeped in the salad an hour or so before serving, do the job nicely.

This salad is likely to appear on Boxing Day or thereafter, at the end of one of the inevitable 'leftovers feasts'. It is somehow both virtuous and celebratory at the same time – which I think is what many of us are attempting to be by this point in the Christmas proceedings.

It's also very welcome at the buffet 'fumble station' or 'trifle range'. This is a cunning and always popular way to offer a delicious range of dessert elements to be assembled ad hoc according to your mood.

The spread could also include a large bowl of Bramley apple compote (my verbena version, if you like, on page 112), or perhaps a plum compote from the freezer, a bowl of yoghurt, another one of cream, a bowl (or jar) of independent crumble (page 112) along with any leftover cakes, puds and mince pies. Meringues, custard and ice cream have also been known to make appearances. So have home-made biscotti and shortbread, and not so home-made amaretti and ginger nuts. All are welcome.

Everyone gets a bowl or a glass and the opportunity to pick and mix their own concoction, with varying degrees of virtue, and indeed virtuosity, along the crumble/fool/trifle axis. A Croofle? A Fimble? A Crumboofle? A Trifumble? It doesn't really matter what it's called, because it's never the same twice, and that's kind of the point.

The other point is that the fumble station feels both considerate and generous. And what more could a host hope to be? **Hugh**

The great outdoors

Getting outside can be a glorious thing to do at this time of year. True, it can be wet, muddy and cold but catch a day when the low winter sun makes the frost sparkle, the air is wasabi fresh or the first snowflakes fall and it's enchanting. So much of the Christmas period is spent inside that we need to remind ourselves, whatever the weather, to take a walk. Striding out does us all good – a change of scenery, working up an appetite and a blast of fresh air to blow away the cobwebs.

'There's no such thing as bad weather, just bad clothing,' is a slightly irritating mantra, but it has a grain of truth to it. If you know that you are under-equipped for enjoying winter days out-of-doors, consider investing in comfortable and functional waterproofs and some good wellies or walking boots, or perhaps put them on your Christmas list. You'll be pleased you did when you get caught in the rain.

Some may need encouragement to hang around outdoors (or to leave the house at all!) so give them something to keep them motivated. The promise of food and drink often does the trick. There is nothing elaborate about my winter picnics. I've learnt from experience not to take food that has too many components or that is too messy or complicated to bring together without stress. It is exactly at that point that the wind whistles from the East, or the threatening rain cloud bursts. Flasks of soup, sausage rolls, pasties, a focaccia stuffed with leftovers – and the last of the Christmas cake – are all great picnic items. As is a hip flask of sloe gin (page 106) or the rummy liquid from the rumtopf (page 50) – a particularly important addition if you are attending Boxing Day pursuits or the mad annual sea swim.

More exciting is the suggestion of a proper outdoor cook-up in the woods or on the beach. It's a brilliant way to catch up with groups of friends without one house having the burden of hosting. It does take a bit of planning (and ideally accurate weather forecasting too), and it needs several of you to willingly carry heavy things in rucksacks to the chosen location. But when we have got our act together, these winter expeditions have made for some of our happiest times as a family.

We are lucky to live on the coast and have access to several lovely beaches, and amazing stretches of beautiful woodland where we are allowed to set up 'camp'. A little fire of driftwood with an old grill or Aga toasting rack works well on the beach. But if the weather has been very wet it's wise to bring your own wood. Beach fires come with all the safety caveats, including a warning about stones overheating and even exploding. My eldest son has a scar on his ankle caused by a popping pebble several years ago.

So, romantic as a 'foraged fire' is, a portable barbecue and a bag of charcoal may very well be the best option. To woods and fields, we often take a small gas camping stove which can boil the kettle or heat a pan of stew in a matter of minutes.

However you cook the sausages or heat up the stew, this sort of endeavour gives a focus to being outside and keeps everyone happily occupied. You can then return to your cosy sanctuary, refreshed and invigorated – and even more grateful for your home comforts.

Outdoor cooking checklist

- Matches
- Water
- Gas burner or barbecue
- Kindling/newspaper
- Firelighters
- Wood or charcoal
- Frying pan/grill or Aga rack
- Knives (a couple)
- Chopping board
- Kettle
- Tea/coffee/milk/sugar
- Enamel mugs/plates/bowls
- Tea towels
- FOOD!
- DRINK!
- CORKSCREW!

And don't forget the garden! This is the one time of year when it demands little of you and, even though it is not bursting with interest and colour, you can still spend time in it. Why not light a bonfire and invite family and friends to join you? Many of us do this pretty religiously on 5 November, and love it too, so there's no reason why we can't enjoy a fire in the garden at Christmas (perhaps for the winter solstice, see page 132).

This is an easy and affordable way to entertain. You can fire up the barbecue, make a bonfire, or if space is tight make your fire in a fire bowl. If actual barbecuing feels a faff, a one-pot supper that you have made earlier and can reheat – a stew, curry, soup or a dhal – are all great options. And better sort some marshmallows for post-supper toasting… you may not get the kids out any other way.

Of course, this is a weather-dependent activity – so some cover may be handy, or you may want to restrict the numbers to a level you can cope with if everyone has to come inside.

Remember that it will be dark early and perhaps plan a day-into-night get-together. After dark will be the most atmospheric time, but people will need to see to move around safely, so prepare plenty of additional outdoor lighting with festoons, fairy lights and blazing torches (safely staked in the ground).

Ask guests to come prepared in wellies, big coats and to bring torches or lanterns. You might even suggest they bring hot water bottles that you can fill up for them as the winter sun disappears. It is such a joy to be outside on a cold clear night, wrapped up around the fire, chatting and waiting for the stars to come out.

Ginger & Honey Switchel

Even though I say so myself, this is a recipe I cannot stop making. I certainly don't want to show favouritism to any dish or drink in this book but if I had to write a poem about just one it would be this beauty. A non-alcoholic refreshment, it was known as haymaker's punch to nineteenth-century farmers, who drank it to quench thirst. A tonic of water, vinegar, ginger and sugar in its basic form, it is less acidic than a shrub but more sour than a cordial. And it tastes just as good served straight up on ice as it does mixed with tonic, gin or vodka.

Makes about 750ml

50g fresh ginger, peeled and
   thickly sliced
100g honey
120ml raw pear vinegar or
   raw apple cider vinegar
1 pear, sliced (if using the pear vinegar)

You will also need:
A medium jam jar
A sterilised 1 litre Kilner jar

Put the ginger into a saucepan, pour on 600ml water and bring to the boil. Remove from the heat and let it sit for 15 minutes.

Meanwhile, combine the honey and vinegar in a jam jar with a screw-topped lid and give it a good shake to combine.

Pour this mixture into your Kilner jar and add the ginger water. Give it all a good stir and add the sliced pear if you're including it. Leave in the fridge for at least 24 hours (up to 48).

To decant, pass the liquid through a sieve into a jug to extract the ginger, pear and any sediment. Pour the switchel into a bottle and store in the fridge. Use within a week.

Here is my promised trio of 'dry' festive cocktails made with kombucha (see page 28). They're a great way to stay in the festive mood while steering clear of the booze, and work best with a nice tart home-made green tea kombucha. Or you can use a shop-bought kombucha that is 'natural' or only subtly aromatised, rather than flavoured with fruits or spices; the River Cottage Meadow kombucha is ideal. **Hugh**

Three Kombocktails

Chilled mulled kombucha

This lightly spiced, tangy kombucha blend is refreshing but still festive – a great 'dry' tipple for evenings when you or your guests aren't drinking.

Serves 5–6
2–3 x 3cm nuggets of fresh ginger
1 cinnamon stick, broken in half
2 cloves
1 scant tsp soft brown sugar or honey
500ml kombucha, chilled
5 or 6 star anise, to serve (optional)

Bash the ginger with a pestle or rolling pin to release the aroma, then tip it into a heatproof jug or bowl and add the whole spices. Pour over 500ml boiling water, add the sugar or honey, stir and leave until completely cold.

Strain out the spices. Chill the infusion, then combine with the kombucha and stir gently. Serve in tumblers, topped with a star anise if you like.

Bucha fizz

Replacing the sparkling wine in a classic buck's fizz with kombucha creates a fruity, booze-free but still nicely dry alternative.

Per person
About 150ml kombucha,
* well chilled*
About 75ml orange juice or freshly
* squeezed clementine juice, chilled*

Pour the kombucha into a champagne flute, top up with the orange or clementine juice and serve straight away.

Apple & rosemary fizz

Aromatic from the rosemary, crisp and tart from the cider vinegar, this is a very sophisticated kombocktail.

Per person

A small sprig of rosemary
25ml raw cider vinegar or
  lemon juice

A few ice cubes
150ml cloudy apple juice, chilled
Kombucha, chilled, to finish

Lightly bash the rosemary with a rolling pin or pestle to bruise the leaves and put into a tall glass. Add the cider vinegar or juice and leave for 15 minutes or so to macerate.

Add the ice cubes and then the apple juice and mix gently. Top up with chilled kombucha and serve.

Mulled Cider

At River Cottage we start making mulled cider around bonfire night and continue serving it through Christmas and beyond to Twelfth Night. In the past, it was drunk in the apple orchards as part of the pagan wassailing rituals, to ask the gods for a successful apple harvest. These days we are more likely to enjoy it in front of a fire, inside or out. It makes a great party drink too, as it can sit and wait for your guests and doesn't mind a slow bit of reheating.

6–8 servings

1 litre still cider
300ml good-quality apple juice
6 cloves
4 cinnamon sticks
2 star anise

1 orange, sliced
200ml sloe gin (page 106)
  or brandy
Honey or sugar, to taste

Pour the cider and apple juice into a big pan. Add the spices, cover and bring gently to just below the boil. Take it off the heat and it can happily sit for a couple of hours.

When you are ready to serve your mulled cider, put the pan back on the hob and bring to a simmer. Add the orange slices, pour in the sloe gin or brandy and give everything a good stir. Remove from the heat.

It may need a little sugar or a couple of spoonfuls of honey or sugar to soften the acidic appley hit, so taste and adjust accordingly.

Mulled Wine

Mulled wine seems like the simplest thing in the world to make (and it really is) but it's so often a disappointment. Ignore the ready-made versions, the prepped spice muslin bags or the market sellers who tempt you with their steamy urns. Instead take a look at the below recipe, an amalgamation of several (I may have lost count) tried-and-tested recipes including one from my editor at Bloomsbury, Kitty Stogdon, whose parents sound like consummate hosts.

It's all about the balance of ingredient quantities. I like my mulled wine to be warmly spiced with hints of citrus, a gingery heat and a soft jab in the ribs from a feisty spirit. I don't want to be floored by it, I want to be hugged.

6–8 servings

750ml bottle red wine
250ml ginger wine
1 orange, halved, each half
  studded with 4 cloves
3 strips of lemon zest
2 cinnamon sticks

2–3 star anise
A good grating of nutmeg
75g caster sugar
A shot of ginger liqueur or
  brandy (optional)

Put all the ingredients, except the sugar and liqueur or brandy, into a large pan. Bring to a simmer but do not allow it to boil. Add the sugar and the optional alcohol and give it a stir.

Turn off the heat and leave until you are ready to serve it. It tastes even better after a few hours of sitting. It will just need a gentle reheat. It's that easy.

Grissini

I try to bake these Italian breadsticks in secret and store them in a tin on a high shelf because otherwise they are the sort of snack that gets picked at as people walk past. If they don't disappear instantly they should keep fresh for several days. They can be pulled out as an accompaniment for dips, soups and the cheeseboard, or a quick snack in their own right. You can vary the toppings as you like – try toasted fennel seeds, sesame seeds, cayenne pepper or grated hard goat's cheese.

Makes 14 long grissini

500g strong white bread flour
8g fine salt
8g fast-action dried yeast
Olive oil, for oiling

Fine polenta, to dust
Flaky sea salt and cracked
  black pepper

Mix the flour, salt and yeast together in a large bowl. Add 270ml tepid water and bring together to form a rough dough.

Tip the dough out onto a clean surface and knead for 8–10 minutes (or give it 5 minutes in a food mixer fitted with a dough hook).

Put the dough into a lightly oiled bowl and turn it so it gets a coating of oil, then cover and leave to rise in a warm place until doubled in size; this should take about an hour.

Preheat the oven to 230°C/Fan 210°C/Gas 8. Dust a large baking tray with fine polenta. Take small 50g pieces of dough and roll them out from the centre to form thin, even sticks, the length of the tray. Lay the dough sticks on the tray.

Brush the grissini with olive oil and sprinkle with flaky sea salt and cracked black pepper. Bake for 10 minutes, then lower the oven setting to 200°C/Fan 180°C/Gas 4 and cook for a further 10 minutes until golden brown. Carefully transfer to a wire rack to cool.

Date, Goat's Cheese & Bacon Devils

Just like their cousin, the devil on horseback, this hot canapé is an absolute crowd pleaser. I have made so many, so often, that I could make them in my sleep. My elder son, Rafferty, hovers in the kitchen when he knows they are about to come out of the oven. I don't just make them at Christmas but they do have a wonderfully festive air about them. Aim for 3 or 4 per person, depending on what other canapés you are serving.

Makes 24

24 organic large dates
200g soft goat's cheese
Finely grated zest of 1 lemon
*   or orange*

24 small sprigs of rosemary (5–10cm)
12 rashers of good-quality streaky
*   bacon*
Sea salt and black pepper

Preheat the oven to 200°C/Fan 180°C/Gas 6. Make a slit along the side of each date and extract the stone. Set the dates aside.

For the filling, in a bowl, mix the soft goat's cheese with the citrus zest and season generously with salt and pepper.

Trim the leaves from one end of each rosemary sprig, roughly to halfway along, to make sticks. Cut the streaky bacon rashers across in half.

Spoon a generous teaspoonful of goat's cheese into each date cavity. Wrap a piece of bacon around each date and secure with a rosemary stick. Place on a non-stick (or foil-lined) baking tray.

Bake the stuffed dates in the oven for 20 minutes or until the bacon is cooked as you like it. Transfer to a plate and serve still warm... although they are delicious cold too.

Buckwheat Blinis
with Labneh & Pickled Celery

These buckwheat blinis make perfect little pads for salty fresh labneh (a strained yoghurt 'cheese') and pickled celery. The labneh should be made at least a couple of days (up to a week) ahead and the pickles at least a week (up to 4 weeks) in advance, so this is a canapé that you can prep long before you need it.

The blinis can be frozen ahead of time and then defrosted and gently reheated in the oven but they are much nicer made fresh. They are also substantial enough to double up as a starter, so these are my go-to canapé for Christmas Day. Have a production line of willing helpers ready to pile the blinis high with the toppings and see how many make it out of the kitchen.

Makes about 30 good-sized blinis

For the blinis:
250g buckwheat flour
2 tsp baking powder
A pinch of salt
250ml whole milk or oat milk
  (or use the whey from the labneh
  and top up with milk)
2 large eggs
30ml rapeseed or sunflower oil,
  plus extra for frying

For the labneh:
500g organic wholemilk yoghurt
1 tsp salt
Optional flavourings: snipped chives,
  chopped parsley or chervil,
  grated citrus zest, black pepper,
  grated raw garlic, toasted ground
  spices, such as coriander,
  cumin or caraway

For the pickled celery:
400g celery
1 tbsp fine salt
250ml cider vinegar
2 tbsp sugar
1 bay leaf
1 tsp caraway seeds
A few black peppercorns

To finish:
Snipped chives, or finely chopped
  parsley or chervil

You will also need:
A sterilised 500ml jam jar
  with a vinegar-proof lid

First make the pickle. Slice the celery thinly, place in a bowl, add the salt and give it a good mix. Leave for at least an hour. Tip away the liquid from the bowl and spoon the celery into your jam jar.

Put the cider vinegar, sugar, bay leaf, caraway seeds and peppercorns into a saucepan. Bring to the boil, then lower the heat and simmer for a few minutes. Pour the contents of the pan over the celery in the jar. Make sure the veg is submerged in the liquid then screw the lid on tightly. Leave to cool and then store in the fridge. Leave for at least a week before you open it. Once opened, use within a few days.

To make the labneh, put the yoghurt into a bowl and stir in the salt. You can include any flavourings now – the zest of a lemon and 1 heaped tbsp chopped chives works well – or keep it plain. You can also add more flavourings when the labneh is finished, if you feel it needs it.

Line a large sieve with a large piece of muslin or a tea towel and set over a bowl. Spoon in the yoghurt and tie the corners of the cloth together, or tie with string. Leave somewhere cool and dry to drain off the whey, for at least 24 hours (up to 2 days).

The resulting whey can be kept in the fridge and used in your blinis. The labneh is ready to eat straight away or you can pop it into a jam jar, cover with a layer of olive oil and store in the fridge for up to a week.

To make the blini batter, put the flour, baking powder and salt into a large bowl or food mixer and mix to combine. In a separate bowl, whisk the milk (or whey), eggs and oil together. Add to your dry mixture, a little at a time, whisking as you go. You should end up with a smooth batter, the thickness of double cream, or a little thicker, but easy to pour from a jug or ladle.

To cook the blinis, put a non-stick frying pan over a medium heat and wipe a little oil over the bottom. When the pan is hot, pour in 1 tbsp or so of batter from a jug or ladle, creating a blini no bigger than 6cm across. Repeat to cook several together, making sure the edges don't touch.

Cook for a minute or so until the blinis start to rise and turn golden at the edges, and bubbles appear on the surface. Flip them over and cook for a minute or so on the other side. Remove from the pan, wrap in a tea towel and keep warm while you cook the rest of the batter in batches, giving the pan a wipe of oil if needed.

Lay your cooked blinis on a tray or large platter and top with the labneh and pickled celery. Finish with a scattering of snipped chives or chopped parsley or chervil and serve at once.

Potage Bonne Femme

Soup comes into its own during the winter months. A big bowl for lunch with home-made bread, a flask of it when you are out on a frosty walk, or the first course of a feast – it works in all settings. It is also the perfect way to use up any veg and stock lurking at the back of the fridge over the Christmas period. I could have put many soup recipes in this book but I have chosen this one for two reasons – firstly it uses ingredients you will almost certainly always have and, secondly, Elizabeth David liked it. If that doesn't make it a worthy inclusion then I don't know what does.

Serves 4–6

50g butter
2 leeks, thinly sliced
2 carrots, chopped
500g potatoes, chopped
250ml milk or cream
Sea salt and black pepper

To finish and serve:
Thick slices of sourdough or
*   sourdough croûtons (see below)*
A handful of chervil or
*   parsley, chopped (optional)*

Put a cooking pot or large pan over a low heat and add the butter. Once melted, add the leeks and carrots. Sweat for at least 5 minutes to soften, giving the veg an occasional stir. Add the potatoes, stir to mix with the buttery veg and sweat for a few more minutes. Pour in 250ml water, add a pinch of salt and stir.

Cover and simmer for 20 minutes until the potatoes are soft. Take off the heat and blitz with a hand-held stick blender. Add the milk or cream and season with salt and pepper to taste.

Reheat the soup before serving in mugs with slices of sourdough, or in warmed bowls scattered with chervil or parsley and sourdough croûtons.

Sourdough croûtons

Cut the crusts off several slices of sourdough, then cut into 1–2cm cubes. Put these into a roasting tray with a few rosemary sprigs, trickle with olive oil and sprinkle with flaky sea salt. Give it a good shake then bake in the oven preheated to 220°C/Fan 200°C/Gas 7 for 5 minutes. Shake the tray again then give the croûtons another 5 minutes in the oven, until crisp and golden brown. For additional joy, grate cheese on top too.

Beef & Stout Stew

This is a belter of a stew. It is one of those dishes that can be made a couple of days in advance or thrown together and left for an afternoon of simmering. I have been known to travel with this dish, taking it down to the beach or to a friend's fire pit, to reheat on a grill rack over a fire. Once I took it to an off-grid cottage in Cornwall where, after bringing it up to temperature, it sat tucked into the inglenook, keeping warm as we prepped the rest of the meal.

To make it a low-maintenance outdoor choice, make sure it is in an old flameproof pot and eat with hunks of bread to mop up the juices. Alternatively, stick to the conventional serving and ladle it out around the kitchen table over a bowl of greens and spelt or barley.

Serves 8

2 tbsp olive oil

1.5kg chuck steak, cut into chunks

50g butter

4 onions, each cut into 8 wedges

4 garlic cloves, crushed

2 tbsp plain flour

2 carrots, peeled and cut into chunks

300ml stout

1 litre beef or vegetable stock

A small bunch of fresh oregano
  (or 2 tsp dried)

4 bay leaves

250g mushrooms, sliced

Sea salt and black pepper

Preheat the oven to 160°C/Fan 140°C/Gas 3. Put a large cooking pot or flameproof casserole over a medium-high heat and add the olive oil. When it is hot, brown the beef in batches to avoid crowding the pan, turning the pieces to colour all over. As the meat browns, transfer it to a bowl.

Once all the beef is browned, melt half the butter in the pot or casserole. Add the onions and cook over a low heat for about 10 minutes to soften. Add the garlic and cook for a few minutes. Return the meat to the pan and sprinkle in the flour, giving everything a good stir to make sure it is coated. Throw in the carrots too.

Now add the stout, a little at a time, stirring and scraping the bottom of the pan to deglaze as you do so. Pour in 600ml of the stock and give everything a good stir. Add the herbs and season generously with salt and pepper.

Bring to a simmer, put the lid on the pot or casserole and place in the oven. Cook for about 2 hours until the meat is tender, checking every 45 minutes or so and adding the rest of the stock bit by bit to keep the meat covered.

If you are cooking the stew ahead of time, take it out of the oven at this point and leave to cool, then place in the fridge (ready to reheat and finish before serving).

If you are planning to serve the stew immediately, melt the rest of the butter in a frying pan, add the sliced mushrooms and sauté for a few minutes to colour lightly, then add them to the stew. Give everything a good stir and return the pot or casserole to the oven without the lid. Cook for a further 30 minutes before serving.

Roasting is one of the simplest ways to cook winter veg – great when you're catering for a crowd – and you can have a lot of fun with the seasonings and flavourings you add. I love the prunes roasted with these earthy vegetables – along with the shallots and balsamic vinegar, they add a subtle, tempting sweetness.

Fill your largest roasting tray – ideally one that spans the whole oven shelf – or you can use a couple of smaller trays. It's a lovely festive side dish that can also serve 4–5 as a veggie main course, with a generous sprinkle of dukka (see page 111) if you like. **Hugh**

Roast Winter Veg with Herbs & Prunes

Serves 8

½ medium celeriac, about 300g
1 small swede, 250–300g
2 large carrots, peeled
5 tbsp olive or rapeseed oil
A few sprigs of thyme, roughly torn
A few bay leaves
1kg Brussels sprouts

12 small or 6 large shallots, thickly sliced
250g pitted prunes, halved
1 garlic bulb, cloves separated, peeled and bashed
2 tbsp balsamic (or red wine) vinegar
Sea salt and black pepper

Preheat the oven to 190°C/Fan 170°C/Gas 5. Peel the celeriac and swede and cut into 2cm chunks. Cut the carrots on an angle into 3cm chunks. Put these roots into a very large roasting tray, or divide between two trays. Trickle over 3 tbsp oil and scatter with the herbs. Add some salt and pepper and toss everything together. Roast in the oven for 20–25 minutes.

Meanwhile, peel away any dirty or damaged outer leaves from the Brussels sprouts, trim the stems if necessary, then cut each one in half. Put the sprouts into a bowl with the shallots, prunes and bashed garlic cloves. Add 2 tbsp oil, the vinegar and some salt and pepper. Toss together well.

Take the root veg out of the oven and give them a good stir, then scatter over the sprouts, shallots and prunes, along with any vinegary juice from the bowl. Return to the oven for another 20–25 minutes, until all the veg are tender and golden brown in places. Serve hot.

Variations
You can use almost any winter root veg – try parsnips, potatoes, beetroot, Jerusalem artichokes, or any combination thereof. And chunky florets of cauli or broccoli, or even wedges of winter cabbage, can replace the sprouts.

Curried Potato Tart

This isn't really a tart, or a quiche, it's a delicious one-crust pie, which makes it so much easier to pull together. It works just as well as part of a buffet as it does the centrepiece of a festive lunch. The filling can be adapted to take in leftover veg, and the mozzarella swapped out for the ends of mild cheeses that may be lurking.

Serves 6–8

For the shortcrust pastry:
340g wholemeal flour
A pinch of salt
170g cold butter, cut into small
    cubes, plus a little melted butter
    to finish
2 medium eggs, beaten

For the filling:
550g potatoes, peeled
20g butter
1 onion, chopped
2 tsp cumin seeds, plus extra to finish
200g spinach leaves
2 x 125g balls of mozzarella
Sea salt and black pepper

For the pastry, sift the flour and salt into a large bowl, add the butter cubes and rub into the flour with your fingers until the mixture resembles fine breadcrumbs. Add the beaten eggs and incorporate them into the mixture using a round-bladed knife.

Bring the dough together with your hands, being careful not to overwork it. If the pastry still feels dry and does not hold together, add a little cold water (just a dash at a time). Shape the dough into a disc, wrap in greaseproof paper and leave to rest in the fridge for an hour while you make the filling.

Preheat the oven to 200°C/Fan 180°C/Gas 6. Cut the potatoes into 3cm cubes and cook in a pan of salted boiling water for 7–10 minutes to soften slightly; they should retain their shape and still be a little firm.

While the potatoes are cooking, melt the butter in a large frying pan, add the onion and sauté gently for about 10 minutes until soft and translucent. Stir in the cumin seeds and cook for a few minutes. Drain the potatoes, tip them into the frying pan and stir well. Now add the spinach, a couple of handfuls at a time, stirring to wilt. Remove from the heat and leave to cool.

Take the pastry dough out of the fridge. Line a baking tray with baking paper. Roll out the dough on a lightly floured surface to a large circle, about 30cm in diameter and roughly the thickness of a £1 coin. Lay the pastry on the lined baking tray.

Cut the mozzarella into 3cm cubes and stir through the cooled potato and spinach mixture. Season generously with salt and pepper. Pile the filling onto the pastry, leaving a 3cm clear margin around the edge. Fold the pastry up around the edge and slightly over the filling to form a rim.

Brush the pastry rim with melted butter and sprinkle with cumin seeds. Bake in the oven for 25 minutes until the pastry is golden and crisp. This tart is delicious served straight from the oven but also works well as a cold buffet option.

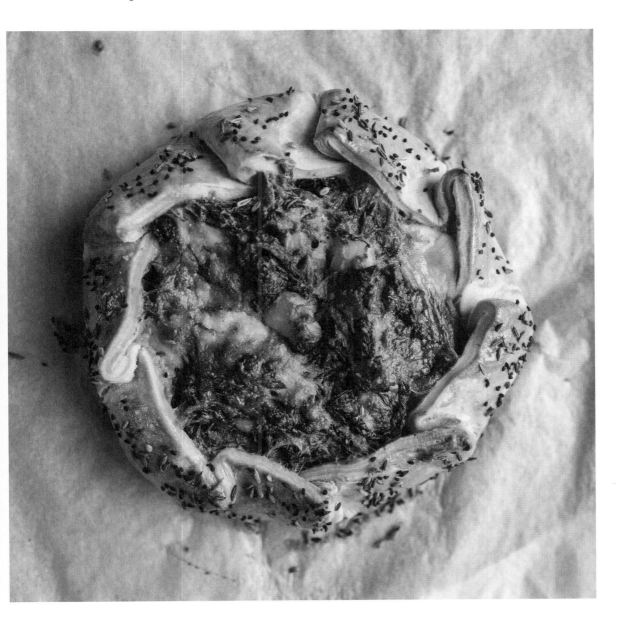

Midwinter Vegan Tart

In recent years Hugh and the River Cottage team have been making plant-based meals a more substantial part of their diets. It doesn't mean meat is off the menu, or that anyone has made the leap to a fully vegan lifestyle, but we are much less reliant on animal-based products.

Like its vegetarian friend on the previous page, this River Cottage recipe does not need a tart tin or a complicated pastry process. Keep a packet of ready-made filo pastry (most are vegan) in the fridge over Christmas and you are only ever one step away from a celebratory midwinter veg tart.

Serves 6–8

For the filling:
300g small cauliflower florets
2 tbsp rapeseed oil
20g pumpkin seeds
60g kale, shredded
300g potatoes, such as Maris Piper, cubed (or cooled cooked leftovers)
Juice of ½ lemon
Sea salt and black pepper

For the cauliflower purée:
250g cauliflower florets
2 garlic cloves, peeled
1 tbsp extra virgin rapeseed oil

To assemble:
2 sheets of filo pastry (about 48 x 25cm)
Extra virgin rapeseed oil, to brush

Preheat the oven to 200°C/Fan 180°C/Gas 6.

To prepare the filling, put the cauliflower florets into a roasting tray and trickle over 1 tbsp rapeseed oil. Scatter over the pumpkin seeds and stir to give everything a good coating of oil. Roast in the oven for 10 minutes then stir in the kale with another 1 tbsp oil. Return to the oven for a further 10 minutes until the cauliflower is cooked and the kale is a little crispy.

Meanwhile, boil the potatoes until tender; drain. Remove the roasting tray from the oven when the cauliflower and kale are ready, add the potatoes and set aside. Lower the oven setting to 180°C/Fan 160°C/Gas 4.

To make the cauliflower purée, put the cauliflower florets and garlic cloves in a saucepan and pour on enough water to cover. Bring to the boil and simmer for 10–15 minutes until soft. Drain well and put into a blender with the extra virgin rapeseed oil. Blend until smooth.

Combine the veg mix and cauliflower purée, add the lemon juice and season with salt and pepper to taste.

Lay the filo pastry on a non-stick baking sheet, overlapping the sheets about halfway across and brushing the bottom layer of the overlap with rapeseed oil. Trim the corners, to form a rough round. Pile the filling mixture evenly on top, leaving a 5cm clear margin along the edges of the pastry.

Fold the uncovered pastry up over the edges of the filling and brush with more rapeseed oil. Bake in the oven for 15–20 minutes until the pastry is golden and crisp. The tart is best served straight from the oven but also good to eat warm.

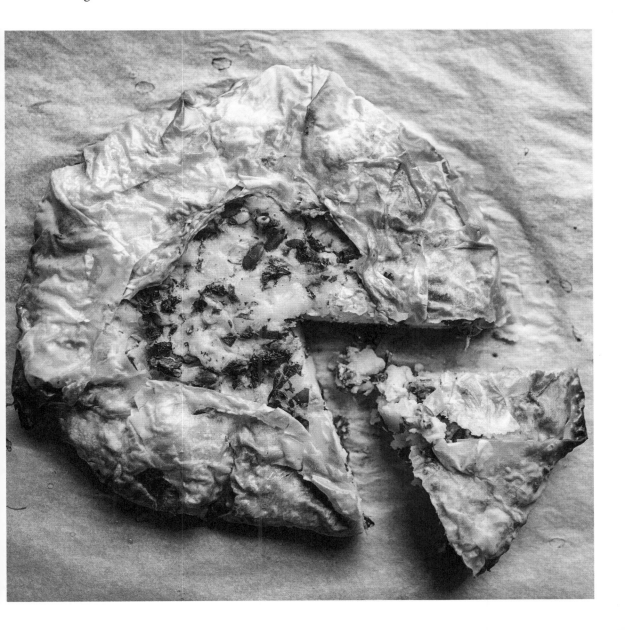

Lentil Salad with Herby Dressing

In some parts of Italy, it is customary to eat lentils on New Year's Day. They are thought to signify good fortune: a humble store-cupboard staple that, once cooked, seasoned and dressed, can be magically transformed into a glistening pile of tiny coins. I think it's a fine idea, not least because lentils are a welcome contrast to the rich meats of Christmas. This salad is lighter on the lentils – as it includes kalettes and spinach. In truth, the real star of this dish is the dressing.

Serves 8 as a side

200g Puy lentils
2 garlic cloves (unpeeled), bashed
2 bay leaves (optional)
A large handful of chervil and parsley stalks (optional)
250g kalettes
100g spinach, shredded
Sea salt and black pepper

For the dressing:

8 tinned anchovy fillets
2 tbsp chopped chervil
2 tbsp chopped parsley
2 garlic cloves, crushed
4 tbsp plain wholemilk yoghurt
6 tbsp mayonnaise

Put the lentils into a saucepan and pour on enough water to cover. Bring to the boil, cook for 1 minute and then drain. Return the lentils to the pan and add the garlic and herbs, if using. Barely cover with water. Simmer gently for 20 minutes or so, until cooked but not mushy, topping up the water if necessary.

Meanwhile, to make the dressing, blitz the anchovy fillets, chervil, parsley, garlic and yoghurt in a blender or food processor. Add the mayonnaise and blitz briefly to combine. Season with pepper and a little salt if needed (check the anchovy hasn't done that job for you). Transfer to a jar or bowl.

Once the lentils are cooked, drain them thoroughly and discard the garlic and herbs; set aside.

Bring a pan of salted water to the boil, drop in the kalettes and cook for a few minutes, then drain. Return the pan to the heat, add the hot kalettes and then the shredded spinach to wilt it quickly. Drain off any excess liquid from the pan before folding in the lentils.

Serve the lentil salad with a generous helping of dressing trickled over.

There's nothing more festive than a plate full of colour and crunch, and there are plenty of winter veg that can deliver that. This hearty salad combines crisp, raw red cabbage and carrot with the sweet juiciness of clementines and the crunch of walnuts. To dial up the colours even further you can scatter with lots of freshly chopped parsley.

Serve it up as part of a spread – it's a great complement to potato-based dishes or anything meaty – or with leftovers. It's also brilliant with my confit of duck legs (see page 37) in which case you can leave out the walnuts. **Hugh**

Red Cabbage, Carrot & Clementine Salad

Serves 8–10

1 medium red cabbage, about 750g
125g raisins
4 tbsp raw cider vinegar
8–10 clementines (or 'easy-peelers'),
   or 4 medium oranges
500g carrots, scrubbed

150g walnuts, bashed or very
   roughly chopped
Sea salt and black pepper
Extra virgin olive oil, to finish
   (optional)

Quarter and core the cabbage, then use a very sharp knife (or a food processor) to shred it as thinly as possible. Place in a large bowl.

Add the raisins and cider vinegar. Squeeze in the juice of 2 or 3 clementines (or 1 orange) and add some salt and pepper. Tumble everything together and leave to stand for 15–20 minutes. This will slightly soften the cabbage and plump up the raisins.

Grate the carrots coarsely and scatter them in a large serving dish or over a big serving platter. Give the cabbage and raisins a good stir, pile on top of the carrots, and pour over any juice left in the bowl.

Peel the remaining clementines or oranges and use a very sharp knife to slice them into 1cm thick rounds (don't worry if some of the rounds fall apart). Lay the fruit over the top of the cabbage and scatter over the walnuts. Finish with a good trickle of extra virgin olive oil, and serve.

Variations
You can, of course, swap white cabbage for red; celeriac or beetroot can replace the carrots; and pumpkin seeds, almonds, hazelnuts or pecans are all good swaps for the walnuts.

This is one of my family's favourite chocolate 'pudding' cakes, and I make it at least once every Christmas (and not infrequently for birthdays and other celebrations too). It's delectably tender, fudgy and chocolatey, and not too sweet or over-rich. You can serve it warm from the oven, with a dollop of whipped cream or ice cream, but it's also good made a day or two ahead and served cold or at room temperature. **Hugh**

Chestnut & Chocolate Cake

Serves 10–12

250g peeled cooked chestnuts
   (vacuum-packed or tinned are fine)
250ml milk
250g dark chocolate (at least
   70% cocoa solids), broken up
250g unsalted butter, roughly cut up

4 medium eggs, separated
100g caster sugar

You will also need:
A 25cm springform cake tin

Preheat the oven to 170°C/Fan 150°C/Gas 3, and grease and line your 25cm springform cake tin.

Put the chestnuts and milk into a pan and heat until just boiling. Take off the heat and mash well with a potato masher – you are aiming for a creamy purée, with just a few crumbly bits of chestnut. Set aside.

Put the chocolate and butter into a second pan and place over a very low heat. Keeping a close eye, to ensure that the chocolate doesn't get too hot, melt them gently together, stirring now and then. Allow to cool a little.

Whisk the egg yolks and sugar together in a large bowl until blended and creamy (they don't need to reach a 'moussey' stage). Stir in the warm (not hot) chocolate mixture and then the chestnut purée, until evenly blended.

Whisk the egg whites in a clean bowl until they hold stiff peaks. Take one spoonful of egg white and mix it into the batter to loosen it, then gently fold the rest in, trying not to knock out too much air. Carefully transfer the mixture to the prepared tin. Bake for 25–30 minutes until the cake is just set but with a slight wobble still in the centre.

To serve warm, leave to cool a little then release the cake from the tin. Slice carefully – it will be very soft and moussey. Alternatively, leave the cake to go cold, when it will have set a bit firmer.

Spelt Digestives

In the early days of River Cottage HQ, when there were just a few of us and the office cat, the kitchen chefs made these biscuits every day. They were given to the team after rigorous orchard planting, served to guests as they arrived to take part in a course, and piled up on the cheeseboard at the end of a feast. They are the most versatile biscuit of all – savoury or sweet depending on the amount of sugar you choose to add – and they are the very essence of River Cottage. To me, they taste of 15 years of memories.

Makes about 16

120g cold unsalted butter, cubed

120g wholemeal spelt flour, plus
   extra to dust

120g medium oatmeal or
   60g puffed quinoa

60g soft brown sugar
   (40g if you want a less sweet biscuit)

6g salt

1 tsp baking powder

A few drops of milk (if needed)

Rub the butter into the flour – either the old-fashioned way with fingers, or in a food processor – until it resembles fine breadcrumbs. Add the oatmeal (or puffed quinoa), sugar, salt and baking powder and mix together until evenly combined. You may need to add a drop or two of milk at this stage to bind everything together and form a slightly sticky dough.

Turn the dough out on to a lightly floured surface, dust with flour and press into a round. Wrap in greaseproof paper and leave to rest in the fridge for 30 minutes. (It will keep well in the fridge for a few days but will firm up considerably, so take it out to soften about 20 minutes before rolling it out.)

Preheat the oven to 180°C/Fan 160°C/Gas 4. Flour the dough well and lay it between two sheets of greaseproof paper. Roll out to a 3–4mm thickness then remove the top sheet of paper.

Using a 7cm pastry cutter, cut out about 16 rounds and lay them on a non-stick baking sheet. Re-roll any trimmings to cut more. Bake in the oven for 7–10 minutes, checking regularly after 5 minutes – the biscuits should be brown around the edges and lightly coloured on top.

Leave the biscuits on the baking sheet for a few minutes and then transfer to a wire rack to cool. They will keep for several days in an airtight container.

5
Christmas Day

CHRISTMAS DAY is a time for being with those you love. This could mean a jolly family gathering, a joyous collection of good friends or an intimate twosome. It may be a day of traditional celebrations, an exciting combination of global customs, a low-key affair or an emotional struggle. But in most cases, for the home cook, it is one of the biggest undertakings of the year. When all's said and done, it is just a large roast, but on Christmas Day the meal is stuffed with expectation and loaded with tradition. No need to panic, though. There are a few important tricks that will help you not just to survive, but enjoy the day.

• **Keep it simple**. Most of us know what a classic Christmas lunch looks like. A first course of canapés or smoked fish maybe, followed by roast turkey with all the trimmings, roast potatoes and root vegetables, then a flaming Christmas pudding with brandy sauce or a bowl of trifle for those who prefer it. While enthusiastic cooks may be keen to try different flavours, techniques and styles of food throughout the year, there is something sacrosanct about the Christmas meal. It has to live up to hard-wired anticipation and appeal to a spread of generations. The best route is to play it on the safe side, tweaking the odd recipe but creating a menu that embraces all the beloved main elements. Find out if your guests have any dietary requirements or special requests – and don't forget your own favourites. For me Christmas lunch must include a bowl of buttery Brussels sprouts with chestnuts, a clove-scented bread sauce and double helpings of pigs in blankets.

• **Draw up a timetable**. Make a note of what you will be cooking, the timings, the sections of the oven they will need, and then write a schedule. I advise you not to 'wing it'. You may think a relaxed approach will encourage a matching atmosphere but this often backfires. No one will feel chilled out if you are still waiting for the turkey to be cooked at 5 p.m. Organisation will be your friend.

• **You need stamina.** What I really mean by this is that it's wise to limit your alcohol intake until you have finished cooking. It's your Christmas Day too, but as the host you can't treat yourself in the same way as your guests until the food is on the table. Then is the time to top up your glass and leave others to worry about the washing up. Which leads me on to my next trick…

• **Delegate.** Do not feel too uncomfortable about asking others for help, and resist becoming that clichéd Christmas figure, the martyr. Most people actively want to share the load. One idea is to write out small tasks on pieces of paper – wine pouring, fire stoking, washing up, making tea – and put them in a bowl. Each guest plucks one out and has their assigned job. It means that no one has to ask how they can help and you have an instant support system. People may choose to swap around halfway through the day or step in to help with the bigger chores.

• **Let go.** It won't be faultless. Recognise how much you have achieved and do not criticise yourself for anything you have forgotten, burnt or botched. What hasn't been done or hasn't worked doesn't matter. If it really *does* matter to you then I would recommend preparing a small stash of items designed to get you out of a tight spot. It could include a couple of gifts for anyone you may have overlooked (chocolates or beautifully packaged panettone are universal). Have some organic stock cubes to hand in case your gravy needs a boost, perhaps a jar of ready-made cranberry sauce and a couple of packets of bread sauce, plus a small bottle of brandy (in case the other one has been drunk) for the pudding. I have never managed to produce a 'perfect' Christmas Day but I have had many very happy ones.

Note: As yet I have not spent Christmas Day on my own but if I do I am going to copy Elizabeth David and take to my bed with a tray of buttered brown bread, smoked salmon and a bottle of perfectly chilled white wine...

Breakfast

The row of bulging stockings hanging from the mantelpiece never fails to delight, even if I have given Santa a helping hand. Whether you are up with the lark (or small children), waiting for guests to surface, or have a calm house, this is a good moment to get organised before the day takes over. Put the oven and the kettle on. Check your cooking schedule if you have one, make sure all your vegetables are prepped, and fill the big teapot. You are going to need it.

In our family, nobody is allowed in the sitting room (where the stockings wait) until everyone is out of bed, then the smallest one leads, with adults at the rear carrying trays of tea and shortbread. This doubles up as breakfast (including the chocolate coins, mini panettone and tangerines Santa may have brought) while there is a fabulous frenzy of stocking opening.

Gifts always include a book, a pair of socks (matching for every child), a puzzle or game, pencils and a trick of some sort. I love this start to the day. It does mean we don't have time for a luxurious brunch – plus we eat our Christmas feast at lunchtime so nobody needs it – but if we did I would prepare the scrambled eggs with crab on page 287. Perhaps served, stately-home style, under a large silver cloche. Or maybe a skillet of kedgeree. Just enough to get you to aperitif time...

Socks and books

My favourite bit of Christmas day is the same now as it was fifty years ago, and it's the bit where we all get to open our presents. Or 'pressies' as my dad used to call them – and, to my delight, still does.

My favourite presents, however, are *not* the same. The presents I used to scoff at as a child are now among those I'm happiest to receive. They are the soft and squashy ones that are about the size of your foot (because they are socks), and the hard rectangular ones that are about the size of a book (because they are a book).

The reason why these two were so disappointing when I was growing up was, obviously, because they were *boring*! The only exception on the book front was the *Guinness Book of Records*.

There were no exceptions on the sock front. But some time in my teens the threat of socks (and indeed any gifted clothes, especially jumpers and, God forbid, ties) became potentially much worse than boring. There was a very real danger they might be unwearable, embarrassingly so. This agony was hugely heightened if the giver was going to be joining us at some point over the festivities. It was obviously expected that the offending garment would be worn, and worn with a smile, and parental pressure would be applied on both counts...

I got over it though. So much so that a few weeks before Christmas I will make a short list of books I am keen to read (or at least own), and sock-makers whose goods meet with my approval in terms of design and comfort. There are also some stipulations on fabric choice and provenance too (bamboo is currently favoured).

The vicissitudes of books and socks notwithstanding, the thing I've always loved about present-opening is not so much the content of the parcels as the ritual of opening them. I love the way that over the days preceding Christmas day the presents slowly accumulate under the tree (and, in the case of some of the lighter ones, in its boughs).

Going back a few years, that meant splashes of bright colour and the shimmer of shiny paper and ribbons. These days it's a more conscientious mix of brown paper, newspaper, reused tissue paper (sometimes celebrating its fourth or fifth Christmas) and, increasingly, some quite shabby looking tote bags (see page 79). We have moved with the times, but I love the scene no less.

The timing of the present-opening ritual has evolved over the years, taking its form under rulings laid down my parents decades ago. It represents (and this is something I have only come to fully appreciate since I have myself become a parent) the perfect intersection of the moment when the youngest children are on the point of melting down with impatience, with the moment when the adults think it's just about acceptable to start drinking. It's been as early as 11 a.m. in some years, but it's generally considered desirable to get past midday. The pattern that the younger the children the earlier the drinking can start is one that seems to have been passed down the generations. It must be sound thinking.

The present-opening requires all members of the household to be gathered around the tree (and no longer in night attire). The starter gun is the popping of a cork on the chosen bottle of fizz. The youngest will be indulged first, and if they want to start by opening the biggest presents, that's allowed. Ideally, gifts that are being given by those gathered will be handed personally to the giftee. But if a young one has ripped off the wrapping before the giver has had a chance to formally hand it over, that's fine too...

It all gets quite chaotic, quite quickly, as parcels are passed, fingers fumble at the tape and string, paper flies around, eyebrows are raised, hugs exchanged, glasses topped up, and variations on the theme of 'just what I wanted' expressed (with varying degrees of sincerity). Labels will be lost, for sure, and the more responsible parent will make a list of who gave what to which child, so thank you letters can be monitored, and ideally completed before the beginning of term, or Twelfth Night, whichever is the later.

It's over far too quickly, but everyone is left with a warm glow, and there is still the feast to look forward to. **Hugh**

Drinks

This is a moment of sheer Christmas pleasure: the joy of an aperitif and the salty snackiness of a canapé or two. There is always a point, when everything is in the oven and on the stove top bubbling away happily, where you can take a break. This may coincide with guests arriving so it is a great way to welcome them. If everyone is already with you then it's an opportunity to congregate and toast the day.

An aperitif was originally a medicinal, slightly bitter herbal recipe which led the way to vermouth. Now it means any alcoholic drink that sharpens your appetite for what is next. It may be a glass of champagne, a small sherry (on ice for me please), a gin and tonic, or a bespoke Christmas cocktail.

Components for a cocktail can be made ahead of time, perhaps incorporating something preserved from the garden during the summer months. Or focusing on seasonal flavours like ginger, cinnamon, apple and clementine. I would suggest making the base non-alcoholic – whether it is a syrup, cordial or purée – so a booze-free version can be offered. Christmas is a difficult time for those who do not drink, as the alternatives can be dull and unconsidered. It is also good to have a version to offer young people.

Once the cocktail glasses have been emptied, encourage guests to help themselves to further drinks, setting up a drinks tray, jugs of water, a space in the fridge for beer and wine, and nominating someone to oversee this. As well as the booze, consider the essential equipment needed to knock up a sturdy cocktail, including a full ice bucket, corkscrew with bottle opener, spirit measure, lemons, limes, bitters and a stirring spoon. A cocktail shaker, Worcestershire sauce, salt and a jar of olives are worthwhile additions. If there is space, add appropriate glasses too, or have them in the fridge to chill.

Keep a relaxed eye on the tray in case anything needs replenishing and give someone else the task of refilling the ice bucket. I say tray but you may have a trolley, cabinet or even a bar area at your disposal. I know someone who has a table in her hall known affectionately as the 'grog tray'. Another pal has the prow of a boat but I am not suggesting you go that far. It may be stating the obvious, but only stock the tray with things you will drink. Something strange happens at Christmas and we are tempted by unusual bottles that ultimately get relegated to the back of the cupboard.

If you are tight on space or keeping costs low, you could dedicate your tray to just one particular drink. This works exceptionally well if you are fond of a Bloody Mary or like to choose from a range of gins. You may want to keep your home-steepers hidden in case they disappear before you have had a taste! And then there's wine.

At this point I am going to hand over to Hugh, who talks about wines we can feel good about both before and during the feast.

Wine

Through the year I drink quite a lot of wine, but less than I used to. That's because these days, in an average week, I try and get at least three alcohol-free days (AFDs) in.

At Christmas, my AFDs tend to thin out a bit. There's just too many lovely people dropping by, or being visited, and frankly too much serious cooking going on, which somehow seems to insist on being conducted wine glass in hand. So, although I will try and insert an impromptu AFD or two into the holiday, more practically I will end up congratulating myself on days when I manage to stick to a couple of bottles of cider.

Realistically though, at Christmas I will mostly be drinking wine. And (I know this is not exactly a formula for festive thrift) my basic Christmas commitment is to drink slightly more and slightly better wine. There's always dry January to help me atone...

There's not much ambiguity about the phrase 'slightly more', but what do I mean by 'slightly better'? I already choose mostly organic wines, for the same reasons I choose organic produce. I want to support a sustainable farming system that nurtures the soil and respects and promotes biodiversity on our farmland. A subsection of organic viniculture is the biodynamic system, which involves arguably even greater commitments to ecological and holistic practices – you can find out more at www.biodynamics.com.

The other word that's storming the world of wine is 'natural', which is harder to define because it describes the techniques of wine-making rather than grape-growing, and unlike 'organic' and 'biodynamic' has no certification bodies regulating the use of the term. Many natural wines are organic or biodynamic too, but many are not, although they are still likely to be sourcing their grapes (if they don't grow them themselves) from small-scale growers employing less intensive methods.

But it's the rejection of industrial fermentation and the chemical additives it depends on that really defines natural wine-making. Many wine-drinkers, including me, are excited by this throwing off the shackles of conventional wine-making, and the quirky, characterful (and sometimes cloudy) wines that result. Others are sceptical, which adds a lively controversy to conversations about natural wines.

Another thing that draws me to natural wines, superficial though it may sound, is their label designs. They are often unexpected, arty and witty, expressing the maverick personality of the wine maker, and the wine. A funkily labelled bottle of, for example, an 'orange wine' (an amber-coloured white wine, fermented with the skins left on the grapes to increase structure and complexity) or 'Pet Nat' (short for Pétillant Naturel, which means naturally sparkling) makes an excellent Christmas present for a wine enthusiast.

I am also keen to support the increasingly varied and excellent range of wines produced in the UK from home-grown grapes, and I'll sometimes sample these even if they are not organically grown. English sparkling wines are undoubtedly some of the best in the world, and organic English sparkling wines are some of the finest.

Christmas day is an opportunity to showcase wines that have been exciting me the most in the previous year. Everyone loves a bit of sparkle at Christmas, and the first thing I open (to accompany present-opening) will definitely be 'organic bubbles'. My current top choice would be one of the sparkling organic wines from Oxney – not least because we now have a River Cottage collaboration with this brilliant Sussex wine maker. So, I'm biased, but not so biased that I wouldn't also point you towards top quality English fizz from makers like Limney, The Grange and, just down the road from us in Devon, Castlewood.

As the big feast looms, I'll pop the cork on a few of bottles of red, in time to let them breathe, and these will also be special. They probably won't be from the UK as we really haven't cracked that yet, but they won't be heavy-hitting Bordeaux wines or elegant Burgundies either. They will be organic, and they won't be stupidly expensive. I am increasingly drawn to lighter reds and Spain and Italy are producing some amazing reds at 13 per cent ABV or less that are either natural or biodynamic, or both. If you want to do some online browsing try our River Cottage supplier, vintageroots.co.uk. And if you want a couple of personal recommendations, Bohem Tempranillo-Garnacha is a good red and Meinklang is a crazy Austrian pink fizz which, at 10.5 per cent ABV, will be quite forgiving while you are cooking Christmas dinner. **Hugh**

Beers and cider

At River Cottage we love a diverse range of craft beers, and we make our own too. What started with the legendary Stinger (beer made with nettles from the farm) has grown into a selection of carefully created (and rigorously tested *ahem*) IPAs that we are seriously proud of. At home we also get a box of mixed ales and stout from Gilt & Flint, the brewery at the end of our village. I know how lucky we are to have this on tap (sorry) as well as other entrepreneurial breweries and wine makers.

Cider is another idea – we are swimming in it in the Southwest – and I buy large flagons for mulling purposes. It reminds me of early days at River Cottage and the competitive and wonderful local cider circle.

Festive spirits

It's hard to keep count of the number of gins available and the new or converted distilleries that have sprung up in recent years. The ingredients and mix of botanicals are just as diverse, using fruits, herbs, spices and even seaweeds. Good gin is a great component for many cocktails as well as being a stunner with tonic.

Brandy, whether required for your Christmas pudding, mulled wine or your nerves, is a must for the Christmas drinks cabinet. In Somerset, Julian Temperley makes the most amazing cider brandy. Vodka is another versatile spirit that also makes a brilliant base for home-steeping.

Rum is an instant cockle warmer (I'm thinking specifically of the spiced version), which translates extremely well in a cocktail too. It is also the base of the rumtopf (see page 50). And a wee dram of single malt whisky in front of the fire is the perfect nightcap for some – served warm with ginger wine for a whisky mac.

I always have a bottle of vermouth in the cupboard – not just for the drinks bar but because it is great to cook with. There are many more artisan brands available now. I also like a Spanish fino sherry – dry as a bone and served over ice. It may even be too good for your trifle.

Madeira, port and Marsala – fortified wines named after their place of origin – all do a similar after-dinner job. If I had to pick one, I would choose Marsala for its ability to transform certain dishes and not least to dunk biscotti into.

Christmas lunch

A roast was one of the first things I learnt to cook and I was surprised by how easy it was. It requires very little attention, can adapt to smaller or bigger numbers and, while delicious in its basic form, is outstandingly magic with all the trimmings. The success largely lies in managing the timings and having an oven plan for dishes going in and out, particularly when cooking something like the Christmas lunch. Of course, there are pitfalls but they can be avoided if you do some fancy footwork around what goes in when. It's a good idea to set out a schedule of timings based on the time you intend to sit down for dinner, whether that's around lunchtime or in the evening, or indeed mid-afternoon.

Common mistakes include not checking the weight or size of the meat or poultry, particularly at Christmas when you are likely to be cooking a joint or bird larger than normal. Make sure you have a roasting tray big enough – and you might want to do a practice run with the uncooked bird/joint, just to make sure you can get it through the door of your oven!

The poultry or meat will also need a good half hour to rest and will take time to carve: both points are often overlooked. Decide what you are going to plate up in the kitchen and put the vegetable dishes in the middle of the table or on a side table for people to help themselves. Or set up a buffet system in the kitchen so everyone lines up to fill their plates before taking their seat at the table.

Do remember to warm the dinner and serving plates before serving. Everyone will take twice as long filling their plate as they normally do, and a cold plate will take heat from your food.

Make sure there is space on the table for jugs of water and bottles of wine. If you are feeding a big group it helps to have salt and pepper at both ends of the table, and your gravy and sauces split into a few boats, jugs or bowls, to avoid 15 people waiting for the bread sauce to come around. My mind is always on the bread sauce…

The roast

Poultry/meat To turkey or not to turkey, that is the question. This poor bird gets a bad rap for being dry and tasteless but that does depend on the type of bird you source and how it is cooked. And one of the great things about a turkey is the number of people it can feed and the potential for leftovers.

If you choose a reputable producer who offers the slower growing breeds, like the Norfolk Black or Bronze turkeys, you will get a better bird with a fuller flavour. These are also available organically reared, which is the choice we always make at

River Cottage. Such special birds should be ordered in plenty of time – either direct from the supplier or from your local farm shop or butcher.

If you want to break with tradition, you can tackle the bird a slightly different way with the River Cottage recipe for turkey au vin, where the legs are casseroled and the crown roasted (see pages 242–5). If turkey really doesn't float your boat, then a rib of beef (on page 263) or a side of ham (on page 154) are two fabulous alternatives. Or you might prefer to roast a goose (see page 259) or duck – both are ideal for a smaller gathering where you are feeding 4–6 people.

Veggie/vegan centrepiece We don't need a meat centrepiece to create a magical feast. The old-school nut roast seems to have fallen out of favour in recent years, as the variety and accessibility of ingredients and interesting veggie and vegan recipes have grown. And many of them work well with other elements of the traditional roast. But if goose-fat-roasted potatoes are a must for you, then you can always do a second tray roasted in veg oil. What does make a difference, though, is creating a veg dish with a wow-factor that looks just as festive as the roast. Hugh's lovely stuffed squash on page 265 does the job, along with a knock-out gravy that you will not believe is vegan, but it is. The omnivores will be after it too. Personally, I am always tempted to stick a sparkler in the squash but, I remind myself, I am not Elton John.

Trimmings By this I mainly mean pigs in blankets and stuffing. Organic chipolatas and bacon are readily available and make for happier pigs in happier blankets. I wouldn't advise buying the ready-assembled version unless you can trace the source of both components. It takes a moment to create a pig in a blanket and you can personalise them in the process, maybe marinating the sausages in honey and mustard, or using rosemary twigs as skewers.

Stuffing can be made ahead of time, cooked, frozen, taken from the freezer on Christmas Eve and then reheated for 20 minutes in the oven. You may choose to stuff your bird with it, roll it in balls and roast it in the juices, or butter a dish and pile your mix in. Traditional flavours like sage, onion, chestnut and dried apricot, based on a breadcrumb mix, are safe, beloved options, but my new go-to stuffing is Hugh's fab recipe on page 251.

Potatoes You can cook whatever type of potato you like but I cannot imagine anything other than roast potatoes with Christmas lunch – fat-crisped, crunchy shells with fluffy middles. One of the best potatoes for roasting is the Maris Piper and it's better still when cooked in goose fat, which can be sourced from your local butcher or supermarket (or saved from roasting a goose). For vegetarians and vegans, cook the potatoes in rapeseed oil instead, keeping them separate from your

goose-fat spuds. To save time on the day, you can peel the spuds on Christmas Eve and keep them in a pan of cold water somewhere cool overnight.

Root veg For me, this means parsnips, carrots and swede. You may have grown these yourself; if not they are very likely to turn up in your Christmas veg box. Depending on oven space, I roast this triumvirate together in one tray. Alternatively, chuck the parsnips in with the potatoes midway through their roasting and boil the swede and carrots instead. They are brilliant mashed together with lots of butter and black pepper. As with the potatoes, you can peel roots the evening before and keep them in a bowl of cold water overnight.

Red cabbage Festive, traditional and very forgiving, this can be braised in advance, frozen and heated through at the last moment. Or you can make a quick pickle (see page 104) and pop the jar on the table for everyone to take a forkful from. This is one of few veg dishes that tastes just as good as leftovers.

Cauliflower A much-loved vegetable in my family, although this may have more to do with the creamy, mustardy cheese sauce that often accompanies it. Throughout the year, I serve it gratin-style with the addition of broccoli or Brussels sprouts and maybe a breadcrumb and crispy bacon topping. I may opt for this at Christmas or go for the plainer but tasty version of slicing the cauliflower and roasting it to get a delicious caramelised, slightly smoky result. I draw the line at boiling it. Everyone should draw the line at boiling it.

Brussels sprouts If I could only choose one vegetable at Christmas it would be this one. I blanch sprouts for just a few minutes, so they are still crunchy, and then sauté them in butter along with a couple of handfuls of chopped chestnuts. It's the final dish I make as it is needs to be served immediately. Trying to keep sprouts warm for any length of time turns them soggy and an insipid yellow, which is perhaps how they earned the bad reputation they do not deserve. You can also roast or steam them, or even finely shred them to eat raw – find the recipe that works for your family. Give sprouts a chance...

Sauces Prepare these in advance if you can. Home-made bread sauce (page 249) is the stuff of dreams so always make more than you think you will need and keep a bowl in reserve for Boxing Day. Cranberry sauce (page 247) is another traditional accompaniment, cooked up with little festive berry jewels and perhaps some citrus or herb additions like orange zest and rosemary.

Pudding

I am hoping you have made Hugh's definitive Christmas pud (on page 41) and lined up your chosen accompaniment – the boozy brandy sauce (on the same page) or a generous helping of custard or cream.

We always take a break after the main course and that's when I put the pudding on for a final steam, rather than fight for hob space earlier in the day. It is also when we exchange presents, which have been piled up under the tree tormenting the children (who may have given several of them a furtive prod, shake or sniff).

More drinks are poured – a digestif, a pot of coffee goes on the stove, a brew of good old Assam, and mint tea to cover all bases. When the pudding is finally ready everyone returns to the table while me, my brother and mother usually douse the thing in brandy, not realising the other one has already done it. Invariably, it is a flaming triumph!

The clear up

If you are feeding an army, you should have a legion of willing washer-uppers too. Children can make excellent table-clearers, although the teens have been known to eye up wine dregs, so be alert.

There is a lovely photo at the end of the December chapter of Hugh's first seasonal cookbook. It shows the joyous aftermath of the Christmas dining table, covered in empty glasses, crumpled napkins and the general mess of a happily devoured meal. You can sense those who have just left the table, full of delicious food and festive cheer, and the contentment of Hugh, the chef, as he finishes his wine in front of the fire. It perfectly captures the moment in the cook's day when the meal is done and the memory there to savour.

Supper and games

The pile of cold turkey sandwiches is often what tempts people to cook the bird in the first place. I am a big fan too but I would rather save the leftover bird for the days to come. So, for supper, I like to give the cheeseboard its first outing, with crackers, pickles and fruit.

You could also pass around a plate of mince pies (page 44) and a tower of chocolate tiffin (page 303) for those who prefer it. We end the evening with a family game to avoid everyone slumping in front of the TV.

Turkey au Vin

It is tricky to roast the perfect turkey, with breast meat still succulent yet dark meat properly cooked through, and the bigger the bird the harder it is. Then there's the giblets and the gravy to mess around with. There is an easier way: two dishes from one bird that pleases everyone and gives you a welcome head start on the big feast.

Our turkey 'au vin' embraces legs, wings, and the neck and gizzard if you like. This leaves the 'crown' (the breast on-the-bone) ready to roast fast and easy on the day. The all-important gravy is the full-flavoured liquor from this slow-cooked dish.

Just like the classic coq au vin, this is better made the day before and left to mellow overnight in the fridge. Ask your butcher or supplier to prepare the turkey for you: you want the legs as drumsticks and thighs, and the wings whole.

Serves 6–8 (based on a 4–5kg turkey)

3–4 tbsp vegetable or olive oil
250g belly bacon or pancetta, diced
*2 turkey legs, cut into drumsticks
    and thighs*
*2 turkey wings (plus neck and gizzard,
    if you have it)*
2 onions, peeled and cut into quarters
2 large carrots, cut into chunks
4 celery sticks, cut into 3cm lengths
4 garlic cloves, crushed
150ml cider brandy

500ml red wine
2–3 bay leaves
A sprig of thyme
Sea salt and black pepper

Saucey treats (optional):
A dash of soy sauce
2–3 tsp strong coffee
½–1 tsp redcurrant jelly
*A knob of softened butter mixed with
    2–3 tsp plain flour (to make a roux)*

Preheat the oven to 140°C/Fan 120°C/Gas 2. Heat 2 tbsp of the oil in a large frying pan, add the bacon and cook, stirring, until it takes on a little colour. Transfer to a flameproof casserole dish or large saucepan.

Now brown the turkey pieces in the pan (including the neck and gizzard), turning to colour them evenly. You'll need to do this in a couple of batches. Transfer the turkey to the casserole. Add a dash more oil to the pan and brown the onions, carrots and celery; add those too.

Add the garlic to the frying pan, then pour in the cider brandy to deglaze, stirring and scraping up the bits, then carefully add the wine. Pour the hot booze into the turkey pot, adding the herbs and some salt and pepper. Cover and cook in the oven for at least 2 hours until the meat is tender and almost falling from the bone. (Or simmer very gently over a low hob.)

Strain the liquor into a separate pan so you can tweak and perfect your 'gravy'. If you want more 'depth', add a dash of soy and a splash of coffee, but not so much that you actually taste either of those things. If you want a touch of sweetness, add a little redcurrant jelly.

If you are happy with a thin (but tasty) jus, pour it back over the turkey pieces now. If you want it a bit thicker, bring to a gentle simmer, then add the roux, a small piece at a time, whisking as you go. It doesn't take much to thicken the sauce, so go carefully and let it simmer for a minute before adding more roux. When you have sauce perfection, pour it back over the turkey and leave to cool. Keep in the fridge until the Christmas feast.

Gently reheat the turkey in the sauce, and serve everyone the tender meat (on or off the bone), alongside the carved meat from the crown, with lots of the liquor/gravy/sauce to accompany both.

Roast Turkey Crown

This is the 'fast roast' companion to the turkey au vin on the previous pages, allowing perfectly cooked breast meat and golden roast skin to be served with the tender legs in their rich, winey gravy. If you've got ahead and cooked the legs the day (or two) before, then you have a lot less to stress about on the big day.

Serves 6–8

The crown of your 4–5kg whole turkey
75g butter, softened, in pieces
A few sprigs of thyme
A few sprigs of rosemary

2–3 bay leaves
A small glass of wine
Sea salt and black pepper

Take the turkey crown out of the fridge a couple of hours before you start to cook it, to bring it up to room temperature. (Or even the night before, though don't leave it in a too-warm kitchen.)

Preheat the oven to 180°C/Fan 160°C/Gas 4. Rub the turkey crown all over with the butter, season well with salt and pepper and put any extra butter into the cavity with the herbs and most of the wine (sprinkling the rest over the bird). Place in a roasting tray.

Cover the bird loosely with a sheet of greaseproof paper and then a layer of foil. Cook in the oven for 1¾ hours. Carefully take the tray out of the oven and turn the oven up to 200°C/Fan 180°C/Gas 6.

Uncover the turkey crown and baste with the buttery, herby juices. Return it to the oven and roast for a further 30 minutes or until it is a tempting golden-brown colour and cooked through. To check it is done the old-fashioned way, push a skewer or fork into the thickest part of the breast and leave for just a couple of seconds then remove. The tip of the skewer should be hot and the juices running clear. You can also insert a digital probe thermometer into the thickest part – it should register 68°C (and again, check the juices run clear).

If your bird is not quite there, pop it back into the oven and give it another 15 minutes before checking again.

Re-cover the turkey crown with foil and leave it to rest in a warm place for a good 30 minutes before you carve and serve it, alongside the richly sauced turkey au vin (to which any roasting juices can happily be added).

The Trimmings

A basic roast is transformed into a Christmas delight by the inclusion of trimmings. Up until then, it is a nice bird, some roast potatoes and a selection of vegetables: no complaints from me. But add a few pigs in blankets, a wedge of herby stuffing and a scoop of bread sauce and I am wearing lipstick and singing Jingle Bells. For me, and my brother Rob, these are the main elements of the Christmas roast; it's everything else that are the trimmings.

Pigs in blankets

However many little sausages I wrap in bacon and pop in the oven, it's never enough. I work out the numbers based on 2 or 3 per person for lunch with the same again for Boxing Day leftovers. Then I consider the couple I snack on as the cook's perk, a few that will be stolen by brazen guests as they pass through the kitchen and then the late-night return to the kitchen where I may use one to scoop up cold bread sauce… then a few more for luck. To be on the safe side, I will at least double up this recipe.

Serves 8
12 thin slices of streaky bacon
24 organic cocktail sausages or
  12 chipolatas
24 (or 12) rosemary twigs (optional)

Preheat the oven to 200°C/Fan 180°C/Gas 6. If you are using cocktail sausages, cut each slice of bacon in half widthways. Wrap a piece of bacon around each sausage and place on a non-stick baking tray, with the join underneath. Alternatively, secure the bacon with a rosemary twig or cocktail stick.

Roast the bacon-wrapped sausages in the oven for 15–20 minutes until golden brown and cooked through. Serve hot, alongside your roast or as a party snack.

Cranberry sauce

My mother adores Christmas and cooking in equal measure. My father, on the other hand, is deeply uninterested in both but he would always take charge of the cranberry sauce. I think this may have had something to do with how much he liked it and how easy it was to make. Two good reasons to give these small red bursts of tartness pride of place next to the turkey.

It is possible to grow cranberries in the UK but most fresh and frozen cranberries are imported and easy to get hold of from November. You can make this sauce several days before and pop it in the fridge. I have heard talk of heating it before serving but that's a step too far for me on Christmas Day.

10–12 servings

*500g cranberries (fresh or frozen
    and defrosted)*
*Finely grated zest and juice of
    1 large orange*
45g sugar

100ml apple juice
100ml Port (optional)
A sprig of thyme
A pinch of salt

Put all the ingredients into a large saucepan and bring to the boil. Lower the heat and simmer, stirring occasionally, to prevent the mixture from sticking, for about 10 minutes until the cranberries start to burst.

Transfer the cranberry sauce to a bowl or clean jam jar and allow to cool, then cover and refrigerate. Bring back to room temperature before serving.

Bread sauce

I had half a mind to dedicate this book to bread sauce, such is my passion for it. My niece Missy feels the same way – we could bury our faces in it. Conversely it is not something I make a lot during the year. Maybe I should and then I wouldn't make such a big fuss about it at Christmas. Ignore this sauce at your absolute peril.

To save time on the day, make your bread sauce on Christmas Eve and keep it in the fridge in a sealed tub or cover the surface with a piece of greaseproof to stop a crust forming. It will just need reheating to serve.

Serves 8

450ml milk
50ml double cream
1 onion, peeled and halved
4 cloves
1 bay leaf

125g breadcrumbs, ideally sourdough
Nutmeg, for grating
40g butter
Sea salt and black pepper

Pour the milk and cream into a saucepan and place over a low heat. Stud the onion halves with the cloves and add them to the pan with the bay leaf and a good grinding of pepper. Bring to the boil and then immediately take off the heat. Leave to infuse for an hour.

Take out the onion and bay leaf, add the breadcrumbs and put back on the heat. Grate a little nutmeg into the mix and simmer gently for 3 minutes, giving an occasional stir. Take off the heat, stir in the butter and serve.

To reheat leftovers, return to the pan, add a dash of milk and warm through, stirring often. Or rejoice in the sauce being cold and solidified and slice for sandwiches, or to accompany cold meats.

This wonderfully savoury chestnut and celery stuffing is delicious with roast meats – especially poultry – but as it is vegan, I serve it increasingly often alongside veg dishes and vegan gravy (see page 269) for a meat-free feast. It's great to serve with the stuffed squash on page 265 (even though that's already stuffed with lovely veg!) **Hugh**

My Favourite Stuffing

Serves 6–8

500g fresh or vac-packed chestnuts
2 tbsp rapeseed or olive oil, plus extra
  to trickle
1 onion, finely chopped
1 head of celery, tough outer stems
  removed, finely chopped
12 plump prunes, stoned and
  roughly chopped
6–8 sage leaves, chopped

A couple of sprigs of thyme,
  leaves picked
A small bunch of parsley, leaves picked
  and chopped
100g fresh (or stale) breadcrumbs
50g hazelnuts, roughly bashed,
  and/or pumpkin seeds (optional)
Sea salt and black pepper

If you are preparing whole chestnuts from scratch, make a small slit in the skin of each one, then blanch in boiling water for about 2 minutes to ease peeling. Drain and, once cool enough to handle, peel off both the tough outer skin and the thin, brown inner skin. Now simmer in unsalted water for 15–20 minutes, until completely tender. Drain and leave to cool. Put the chestnuts (home-cooked or vac-packed) into a bowl and break up roughly with a fork – they should be crumbled rather than puréed.

Heat the oil in a large frying pan over a medium heat. Add the onion and celery and sweat for 10–15 minutes, until softened and golden. Add the prunes, chestnuts, herbs and some salt and pepper. Mix well and cook for another 8–10 minutes, stirring occasionally. Remove the pan from the heat.

When the mixture has cooled a little, mix in all but a good handful (about 20g) of the breadcrumbs until well combined. You can add a dash of warm water or veg stock if that's needed to bring it together.

Preheat the oven to 190°C/Fan 170°C/Gas 5. Oil an ovenproof dish and pile in the stuffing, packing it down fairly firmly. Rough up the surface a bit with a fork, then scatter over the reserved breadcrumbs and hazelnuts and/ or pumpkin seeds if including. Trickle over a little more oil, and bake for about 30 minutes until nicely browned and crisp on top. Serve hot.

Classic Roast Potatoes & Parsnips

You could take different routes here – adding garlic and rosemary to the tray, or roasting the parsnips separately with a spicy mix of cumin, coriander seeds and fennel – but for Christmas lunch I like to keep it classic. It also helps your kitchen space, and your head space, if you combine these two roots.

Serves 6–8

1kg potatoes, ideally Maris Piper
125g goose or duck fat,
  or 125ml rapeseed oil

500g parsnips
Sea salt and black pepper

Preheat the oven to 200°C/Fan 180°C/Gas 6. Peel the potatoes and quarter if large, or cut into thirds if medium sized.

Bring a large pan of water to the boil and add a couple of pinches of salt followed by the potatoes. Let it return to the boil and boil the spuds for 5 minutes, then drain off the water (saving some in a jug to use in your gravy). Allow the potatoes to 'steam dry' for a couple of minutes, then give them a quick bash around the pan to roughen up their surfaces.

Put the fat or oil into a large roasting tray and place in the oven to heat up for a few minutes – it should be sizzling by the time you take it out.

Tip the potatoes into the roasting tray and turn them to give them a good coat of hot fat, then sprinkle with salt. Put the tray back into the oven for 10 minutes, then turn the potatoes and return to the oven for another 10 minutes. Meanwhile, peel the parsnips and halve them lengthways.

Now add the parsnips to the roasting tray and give everything a good baste with the fat. The veg shouldn't be crowded or they won't crisp up so, if you cannot fit them all in one tray, heat a second tray and split the potatoes and parsnips between them.

Return the tray(s) to the oven and roast for another 30 minutes until the potatoes and parsnips are golden. If they are not quite crisp enough, leave them in for another 10 minutes. Serve straight away.

Brussels Sprouts & Chestnuts

Love them or hate them, Brussels sprouts are *the* vegetable of Christmas. They get such a bad press after decades of being over-boiled, but I could start a campaign in praise of sprouts and the variety of ways they can be cooked: roasted, baked in gratins, fermented or shredded and eaten raw. Nevertheless, the recipe I include here is straightforward, to minimise stress on Christmas day, and showcases the classic sprout and chestnut combo.

Serves 6

800g Brussels sprouts
50g butter
200g cooked chestnuts, peeled and chopped

A generous sprig of thyme
Juice of ½ lemon, or to taste
Sea salt and black pepper

Put a large saucepan of salted water on to boil. Trim the base of your sprouts. Add them to the boiling water and cook for 5 minutes.

Meanwhile, heat a large frying pan and add the butter. Drain the sprouts and tip them straight into the frying pan. Add the chopped chestnuts and thyme and stir-fry for several minutes.

Take the frying pan off the heat, give the mix a good squeeze of lemon and a liberal seasoning of salt and pepper and the dish is ready to serve.

Variation
If you have enough oven space you could roast the sprouts and chestnuts together with a couple of chopped garlic cloves, 2 tbsp oil and the thyme, for around 20 minutes.

Carrot & Swede Mash

Swede is often overlooked but all it needs is a chance – and a generous amount of butter. This is a dish that can also be made earlier in the day and then reheated at the last moment. It captures the sweetness of the root veg and adds a vibrant splash of orange to the plate. I add any leftovers to the Boxing Day bubble and squeak.

Serves 6

500g swede
500g carrots

50g butter
Sea salt and black pepper

Peel the swede and carrots and chop into 1cm cubes, keeping them separate. Bring a large pan of salted water to the boil and add the swede. Bring to a simmer and cook for 20 minutes before adding the carrots. Cook for another 10 minutes until both veg are soft but not collapsing.

Drain off the water, then add the butter to the pan with plenty of pepper and mash with a potato masher. If you want a smooth purée, then give it a final blitz in the food processor. Taste to check the seasoning and reheat to serve.

Roast Goose

Traditionally goose was eaten at Michaelmas after it had been fattened on the stubble of the year's harvest. Luckier geese managed to hang on until Christmas, when they were killed and given out at The Goose Club, a savings plan that enabled the poor to deposit a few pennies each week towards their Christmas lunch. They were a popular choice, long before turkey squawked into the picture.

Whether you cook your goose for Michaelmas or Christmas Day, a good place to start is with the British Goose Producers Association who can direct you to farmers who rear their geese sustainably outdoors, feeding them on a diet of grasses, herbs, wheat and sun. Alternatively, you could go to a trusted local butcher and ask for a free-range or organic goose. Other than the occasional diversion of an excellent rib of beef, this is Hugh's favourite Christmas lunch.

Serves 6

1 free-range or organic goose,
  about 4–5kg
2 onions, sliced
1 carrot, roughly chopped
A small bunch of thyme
A few bay leaves

For the giblet stock:

A little oil
The goose giblets (except the liver),
  the neck chopped into 4 pieces
1 onion, roughly chopped
1 carrot, roughly chopped
1 celery stick, finely chopped
A bay leaf

For the gravy:

About 400ml giblet stock
1 rounded tsp plain flour
A glass of red wine
Sea salt and black pepper

Saucey treats (optional):

A splash of strong coffee
A dash of soy sauce
½ tsp redcurrant jelly
A dash of cider vinegar or wine
  vinegar

Take your goose out of the fridge the night before you are going to cook it to bring it to room temperature.

You can make the giblet stock for the gravy in advance or, if you're attentive, while the bird is roasting. Heat a little oil in a medium saucepan. Add the goose giblets, except the liver, along with the veg and bay leaf. Pan-fry over a medium-high heat, stirring often, to caramelise (but not burn) both veg and giblets. Pour on 600ml water to just cover, bring to the boil, then lower the heat and simmer very gently for 1 hour, or a bit more if you are doing this in advance. Strain and set aside to cool. You should have about 400ml of well-flavoured stock. There's good meat on the neck and the gizzard too, so both can be served up with the goose.

Before cooking, make sure the skin of your goose is dry to touch, so it will crisp up nicely in the oven. Calculate the cooking time at this stage: as a guide, the bird needs about 20 minutes in the oven for every 1kg with an additional 20 minutes at the end. So, a 5kg bird should take no more than a couple of hours. That said, ovens and geese differ so do not slavishly follow timings but have a meat thermometer handy.

Preheat the oven to 220°C/Fan 200°C/Gas 7. Roll up your sleeves and reach into the goose cavity to remove the fat. (This sits thickly around the cavity opening and will be easy to peel away from the carcass.) Set this fat aside.

Using a skewer or sharp knife, prick the skin of the bird all over, making sure you double up your efforts around the thighs and wings. This will help release the fat as it is cooking.

Pull the legs a little away from the body. Put the onions, carrot, thyme and bay leaves into the cavity (it must be no more than half-full); they are going to give your gravy a boost later. Place the bird, breast side down, on a wire rack over a roasting tray.

Roast the goose in the hot oven for 20–30 minutes (Hugh calls this the half-hour sizzle) then turn the oven down to 170°C/Fan 150°C/Gas 3 and carefully take the bird from the oven. (You will need to use oven gloves for this because the fat will be scorchingly hot.) Lift the goose off the rack for a moment and pour the excess fat from the roasting tray into a bowl. Be aware, it will continue to spit.

Now put the goose, breast side up this time, back on the rack over the roasting tray and into the oven. Cook for the remainder of the calculated time at the lower heat or until it is cooked through (see opposite). You will need to baste the goose every 20 minutes, at the same time checking that the skin is not becoming too dark (cover with foil if it is) and draining off the fat. Either spoon the fat out of the tray or use a baster to suck it up safely, and transfer it to a bowl. Alternatively, you could take the entire tray out of the oven, lift the bird off and pour the fat into a bowl before returning the bird and tray to the oven. Try to leave any meat juices behind in the tray though.

When you estimate your goose is ready, check that the bird is cooked as you would other poultry: pierce the thickest part of the thigh, where it meets the body, with a skewer – the juices that run out should be clear, not pink. You can also use a meat thermometer: inserted into the thickest part of the meat, it should register 65–70°C. Once the goose is ready, transfer it to a warmed platter, cover loosely with foil and leave to rest in a warm place for at least 30 minutes.

While the goose is resting, finish the gravy. Heat up the giblet stock in a small pan (gently reheating the neck and gizzard in it if you want to serve them). Pour off most of the residual fat from the roasting tin, leaving behind just a little fat with any meat juices and 'burnt bits'. Put the roasting tin over a low heat. Add the veg from the goose cavity. Shake 1 rounded tsp flour into the tray, and use a spatula to mix it with the burnt bits, juices, veg and fat, scraping and stirring. Add half your glass of wine and keep scraping. When all is well mixed and bashed up, pour the hot giblet stock into the pan (first placing the hot neck and gizzard with the goose, if serving). Keep mixing vigorously, swapping the spatula for a wooden spoon. The flour and bashed veg will help thicken the gravy.

Strain the gravy into a small pan. Bring to a simmer, taste and make final adjustments, if needed, with another splash of wine, coffee and/or soy, even a little redcurrant jelly if you think it needs sweetness, and a splash of cider vinegar to sharpen. It should be richly flavoured and well balanced.

To carve the goose, take the legs off first and then take the breasts off and cut into thick slices. Serve on warmed plates, with the gravy and your chosen accompaniments.

Note: You may end up with as much as 1 litre of goose fat in total, including the fat that you took out of the carcass right at the start. You can render this down by heating it in a saucepan before passing it – along with the fat you have taken through the cooking process – through a sieve into sterilised jars. It lasts for several months if stored in the fridge and makes the very best roast potatoes.

Roast beef is a celebration of all that is exciting about good meat. And as I raise some very special beef of my own, from my 'micro-herd' of North Devon cattle (aka Ruby Reds), for me it really is the most special thing I can put on the table at Christmas.

You don't have to raise your own beef to have a very special joint, but I would recommend talking to your butcher or, better still, a beef farmer who sells direct, to procure a well-aged (hung for at least 3 weeks) piece of 'well-covered' (nice and fatty) fore-rib on the bone.

It's actually quite a forgiving joint, as you can roast it pretty fiercely to get the outer muscles well done with a nice, crisp, almost-burnt exterior, while the eye of the joint stays lovely and pink.

Trimmings should include roast spuds and parsnips (see page 252) which you may want to roast in beef fat, home-made horseradish sauce and a knockout gravy, as well as a nice pile of winter greens (cabbage or kale). If you want to serve some Yorkshire puds, be my guest, but with Xmas pud to come I don't think they are vital (unless, of course, you are reading this in Yorkshire – in which case you won't need my instructions). **Hugh**

Rib of Beef

Serves 8–10 with leftovers

A joint of aged rib of beef (3–4 ribs), about 4–6kg
A little olive oil or rendered beef dripping
Sea salt and black pepper

For the gravy:
1–2 tsp plain flour
A glass of red wine
Up to 500ml beef stock

For the horseradish sauce:
50–75g piece of fresh horseradish, peeled and very finely grated
1 tbsp cider vinegar or wine vinegar
1 tsp English mustard
A pinch of sugar
150–200ml crème fraîche

Make the horseradish sauce ahead (the day before is fine). Combine all the ingredients except the crème fraîche in a small bowl, and leave to macerate for an hour or two. Then stir in the crème fraîche. Cover and keep in the fridge, removing it an hour before serving to bring to room temperature.

Ideally, take the joint of beef out of the fridge the night before you intend to cook it and keep it in a cool larder overnight, then leave it in the kitchen for a couple of hours before roasting.

Preheat the oven to 220°C/Fan 200°C/Gas 7. Massage the beef joint with olive oil or dripping and season lightly all over with salt and pepper. Place in a roasting tray and put into the hot oven to cook for 30–40 minutes, until the meat is well browned and sizzling.

Turn the oven down to 160°C/Fan 150°C/Gas 3 (leave the oven door open for half a minute to help it cool quickly). I don't want to be over-prescriptive about timings. You have a nice buffer of fat on one side and bone on the other, and you actually want the outer muscles to be well done. For the full 4 ribs and a joint that's over 5kg, give it another 1 hour 20 minutes for a very rare 'eye' and up to 2 hours for 'still just pink in the middle'. For 3 ribs, or a less well covered joint, the range is more like 1 hour 10 minutes– 1 hour 40 minutes. You can also use a digital probe thermometer to check the cooking, inserting it into the thickest part of a central rib: a reading of 55°C indicates very rare meat, while 65°C will be just pink.

When the meat is cooked to your liking, remove it from the oven, transfer to a warm serving plate or carving tray and cover loosely with foil. Leave to rest for *no less than half an hour* before carving and serving.

While the meat is relaxing, make your gravy. Carefully pour off almost all the fat from the roasting tray, without losing any juices or burnt bits. If it's not too flimsy, you can place the tray over a medium heat and bring the juices to a sizzle. Sprinkle over 1 tsp flour and rub into the juices with a spatula. Work the spatula into the corners, scraping up all the burnt and sticky bits and sloshing in the wine and some of the stock as you go. Strain it through a fine sieve or chinois into a small saucepan for the final tweak.

Bring your gravy to the boil, whisking to emulsify and thicken it. Taste and add a bit more stock, salt and pepper if needed, as you like. You can make it thicker by whisking in a little more flour, but go carefully, and always bring back to the boil, stirring, to cook out the flour. Keep the gravy warm over a very low heat.

Bring the joint to the table to show everyone, even if you are going to carve it on a another surface. Slice all the meat away from the bones. Then release the central muscle that is the 'eye'. Thickly slice the outer layers, and thinly slice the eye. Everyone can have something almost burnt, and something pink or rare, or even a rib to gnaw on, according to preference.

Serve up the meat on warm plates, with roasties and greens, and pass around the gravy and horseradish sauce at the table.

I devised this dish a few years ago to create a great Christmas centrepiece for vegetarians and vegans. It looks celebratory and tastes of all the festive flavours. Served with the lovely vegan gravy that follows, it is also a dish which omnivores will enjoy, and so it makes for a wonderfully inclusive feast. The stuffing on page 251 can also be served on the side, for a full-on vegan celebration. **Hugh**

Stuffed Squash

Serves 6–8

1 medium sweet-fleshed squash,
    about 2kg (Crown Prince works
    particularly well)
About 4 tbsp olive or rapeseed oil
8 garlic cloves, peeled and bashed
2 medium onions, quartered
About 350g parsnips, peeled and cut
    into pointy chunks
1 orange
2 eating apples, cored and cut into
    chunky eighths
150g cooked chestnuts, roughly
    chopped
3 chicory bulbs, quartered lengthways
A squeeze of lemon juice
Sea salt and black pepper

For the spice mix:
2 tsp fennel seeds
2 tsp coriander seeds
1 tsp sweet smoked paprika
A good pinch of dried chilli flakes
1 tbsp chopped rosemary leaves
Zest of the orange (see left)

For the Brussels 'slaw' (optional)
150g Brussels sprouts, trimmed of
    any tired outer leaves
½ lemon
½ clementine

To finish and serve
50g pumpkin seeds, toasted
Vegan gravy (page 269)

Preheat the oven to 190°C/Fan 170°C/Gas 5. Slice the top quarter or third off the squash and set it aside. Scoop out the seeds from the 'bowl' that's left and scoop out or trim some of the flesh around the inside of the opening to make it wider. Cut away the peel from the top then cut the flesh from this piece into chunks; save these with the trim from the bowl.

Brush the inside of the squash with a little oil, season well with salt and pepper and add half the bashed garlic cloves. Place the squash on a baking tray and roast for 1–1½ hours, until the flesh is tender.

Meanwhile, prepare the spice mix. Toast the fennel and coriander seeds in a dry pan for a minute or two until fragrant, let cool slightly then crush to

a coarse powder, using a pestle and mortar. Add the paprika, chilli flakes and chopped rosemary. Finely grate the zest of the orange and add this too. Season with some salt and pepper and mix well.

Put the reserved squash into a large roasting dish, along with the squash pieces. Add the onions, parsnips and the rest of the garlic. Add 2 tbsp oil and toss the veg in it, then add the spice mix and stir well so that the veg is well coated with spices. Put into the oven (above the squash if that fits) and roast for 20 minutes, until starting to colour. (If the squash is cooked before the rest of the roasted veg, cover it with foil to keep it warm.)

If you are serving the slaw, prepare it while the veg are roasting. Slice the Brussels sprouts very thinly and put them into a bowl. Trickle over a little oil and give them a squeeze each of lemon and clementine juice. Season with salt and pepper and toss together well, breaking up the sprout leaves a bit as you go. Put to one side.

Slice the zested orange into 8 wedges. Take the roasting tray from the oven and add the apples, orange wedges, chestnuts, chicory and lemon juice. Stir, so that all the ingredients get a coating of spice. Return to the oven for 25–30 minutes or until everything is tender and starting to turn golden. Remove the roasted orange wedges and set aside.

When the squash is tender, place it on a warmed large serving platter and heap the roasted veg, chestnuts and apples into it. (Any spare veg can be served on the side.)

Scatter the toasted pumpkin seeds over the top of the filled squash. Serve with the roasted orange wedges for squeezing over, and the slaw on the side if serving. Pour the vegan gravy into a jug to pass around.

A great vegan feast deserves a great vegan gravy, and here it is. The rich umami flavours come from the mushrooms, and the thorough browning of all the veg, plus a cunning tweak with a dash of coffee and soy. As it can be made in advance and kept chilled for up to a week, or frozen, it's a great thing to tick off your list ahead of the big day. **Hugh**

Vegan Gravy

Serves 6–8

2 tbsp rapeseed oil

About 100g large chestnut or open
 cap mushrooms, roughly chopped

200ml red wine

1 medium onion, roughly chopped

1 medium carrot, halved lengthways
 and thickly sliced

1 celery stick, roughly chopped

About 1 tsp plain flour

About 500ml hot light vegetable stock
 (or water)

2 bay leaves

1 large sprig of thyme

1 tbsp strong coffee (espresso or similar)

1 tbsp tamari or soy sauce

Sea salt and black pepper

Heat 1 tbsp oil in a wide, heavy pan over a high heat. Add the mushrooms and fry 'hard' for 7–8 minutes, without stirring to start with to develop some colour, then stir from time to time. They will release some liquid; keep cooking until this is evaporated and the mushrooms are well reduced. Loosen any bits sticking to the base of the pan with a wooden spatula from time to time. Keep going until the mushrooms are thoroughly browned and caramelised then tip them into a bowl. Add a splash of the wine to the pan, scraping to deglaze it, then add this liquor to the mushrooms.

Give the pan a wipe and add the remaining 1 tbsp oil, then the onion, carrot and celery. Sizzle pretty hard until the veg are well browned. Add another splash of wine, giving the pan a good stir-and-scrape with a spatula. Now add a sprinkling of flour and cook, stirring, for a couple of minutes.

Add the stock, remaining wine and herbs. Bring to a simmer and cook for 6–7 minutes until the veg are just tender. Add the coffee and tamari/soy and return the mushrooms to the pan. Take off the heat, discard the herbs and tip the contents of the pan into a blender. Blitz to a smooth gravy, adding a little extra stock if needed. Add salt and pepper to taste if required.

Serve straight away or cool and chill until needed. It may separate a bit on cooling, but will come back together if you give it a whisk as you reheat it.

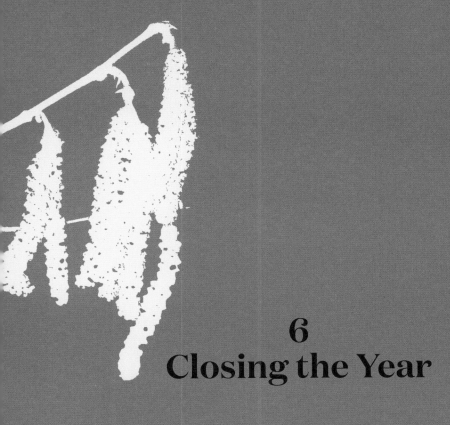

6
Closing the Year

THE QUIET DAYS BETWEEN Christmas and New Year, now sometimes referred to as 'betwixmas', are a blessing. They give us the perfect opportunity to pause, if we can, and catch our collective breath after a busy year. Released from the traditions of the preceding days we are free for revelry or retreat. I prefer the latter approach, finding a new, slower pace with my family. We gravitate to a jigsaw in a cosy corner, the record player is hauled out, there are old and new games to compete over, dogs to be walked across frosty fields and a pile of books to read by the fire. The fridge and larder are well stocked, the drinks tray replenished and forty winks encouraged. The idea of breaking this harmony to queue outside a store for the Boxing Day sales or hovering over the laptop for online deals makes me anxious.

The heroes of these quiet, in-between days are leftovers from your festive feasting that are just as delicious second time around. It is worth building them into your Christmas cooking plans – to ensure you have plenty of them. These rich pickings can be the basis of an entirely new meal and can save you from any kind of strenuous cooking. 'Factoring in' leftovers, as Hugh likes to put it, is an art form in itself.

I return to the kitchen with a different attitude during the lull days. The food we make and eat after Christmas takes on a new, creative significance, whether we are rustling up something slow and considered like a stew, or quick and crunchy like a raw vegetable slaw. This is the time to fully reap the rewards of planning and preparation – transforming leftovers, pulling things out of the freezer, rummaging in the store cupboard and plundering the preserves. It can be a very creative time: when I don't have to cook, I often find that I really want to!

If the very idea of getting back in the kitchen makes you feel like throwing this book across the room then focus instead on the quick fixes with pre-prepared ingredients or pass the cookery baton to others in your household. Point them in the direction of the larder you have diligently stocked and let them take over.

It's not all rest and quiet: there is a flurry of significant days towards the end of the holiday, starting with the high expectations of New Year's Eve, that blend into New Year's Day, an excuse for final indulgence before resolutions and a return to the routine. Twelfth Night, on 5 January, marks the official end of Christmas and carries with it the ominous tradition of putting the decorations away or risk being cursed with bad luck for the rest of the year. I am often one step ahead because I take the tree down by New Year's Eve, refresh the greenery and string the fairy lights around the room, maintaining a little natural beauty and sparkle as we head into January.

So, do a quick stocktake after the main celebration to make sure no leftover is a 'left-behinder'. Check your fridge in case anything has been pushed to the back. Do the same with your store cupboard to remind yourself what you have and if any of the basics need replenishing, and you are all set. There is a true sense of peace during these in-between days, so I hope very much that you find it.

Factoring in festovers

For me, pretty much every meal over the holiday that isn't a 'set piece' feast is going to be some kind of smörgåsbord of the left over and the thrown together. That's how I love to feed the family, and it's how we all love to eat. This means that at Christmas I will be, even more than usual, in a kitchen mode that I can best describe as 'conscious over-catering'. It's where Gwyneth meets Fanny.

This penchant for factoring in 'festovers' means that every stew will be made as if four more people might drop by unexpectedly just as I'm dishing it up. They probably won't. And when it comes to putting lunch together the following day, we'll all be glad they didn't. Because we all know second-day stew is even better than first.

Roast meat has a special status as a leftover. It's delicious served cold, and pretty much straight up, with just a little something to help you relish it. It may be that mustard or mayonnaise is all you need to 'relish' it good and proper, in a sandwich perhaps. But something a shade more elaborate, like my caper and parsley dressing, plus a smattering of lentils (see page 290) will give it a damn good relishing, and resuscitate the roast as not just a snack, but a second feast.

And it's not just my meaty mains that get deliberately left over. My children can eat a lot of mashed potatoes at a sitting, but over time, I have learnt to out-mash them. Because we all like a bubble and squeak too. They may not be quite so enamoured of lentils, but they like them well enough. So, I find it very useful to have a tub of them cooked, in the fridge, and ready to deploy in non-meaty contexts too: tossed with thin slices of apple and raw celeriac, and again parsley, they make for a quick and easy but really special winter salad, for example.

The tins and jars in the larder must also be mentioned in Christmas despatches. They are 'territorial leftovers' – being already cooked, and on permanent standby. They are ready to be pressed into service to stand shoulder to shoulder with the finest perishable leftovers from the fridge. The balance of the over-catered stew becomes a top-drawer chilli con carne with a couple of tins of beans, a jar of passata and a generous pinch of cayenne. (Tip: chop up the meat in the stew so it's roughly the same size as the beans.)

Tinned fish is not to be overlooked either. At some point over the holiday, often when a mild hangover is asking to be comforted, I am likely to rustle up a sardine omelette – topped with finely sliced raw onion, and a dash of Tabasco. Gosh, I never thought I would reveal details about my secret self-treats. Well, it's a sentimental time... Happy New Year everyone. **Hugh**

Boxing Day

There are very few days I anticipate and enjoy more than 26 December, St Stephen's Day (in honour of the saint), or Boxing Day as it has been known since the 1800s. The name is thought to come from the alms boxes in church, put out to celebrate the Feast of Stephen, as well as from the tradition of the rich giving boxes of gifts and money to the poor. 'Leftovers day' would be another appropriate name, as many of us tuck into the cold spoils from the previous day's roast. It's the simplest day for the cook after one of the busiest in the calendar and a time I can truly savour.

Planning the food

Make it easy on yourself by over-catering on those dishes you know you will want to see again on Boxing Day. Choosing a bird that serves more than those around your Christmas Day table, cooking extra pigs in blankets and additional roast potatoes for example, will pay dividends the following day.

Cold meat A succulent home-cooked ham is the perfect centrepiece for the Boxing Day spread and you can cook it (and enjoy it hot) a few days ahead (see page 154). Leftover roast meat from the Christmas Day meal is incredibly useful, and you should not waste a delicious morsel from whichever bird or beast you have chosen. Serve it cold alongside leftover trimmings, bubble and squeak, salads and pickles. If you are lucky there will still be enough for a few slices sandwiched between sourdough later in the week and a fragrant curry on New Year's Eve. Making a stock or broth with the carcass or bones is the final mark of respect and will reward you in the days ahead.

Roast potatoes Incorporate them in your bubble and squeak, slice and fry them with eggs for a late breakfast or serve them cold with an aïoli or beetroot hummus. In my house they don't hang around long so if you are only left with a handful save them to press into focaccia dough, along with the last of the stuffing, sprouts and chestnuts (see page 284). The result is more than bread, it's a complete lunch and makes the ideal walking snack.

Vegetables I don't actively plan to have veg as leftovers because I prefer to cook from scratch and eat them fresh. However, surplus brassicas and roots can be turned into a soup, added to a frittata (see page 293), layered in a gratin, fried in a bubble and squeak or puréed into a dip.

Sauces Gravy can be reheated the following day or frozen if you find yourself with excess. I always make double helpings of bread sauce and hide a bowl in a secret place to ensure there will be enough for Boxing Day. Sometimes one has to resort to these measures…

Christmas pudding Leftovers work beautifully fried briefly in a little butter, broken up and swirled through ice cream or deployed as a luxurious base for a trifle.

Cheeseboard If this hasn't had its first outing already then now is the time to reveal it in all its glory. From Boxing Day onwards, it features daily in our house until we finish the cheese or the cheese finishes us. If you feel overwhelmed by your cheeseboard then you can see off that wheel of Stilton or Cheddar truckle with a retro fondue, soup or salad. Turn to page 299 for one of our favourite winter salads comprising radicchio, chicory, blue cheese, parsley and toasted nuts and seeds.

Table of joy At home we have an old wicker shopping trolley to store our treats in with wheels for easy transportation to table or sofa. I have also been inspired by my friend and River Cottage colleague Jessamy, who sets up a table of treats every Christmas. Her buffet of small bowls includes her favourite sweet and savoury snacks and makes the ideal grazing place with a cup of tea or glass of wine. There is always Turkish delight, lebkuchen, candy canes, mixed toffee assortment in shiny paper, peppermint creams, humbugs, tangerines, cheese straws, chocolate orange and nuts. You can construct your own selection, storing anything that goes stale quickly in glass jars or tins.

I create my own version including grissini (page 201), biscotti (page 169), roasted nuts and seeds (page 137) and tiffin (page 303). This table is an excellent device when you have guests and helps avoid constantly checking if anyone needs anything. Just point to the table of joy.

New Year's Eve

I have had some wonderful (and disappointing) New Year's Eve celebrations over the years. From student parties and pre-children cottage rentals with my best pals to the special family dinners of recent times, there has been much to recommend Old Year's Day.

It is a significant date in the River Cottage calendar too, the finale of another busy year and the opportunity to party before the dark, quiet days of January. We throw a huge communal feast, probably the biggest of the year (if we don't include the private events and weddings we host). The kitchen team spend days prepping a seasonal menu of incredible courses, matched by an expansive drinks list. The fires are lit so as guests arrive they are greeted by warmth, boards of canapés and a pre-dinner sharpener – a mulled cider or kombucha cocktail perhaps – before they take their seats. There is always live music from a local band or musicians, who save their most rousing numbers for a post-dinner shindig, when the barn is transformed into a dance space and the English sparkling is on ice, waiting for midnight.

There can be huge significance pinned to the way we say goodbye to one year and welcome the next. For many of us, food and drink play a crucial part in the success of the evening, whether we are throwing a big party (head back to the chapter on Feeding a Crowd for ideas), a small gathering or a family supper. There is no need for a culinary fuss – particularly if you are still recovering from a mammoth kitchen stint over the main Christmas days.

A few canapés, like my version of devils on horseback (on page 202) and a pile of crackers with a bowl of Hugh's divine brandade (page 146), can be prepared in advance and set the celebratory tone, however many you are entertaining. As does a ginger and honey switchel (page 192), which transforms into a cocktail with a shot of freezer-chilled vodka (get your glasses cold too if you have space in your ice box). Or Hugh's kir royale, made extra special if you are using home-made cassis (page 53) and local fizz, or with a kombucha twist one of his kombocktails (on pages 194–5).

What you do next depends on the number of guests you have but a one-pot wonder or a tray of roast veg are fail-safe choices, as they can be flexible and easy to prep ahead of time. That may leave you more energy to make a pudding – perhaps a sumptuous trifle of cream, custard, booze-soaked sponge and pear compote layers, or a lovely mincemeat frangipane tart (page 300) to slice and pass around before Big Ben strikes twelve.

For myself, I like a celebratory curry, served with fizz and eaten in my pyjamas…

A wild winter walk

A walk is a fine thing at any time of year, but it somehow takes on an extra mantle of virtue and reward in the days following Christmas. The days are already lengthening, we are looking forward to the year ahead, and even if spring is still some way off, we have seasonal change, and perhaps some changes we are planning to make for ourselves, in our sights.

Being outside, in nature, is a good way to let those thoughts and feelings play out. The rhythm of putting one foot in front of the other, the open sky above us, and the sound of birds and rustling branches, is conducive to subliminal percolation. Stuff quietly gets settled. So, I think it's a good rule to make a daily walk in the days before and after Christmas and before the return to work compulsory – for myself, if not for the rest of the family.

Of course, in the closing days of the year there may be different weathers to walk in. I have what I need to make pretty much everything except my face rainproof, and I can live with having wet glasses long enough to notch up some self-awarded brownie points. Though I draw the line at walking through the woods in very high winds. We'd all do well to draw that line.

Sometimes heading out into a chilly, gusty drizzle is its own reward, as your senses get scrubbed and scoured, your hands and feet nipped and numbed. Back inside you shut the door on the wild weather and the slow re-heat after taking off wet things becomes a deliciously tingling affair: the toasting of toes in front of the fire, the cuppa, the well-earned slice of cake.

Other times, a winter walk can be uplifting in the moment, and beyond all expectation. Clouds part and the light does something extraordinary, almost biblical, that wows us. The blue of the sky on a still clear day allows us to feel the warmth of the sunshine of spring two months ahead of time. A jagged hoar frost sharpens sights and sounds into crystalline precision. A full blanket of snow summons up childish glee.

I usually take binoculars – a small pair that fits in my pocket. I'm not birdwatching, just looking out for things. I might see a bullfinch on a branch of hawthorn, and get a gorgeous close up of its rose-pink chest. Or I might watch a distant kestrel, balancing on an invisible pole that's been photo-shopped out of the sky, head into the wind.

But sometimes the joy comes from something close by that demands your attention like a tug on your scarf. The first spray of snow drops will do it, arresting you in their spotless, guileless little aprons. Their white gives permission to the colours that follow, tagging the crocuses, the first primroses, but staying true and pure until the riot of the daffs takes over. Then we'll be home and dry. **Hugh**

New Year's Day

It's the day of the big walk, the freezing swim or the last feast of the festivities, depending on your preference: a good day to get everyone out of the house with the encouragement of a flask and a treat. Either take your lunch with you or come back for a long, leisurely meal. However you choose to spend the first day of the New Year, it is likely to be a last hurrah before everyone returns to work and school. It is also the day to establish resolutions – if you believe in that sort of thing.

Twelfth Night

After the twelve glorious days of Christmas, Twelfth Night signifies the close of the festivities. Superstition dictates that the decorations must be down by this day and this usually coincides with a return to work and school. It feels like a sad but necessary step into the New Year. However, historically Twelfth Night was considered an important date and celebrated as the day the Wise Men arrived at the stable to visit the baby Jesus. The finale of twelve days of feasting, it's a date we often observe at River Cottage. We toast the year ahead with mulled cider – a traditional wassail drink, symbolising a healthy future harvest – and eat slices of warm almond cake.

Back to the beginning

Winter is a time of hibernation, an opportunity to stop and take stock of the year that has passed before we forge ahead into what is to come. There is a gloomy, anti-climactic feeling that can hang around after the holiday and sometimes the best way to beat this is to plan the next one. This is one of the great appeals of the pagan year – there is always something to look forward to and celebrate. So, too, in nature and seasonal bounties. We don't have to wait long for the cycle to begin again and in early January the Seville oranges will appear, piled up in greengrocers and farm shops, ready for a weekend of marmalade making. A bowl of vibrant orange fruits and the smell of citrus in the kitchen cuts through the damp, grey days.

Now is the ideal time to think about what you want to grow and preserve in the months ahead. I keep a notebook to remind myself what worked (and didn't) in the previous year. This is the time to garden without even going outside, although I like to wrap up and potter about in the low winter sun. I'll feel less guilty about settling by the fire with seed catalogues, cookbooks and the dregs of the home-steeped booze, to dream of the spring and summer to come. And so, the year begins again...

Mermaid's Hot Chocolate

I don't like to go on about my obsession with early morning sea swimming. Much. Hugh is also a big fan of cold water and takes a daily dip in his pond, sometimes breaking the ice when it is safe to. He and I are not alone in this year-round activity, although it is definitely quieter over the winter.

In the colder months my sea swim pals often take it in turns to bring a flask of something hot and a tin of something baked. The hands-down winner is always Tracy's hot chocolate. When I asked her if I could include the recipe she sent me a vague note about chucking stuff in, judging by eye and adapting to ingredient availability. Less a recipe, more a work in progress. She has even been known to include the dregs from the coffee pot. Here I have tried to tie the basic recipe down to capture the spice, heat, sweetness and rich darkness of what can only be described as rocket fuel when it is drunk at 6.30 a.m.

Serves 2

*4–5 heaped tsp raw cacao powder or
   unsweetened cocoa powder*
*A good grating (1 heaped tbsp) dark
   chocolate (at least 70% cocoa solids)*
1 tsp ground cinnamon
½ tsp ground ginger
½ tsp ground cloves

½ tsp ground mixed spice
*½ tsp chilli powder or a good pinch
   of dried chilli flakes*
A knob of preserved stem ginger
*2 tsp honey, maple syrup or syrup
   from the ginger*
500ml whole milk or oat milk

Put the cocoa, grated chocolate, spices, stem ginger and honey or maple syrup into a blender. Add about 2 tbsp boiling water from the kettle and blitz until smoothly combined.

Add the milk and give it another blitz. Taste to check for spice, sweetness and heat, and adjust accordingly. Pour into a pan and slowly bring almost to the boil, stirring. Pour into a warmed flask or a couple of mugs.

Boxing Day Focaccia

Focaccia, an Italian-style olive oil bread, is traditionally topped with rosemary and sea salt but it will happily take on countless other flavours and ingredients. Save some of your leftover Christmas dinner for this recipe. A handful of roast potatoes, a few sprouts and chestnuts, some chunks of stuffing – all wedged into this doughy delight – make it much more than the sum of its parts. Cut into chunks, wrap and take it off on a walk with you; I guarantee people will go the extra mile for this.

Serves 6–8

300g strong white bread flour
6g salt
3g fast-action dried yeast
Olive oil, to trickle

For the topping (optional):
Sprigs of rosemary, cooked chestnuts,
*   chunks of stuffing ball and*
*   roast potato, Brussels sprouts*
*   (any combination of these)*

Combine the flour, salt and yeast in a large bowl. Add 225ml water and mix to form a wet, sticky dough. Tip it straight out onto a clean surface and lift the dough up with two hands – don't worry about it sticking to the surface at this stage. Slap the dough hard back onto the work surface and stretch it up and over itself. Now slip your hands back under the dough and repeat this slapping then folding motion. After 5–10 minutes of this kneading technique the dough should become much more stretchy, and less inclined to stick to your surface as you lift it up. Alternatively, you can knead the dough in a food mixer fitted with the dough hook.

Trickle a generous glug of olive oil into your bowl and return the dough to it. Cover with a tea towel and leave to rise until almost doubled in size. This should take an hour or so.

Oil a non-stick baking tray or cast-iron pan. Gently lift the dough into the tray or pan and spread it out with your fingers. Trickle olive oil over the surface and leave to prove for 40 minutes until the dough is risen and puffy.

Preheat the oven to 230°C/Fan 210°C/Gas 8. Oil your hands and press your chosen topping ingredients into the middle of the dough (or leave it plain). Use your fingertips to make dimples in the dough around the filling, pressing your fingers right through to the bottom.

Bake for 20–25 minutes or until golden. Transfer the focaccia to a wire rack to cool for about 10 minutes before serving, or leave to cool completely.

Scrambled Eggs & Crab

This dish makes the most divine celebratory brunch. But it is not just for Christmas and it's not just for breakfast either. It defines the idea of simple luxury – a few excellent ingredients, a little bit of patient stirring and hot, buttered toast to scoop it up with. Crab is one of the more affordable shellfish and a little goes a long way, meaning a single crab can stretch to serve more than one or two if added to egg, pasta or rice or turned into fish cakes.

Serves 6

12 large eggs
1 cooked medium brown crab,
  brown and white meat picked out
  and kept separate
4 tbsp double cream

75g butter
A small handful of chopped mixed
  herbs (parsley, chives, dill)
Sea salt and black pepper
Toasted sourdough, buttered, to serve

In a large bowl, beat the eggs together, then mix in the brown crab meat and cream. Season with pepper (but not salt).

Melt the butter in a large saucepan over a low heat and pour in the egg and crab mixture. Stir the egg gently and consistently, keeping the heat as low as possible. It should take a good 5–10 minutes for the eggs to begin to thicken; do not be tempted to rush this. Continue to cook gently until the eggs develop a velvety texture.

Take the pan off the heat and fold through the white crab meat and chopped herbs. Taste to check the seasoning, adding salt at this point if the dish needs it. Serve right away on toasted, buttered sourdough.

This vibrant hummus takes leftover roast veg on board, to create a tasty, textured, veg-packed dip. It makes a delicious and proteinaceous element in post-Christmas spreads and buffets. For a contrasting texture, serve it with some fancy, seedy crackers or very thin, crisp sourdough toast. You can up the veg quotient further by partnering it with crunchy raw veg too – winter lettuce, carrot, fennel and slim wedges of very fresh cauliflower are all excellent partners. **Hugh**

Curried Leftovers Hummus

Serves 4–6

2 x 400g tins chickpeas (or white beans, or one of each), drained and rinsed

About 250–300g cooked roasted root veg, such as potatoes, carrots, parsnips or celeriac, roughly chopped

2 tbsp (about 50g) tahini or nut butter, such as peanut or almond

1 tbsp of your favourite curry paste or powder

Finely grated zest and juice of 1 lemon

3–4 tbsp extra virgin olive or rapeseed oil

Sea salt and black pepper

Put the drained chickpeas into a food processor with the veg, tahini or nut butter, curry paste or powder, lemon zest and juice, a pinch of salt and a twist of pepper. Blitz to a coarse purée. Now keep blending, trickling in the extra virgin oil. Trickle in a little cold water too, to achieve a loose, spoonable texture.

Taste to check the seasoning and adjust with more lemon, curry spices, salt or pepper, if you need to, then it's ready to eat.

Variation
Leftovers of almost any veg curry work well blitzed into the hummus instead of the roasted veg and curry spice.

This is one of my favourite ways to dress and serve cold cuts of roast meat, especially beef, though it's also excellent with cold duck, goose, lamb and pork. It's always a very welcome platter in any post-Christmas spread. **Hugh**

Roast Beef Salad
with Lentils, Mustard & Parsley

Serves 4–6

About 500–750g leftover cold roast beef (such as the rib of beef on page 263)

100–150g freshly cooked or tinned Puy lentils

For the dressing:

A handful of flat-leaf parsley, roughly chopped (or whole leaves if small)

1 tbsp capers, thoroughly rinsed if salted; well drained if in vinegar

2 tbsp olive oil

Juice of ½ lemon, or 1 tbsp cider vinegar

1 generous tsp English or Dijon mustard

A few twists of black pepper

Trim the beef, removing any very fatty or gristly pieces. Slice it very thinly and arrange overlapping on a large platter, the pink meat in the middle, the more well done around the outside.

For the dressing, in a small bowl mix all the ingredients together thoroughly. Stir through the lentils.

Spoon the dressed lentils generously over the meat just before serving.

Leftovers Frittata

A frittata is a perfect vehicle for leftover veg – anything from roast potatoes and other roots to buttered leeks and greens or a couple of spoonfuls of cauliflower cheese. You can add bits of stuffing, scraps of cold meat and oddments of cheese as well. With this easy oven-baked method, the egg is poured straight into a dish full of hot veg and put back in the oven, so there's no frying or flipping involved. Serve with a crunchy wintry salad, like the red cabbage, carrot and clementine salad on page 221, for complete veg satisfaction.

Serves 4–6

About 500g cooked leftover veg, roughly chopped

Other leftover scraps such as chunks of stuffing, scraps of meat or nuggets of cheese (optional)

1 tbsp rapeseed or olive oil

8 medium eggs

A handful of mixed herbs, such as parsley, chives and thyme, finely chopped (optional)

A good handful (20–30g) of freshly grated or crumbled Cheddar, Parmesan, goat's cheese or other well-flavoured cheese

Sea salt and black pepper

You will also need:

A shallow ovenproof dish or roasting tin, about 27 x 20cm

Preheat the oven to 190°C/Fan 170°C/Gas 5. Put all the veg and any other leftovers into your ovenproof dish or roasting tin and toss with the oil. Add salt and pepper only if the leftovers aren't already well seasoned. Roast for 10 minutes to heat through.

Meanwhile, in a bowl, beat the eggs together with the chopped herbs, if using, and some salt and pepper.

Take the dish from the oven, pour the egg evenly over the veg and scatter over the grated cheese. Return to the top of the oven for 10–15 minutes until the egg is all set and the top is starting to colour. If your oven has a grill, you can use that to accelerate the browning of the top.

Leave to cool slightly, then slide the frittata out onto a plate or board. Serve warm or cold with a big salad… and mustard.

Bubble & Squeak

I love the fact that this dish, dating back to the 1800s, is enjoyed just as much today. The name was originally inspired by the sound of the cabbage cooking and, as now, it was synonymous with the day after a big roast. Serve with cold meats, top with a fried egg, pile a mound of red cabbage sauerkraut on top, or eat it straight out of the pan with a fork.

Serves 6

4 tbsp rapeseed or sunflower oil
2 onions, finely sliced
1 garlic clove, crushed
1 small red chilli, deseeded and
*   finely chopped, or 1½ heaped tsp*
*   of your favourite curry powder*
*   or paste (optional)*

About 600g cold, cooked potatoes
*   (boiled, baked, roast or mashed),*
*   in chunks*
About 300g cold, cooked cabbage,
*   greens, kale or Brussels sprouts,*
*   roughly chopped*
Sea salt and black pepper

Place a large, non-stick frying pan over a medium heat and add the oil. When it is hot, add the onions and cook for 10 minutes, until soft and starting to colour. Add the garlic, along with the chilli or curry powder/paste if you want to spice it up, and cook for another few minutes.

Toss in the potato chunks and cook for a few more minutes, stirring regularly, until it starts to colour. Do add a little more oil if you think the pan needs it. Give the bottom of the pan a little scrape to loosen anything that's stuck, and then add the greens. Cook, stirring frequently, for a few minutes. Season with salt and pepper to taste and serve immediately.

This vegan version of a creamy root gratin, finished off with a crispy, oaty topping, is warming, comforting and very, very tasty. It goes extremely well with simply cooked lentils and/or a salad of bitter winter leaves. **Hugh**

Multi Root Vegan Gratin

Serves 6

2–3 large potatoes, about 500g in total, such as King Edward, thinly sliced, rinsed and dried

½ large celeriac, about 350g, quartered and thinly sliced

3–4 Jerusalem artichokes or parsnips, about 350g in total, thinly sliced

2–3 tbsp rapeseed or olive oil

2 garlic cloves, thinly sliced

½–1 fresh chilli, finely chopped, or a good pinch of dried chilli flakes

350g cashew nuts, soaked in water overnight

1.2 litres hot vegetable stock

4 tbsp jumbo oats

2 tbsp bashed hazelnuts

2 tbsp toasted buckwheat groats

Sea salt and black pepper

Preheat the oven to 180°C/Fan 160°C/Gas 4.

Put all the sliced veg into a large bowl. Drizzle over 1 tbsp oil, add the garlic and chilli and season with salt and pepper. Mix everything together with your hands.

Drain the cashew nuts and put them into a blender. Add just enough of the hot stock to cover them. Blitz until smooth then trickle in the remaining stock, little by little, until you have a smooth, creamy sauce (you might not need it all).

Add the cashew cream to the sliced veg and toss to mix. Transfer to a baking dish and spread out. Grind over some pepper and trickle over a little more oil. Bake for 30 minutes, or until bubbling and golden around the sides and the centre of the gratin yields completely when pierced with a knife.

Meanwhile, make the topping. Mix the jumbo oats, bashed hazelnuts and toasted buckwheat groats together in a bowl, seasoning with a good pinch each of salt and pepper. Add 1–2 tbsp oil, or enough for the mix to start to clump together into a sandy, crumble-like topping.

Sprinkle the topping evenly over the gratin. Return to the top shelf of the oven for 10–15 minutes, until the topping is golden and crisp. Serve hot.

New Year's Eve Turkey Curry

A New Year's Eve curry is a fitting use of the last of the turkey. This recipe is by my husband Steve, a natural cook, who can make something (absolutely delicious) out of very little at all, although he does use every pan to do so. Don't be put off by the list of ingredients – you should have many of them in the store cupboard already – and adjust the chilli according to taste. Make it the day before you plan to eat it to allow the flavours to mingle and deepen before gently reheating. Serve with very cold fizz.

Serves 6–8

For the dry-roast spice mix:
2 heaped tsp cumin seeds
2 heaped tsp coriander seeds
1 heaped tsp fennel seeds
2 tsp fenugreek seeds

For the wet spice mix:
25g fresh ginger, grated
4 garlic cloves, chopped
3 dried red chillies
1 tsp salt
10 black peppercorns
1 tsp black mustard seeds

2 tbsp tomato purée
½ tsp ground cinnamon
1 tsp sugar
5 tbsp rapeseed oil

For the curry:
40g butter
2 tbsp rapeseed oil
2 medium onions, chopped
750g turkey, roughly torn or chopped
2 x 400g tins whole tomatoes
A generous handful of coriander leaves,
  roughly chopped

Heat the oven to 160°C/Fan 140°C/Gas 3. For the dry-roast spice mix, toast all the spice seeds in a dry frying pan for a few minutes until they release their aroma. Take off the heat and grind to a powder, using a pestle and mortar or spice grinder. Tip into a small bowl and put to one side.

For the wet spice mix, using a pestle and mortar, pound the ginger, garlic, chillies, salt and peppercorns to a fragrant mush. Scrape into a bowl and stir in the mustard seeds, tomato purée, cinnamon, sugar and rapeseed oil. Add the dry-roast spice mix and stir to create a well combined paste.

In a large flameproof casserole over a low heat, melt the butter with the rapeseed oil. Add the onions and cook gently for 15 minutes until soft and translucent. Stir in the paste and cook for 5 minutes, stirring regularly. Add the leftover turkey, tinned tomatoes and 125ml water. Stir well, put the lid on and bring to a low simmer. Transfer to the oven for 1 hour, stirring halfway through cooking. Serve with a good scattering of fresh coriander.

Winter Store Salads

Winter salads are all about flavour... and crunch, heat, citrus tang, sourness and punch. You do not want a light, floral, subtle sort of salad on a cold day. These three combos hold their own alongside bold Christmas flavours and keep their seasonal integrity. Serve on their own, as a trio, or lined up on the party buffet table.

Chicory, blue cheese and roasted nut salad A family favourite, this is a speedy assembly. Choose a mix of red and white chicory and radicchio (at least 2 heads in total). Line a salad bowl with two-thirds of the leaves. Shred the rest and place in the centre. Crumble blue cheese (as much as you like) over the shredded leaves, followed by a drizzle of honey (2 tbsp) and the juice of 1 orange. Roughly chop a small bunch of parsley and scatter on top. Finish with 100g roasted nuts and seeds (page 137).

Chickpea, herb and red onion salad An unassuming salad that everyone returns to for second helpings. Drain 2 x 400g tins of chickpeas into a sieve and rinse under running cold water. Tip into a bowl and add a thinly sliced red onion, 4 tbsp drained capers, roughly chopped, and the grated zest and juice of 1 lemon. For those who like a little heat, add a deseeded and finely sliced red chilli. Now add a glug (2 tbsp) of olive oil and give everything a good stir. Scatter over a large handful each of parsley and chervil leaves and toss gently before serving. It doesn't need it, but you could crumble feta over the top if you wanted to.

Roast veg and spelt salad This super-grain makes a great base for a salad. Preheat the oven to 190°C/Fan 170°C/Gas 5 and peel and cut the following veg into chunks: ½ butternut squash (deseed this too), 2 parsnips, 2 fennel bulbs and 4 carrots. In a large roasting tray, toss the squash and parsnips in a good glug of olive oil and roast for 10 minutes. Add the fennel and carrots with 4 peeled and bashed garlic cloves and the finely chopped leaves from 3 sprigs of rosemary. Add another glug of oil and stir to mix. Roast for a further 30 minutes or so until the veg are cooked, throwing in a handful of seeds (sesame or pumpkin) or chopped hazelnuts. In the meantime, cook 150g quick-cook pearled spelt (or pearl barley) in salted boiling water for about 20 minutes until tender but retaining a bite. Drain and let cool slightly for a few minutes, then toss into the roasting tray and combine with the veg. Add a squeeze of lemon and a handful of feathery dill. For a final flourish, you could grate over some hard goat's cheese or tangy Cheddar.

Mincemeat Frangipane Tart

This tart could sit in any chapter but I am including it here because it is a great way to finish a jar of mincemeat. The combination of pastry, almond and spiced dried fruits is sublime and it is an easy assembly job if you have made the pastry ahead of time.

Makes 12 slices

For the sweet pastry:
340g plain flour, plus extra to dust
85g icing sugar
170g cold butter, cubed
1 medium egg
1 egg yolk, beaten, for the glaze

For the filling:
110g butter, softened
110g caster sugar

2 medium eggs
80g ground almonds
30g plain flour
A dash of brandy or whisky (optional)
650g mincemeat
A handful of flaked almonds

You will also need:
A 24cm tart tin

To make the pastry, sift the flour and icing sugar into a large bowl, add the butter and rub in with your fingertips until the mix resembles breadcrumbs. Add the egg and mix until the dough comes together. Knead lightly for 2–3 minutes until the pastry is smooth and 'fudgy'. Flatten into a disc and wrap in greaseproof paper. Chill for 30 minutes (or freeze if making ahead).

Preheat the oven to 160°C/Fan 140°C/Gas 3. Unwrap the pastry and roll out on a floured surface to a 2mm thickness. Use to line a 24cm tart tin, leaving 3cm excess pastry overhanging the edge. Prick the base with a fork.

Line the pastry with a sheet of baking paper and fill with a layer of baking beans. Bake 'blind' for 35 minutes, then remove the beans and paper and bake for a further 10 minutes or until the pastry base feels dry. Using a small, serrated knife, trim away the overhanging pastry. Brush the pastry with egg yolk, then return the pastry case to the oven for 2 minutes to set the egg. Remove and set aside. Turn the oven up to 180°C/Fan 160°C/Gas 4.

For the frangipane, using an electric whisk, beat together the butter, sugar, eggs, ground almonds, flour and booze if using, until smooth and light.

Spread the mincemeat evenly in the pastry case. Spoon the frangipane on top and smooth out. Sprinkle with the flaked almonds and bake for about 25 minutes until golden and firm in the centre. Enjoy warm, with cream.

Christmas Tiffin

Hugh introduced me to this more virtuous version of a tiffin. True, it still has all the joyous flavours and texture of a traditional tiffin or fridge cake but without the sugar overload. It makes an ideal mid-afternoon treat or gift, wrapped in greaseproof paper and presented in a tin. One note of caution: tiffin needs to be kept in the fridge as it will begin to melt a little at warm room temperature. This is another recipe that I make all year round and vary some of the ingredients, depending on what is in the store cupboard.

Makes 12–16

100g dried sour cherries
  (or dried cranberries or sultanas)
1 tbsp rumtopf liquor (page 50),
  cherry vodka or brandy
75g jumbo oats
50g whole hazelnuts, roughly chopped
40g sunflower seeds
35g pumpkin seeds
50g coconut oil

150g plain chocolate (at least
  70% cocoa solids), broken up
2 pieces of preserved stem ginger,
  finely chopped, plus 1 tsp syrup
  from the jar

You will also need:
A shallow baking tin, about
  20 x 15cm

Line your baking tin with baking paper. Turn the oven on to 200°C/ Fan 180°C/Gas 6. Put the dried cherries (or cranberries/sultanas) into a heatproof bowl with the alcohol. Put the bowl in the oven as it heats up to warm the fruit, taking it out after 5 minutes so you don't cook it!

Once the oven is up to temperature, spread the oats, hazelnuts and seeds on a baking tray and toast in the oven for 7–9 minutes, checking regularly. The oats need to be crispy and the nuts slightly browned. Set aside to cool for a few minutes.

Put the coconut oil and chocolate pieces into a saucepan over a low heat and stir occasionally as the mixture starts to melt. Remove from the heat just before the chocolate is completely melted and stir in the toasted oats, nuts and seeds (they can still be warm but not hot). Add the fruit with any boozy liquid, the chopped ginger and syrup.

Spread the mixture evenly in the prepared tin and leave to cool for a few minutes then place in the fridge. Leave until completely cold and set before cutting into squares.

Twelfth Night Cake

Centuries ago, Twelfth Night was considered more important than Christmas day, as the culmination of twelve days of celebration. The centrepiece of the feasting was a cake – sometimes called 'king cake' because it symbolised the day the three Magi reached Jesus. Originally a fruit cake, it evolved into an almondy, buttery sponge or a pastry-based treat, and tradition has it that a bean, trinket or tiny ceramic figure should be hidden in the mixture. I top mine with this snow baby, inherited from my grandmother Doff, my Christmas angel.

Serves 8–10

150g unsalted butter, softened,
  plus extra to grease the tin
150g caster sugar
Finely grated zest and juice of
  1 orange
3 medium eggs

50g plain flour
200g ground almonds
150ml plain wholemilk yoghurt

You will also need:
A 20cm round cake tin

Preheat the oven to 180°C/Fan 160°C/Gas 4. Lightly grease a 20cm round cake tin with butter and line with baking paper.

Using an electric mixer (or hand-held electric whisk), beat the butter until it is soft and light. Add the sugar and continue to beat for a few minutes until creamy. Add the orange zest, followed by 1 egg and a spoonful of flour. Beat together until just combined. Beat in the second egg with another spoonful of flour. Repeat to incorporate the third egg.

Using a large metal spoon or spatula, fold in the rest of the flour, the ground almonds, orange juice and yoghurt.

Spoon the mixture into the prepared tin and gently level the surface. Bake for 25 minutes until golden and firm to the touch. To test, insert a skewer into the middle of the cake – it should come out clean.

Leave the cake to cool in the tin for 10 minutes, then turn out and cool on a wire rack. It can be served still warm or left to cool completely and stored in a tin for up to a week.

Index

Index

T

V

W

Y

Directory

FOOD AND DRINK

Trill Farm Garden
www.trillfarmgarden.co.uk
Market garden, growing a wealth of heritage produce for veg boxes and local restaurants.

Haye Farm
www.hayefarmdevon.co.uk
Mixed organic farm in Devon with a focus on high animal welfare, biodiversity and wildlife.

Riverford
www.riverford.co.uk
Organic veg grower and veg box supplier. Their Christmas larder selection is a treat.

Pipers Farm
www.pipersfarm.com
Award-winning farm embracing sustainable methods. Exceptional quality meat and produce (also Christmas goodies) available online.

Gilt & Flint
www.giltandflint.com
Brewhouse creating organic, modern beers, ciders, soft drinks and vinegars as well their ingenious Christmas hamper – Pub In A Box.

Castlewood
www.castlewoodvineyard.co.uk
Family-run vineyard producing small but delicious pressings of traditional sparkling wines. Organises tours and tastings.

Somerset Cider Brandy Company
www.somersetciderbrandy.com
Award-winning cider, brandy and aperitifs produced from Somerset cider apple orchards. Owned and run by the Temperley family, who also organise regular events and distillery tours.

Vintage Roots
www.vintageroots.co.uk
Online drinks supplier, 100% organic, offering a fantastic selection of wines, beers and ciders delivered straight to your door.

TREES, PLANTS & SEEDS

British Christmas Tree Growers Association
www.bctga.co.uk

Grace Alexander
www.gracealexanderflowers.co.uk
Somerset seed specialist with an online shop of beautiful things and a wealth of inspiration.

Otter Farm Nursery
www.otterfarm.co.uk
Online store, stocked with the best varieties of veg, fruit, herbs, spices and seeds.

Tamar Organics
www.tamarorganics.co.uk
Organic seed merchants focusing on edible produce and practical garden kit.

CRAFT

Molesworth & Bird
www.molesworthandbird.co.uk
Shoreline designed products, including seaweed pressings from regular forages.

Ali Herbert Ceramics
www.aliherbert.com
Exquisite porcelain and stoneware pieces, which are functional as well as aesthetic.

Eleanor Percival
www.eleanorpercival.com
Eleanor makes beautiful cards and prints and sells through her Etsy store.

Simple Shape
www.simple-shape.com
Homewares for inside and outside living, including wonderful present ideas.

Ryder & Hope
www.ryderandhope.com
Thoughtfully designed homewares, including gift ideas and Christmas decorations.

Acknowledgements

It is tempting to take this opportunity to thank everyone who knows me but I must remember this is a place to express gratitude to those who directly influenced this book. That's still a big list.

To Alex Heaton-Livingstone and Katy Shields, for their creative input, friendship and shared recipe passion, my caffeinated thanks. Likewise, the marvellous Fitzpatricks – Anna, Dan, Isaac, Merle and Mack – who ate and lived some of this book and still want a copy. To lovely Maddie Huggins for her extensive garden knowledge and text reminders about what to plant when. And to Grace Alexander for her beautiful hand-dyed fabrics and seed inspiration.

Briny appreciation to my swim pals immortalised in the solstice snap. With special thanks to Ros Byam Shaw, my partner in cold water and pigs in blankets, who makes me laugh every day. To Alice (and Gill) Meller for being prop lending saviours and to Pam 'The Jam' Corbin for her wise words and rumtopf pot. Last, but not least, to Tracy Low for sharing her secret hot chocolate recipe and for culinary excellence on beaches, even cold winter ones.

To the amazing team at River Cottage who continued to shine despite everything a pandemic could throw at them. I'm looking at you, Gelf Alderson, a guiding light who worked tirelessly with me on recipes and photoshoots. To Nikki Duffy, a sublime wordsmith who took my hand and early draft and led me somewhere better. Additional thanks and beers are due to Stewart Dodd, Rob Love and Antony Topping who have all championed me from the start. As have Jessamy Upton and Cat Bugler, two absolute diamonds, who clasped me to their bosoms on the first day of my River Cottage life and still haven't let go 15 years later.

For their encouragement and wisdom, I heartily thank Diana Henry and my old mucker Mark Diacono, two of my food writing heroes. And, through them, I met the Cadhay Crew, a group of talented people who I am lucky to know and be inspired by.

Bloomsbury have been a dream to work with. From the earliest conversations about this book with Natalie Bellos, Lena Hall, Lisa Pendreigh and Xa Shaw Stewart to the actual working on it with the excellent Rowan Yapp and the unflappable, dedicated Kitty Stogdon, it has been a treasured experience of professionalism, care and commitment. And a special mention to Ellen Williams, a cheerleader from the start – I couldn't think of a better person to take this book into the world with.

This book would not be what it is without Will Webb for his beautiful design vision and the wonderful Janet Illsley, who has kept me safe under her expert wing. Or the photographer, Charlotte Bland, whose input in this book has been so much more than the stunning images. Her steadfast and stylish approach combined with an artist's eye has brought the writing alive. I would follow her anywhere, although she still hasn't managed to get me to eat cold pizza for breakfast.

To Hugh, for a fateful fishing trip that led to a titanic life change, I am forever indebted. It has been a sparkling honour to be joined by him on this festive journey. He trusted me with the project from the start and has shown complete respect and support throughout the process. Our next collaboration should be a Lemon Verbena Lovers' Club.

Finally, to my family. The people that make my Christmases past, present and future and who I have thought of as I have written this book. My gorgeous godchildren – Gabriel, Ella, Caro, Chloe and Edith. My extended family – Susan, David, Emma, Mike, Isabella, Olivia, Sophie, Will, Theo, Esther, Angela, Chris, Sharon, Esme, Max, Alwyn, Peter, Ian, Susan and Edie – who weave in and out of festive celebrations. My exceptional parents Ruth and Richard, whose unconditional love, support and work ethic has been the mainstay of my life. My dear-heart brother Rob, sister-in-law Ali, nephew Dodge and nieces Missy and Kitty, for being and sharing the true meaning of Christmas. You five are the magic. And to my beloveds – Steven, my sail and anchor, and our three incredible children – Rafferty, Hebe and Jesse – who make me burst with love, gratitude and pride. Thank you for your unstinting belief in me. How lucky I am.

River Cottage: Food to Inspire Change

From the moment River Cottage came to our TV screens, Hugh has been agitating for a shift in our attitude to food. He wants us to know where our food comes from, and to understand the consequences of our food choices. For almost three decades now, River Cottage and Hugh have been championing the idea that food can inspire change – both in our lives and in the world around us.

Hugh Fearnley-Whittingstall and his partners at Keo films created the original River Cottage television series in 1999. The shows ran on Channel 4 in the UK for the next 15 years. The series charted Hugh's culinary adventures, first as a down-sizing smallholder at the original River Cottage in West Dorset, and later at more expansive Park Farm in rural East Devon. There are over 80 River Cottage TV shows that are still regularly repeated on Channel 4 and other platforms all over the world.

In 2006, Hugh and his team established River Cottage HQ at Park Farm, a 90-acre property in an Area of Outstanding Natural Beauty on the Devon/Dorset border. The site was developed and designed under the guidance of architect and sustainability specialist Stewart Dodd, now Chief Executive at River Cottage. It is home to an award-winning cookery school where guests from all over the world learn not only how to improve their cooking techniques and artisan food skills, but also how to grow their own ingredients and source food in an ethical and sustainable way. River Cottage HQ has won many awards including 'Best Cookery School' in the Great British Food Awards, for the past 4 years running. Recently, the River Cottage Online Cooking Diploma was launched.

Guests can also stay at Park Farm's beautifully restored seventeenth-century farmhouse and feast on seasonal, local, organic and wild food in the threshing barn. In nearby Axminster, the River Cottage Kitchen, recently awarded a Michelin Green Star, offers an outstanding menu created from locally sourced produce.

Hugh and River Cottage have published 34 books, including the popular River Cottage Handbook series of practical manuals on artisan cooking techniques, gardening, smallholding and foraging. These books have sold over 2 million copies and won multiple awards, including the Glenfiddich Award, the André Simon Award and, in the US, the James Beard Award.

River Cottage also produces a range of ethical and organic products including yoghurt, kombucha, kefir, sauerkrauts, stocks, sauces, wines, beers and ciders.

BLOOMSBURY PUBLISHING
Bloomsbury Publishing Plc
50 Bedford Square, London, WC1B 3DP, UK
29 Earlsfort Terrace, Dublin 2, Ireland

BLOOMSBURY, BLOOMSBURY PUBLISHING and the Diana logo are trademarks of
Bloomsbury Publishing Plc.

First published in Great Britain 2021

A catalogue record for this book is available from the British Library.

ISBN: HB: 978-1-4088-7356-4; eBook: 978-1-5266-3062-9

10 9 8 7 6 5 4 3 2 1

Project Editor: Janet Illsley
Designer: Will Webb
Photographer: Charlotte Bland
Indexer: Hilary Bird

Printed and bound in Germany by Mohn Media

MIX
Paper from
responsible sources
FSC® C011124

To find out more about our authors and books visit www.bloomsbury.com
and sign up for our newsletters.